NICHOL

GUIDE TO THE WATERWAYS 3

Birmingham &
the Heart of England

Nicholson

An imprint of HarperCollins*Publishers*

Also available:

Nicholson Guide to the Waterways

1. **London, Grand Union, Oxford & Lee**
2. **Severn, Avon & Birmingham**
4. **Four Counties & the Welsh Canals**
5. **North West & the Pennines**
6. **Nottingham, York & the North East**
7. **Thames, Wey, Kennet & Avon**

Nicholson Inland Waterways Map of Great Britain

Published by Nicholson
An imprint of HarperCollins*Publishers*
77–85 Fulham Palace Road
Hammersmith, London W6 8JB

www.**fire**and**water**.com
www.bartholomewmaps.com

First published by Nicholson and Ordnance Survey 1997
Reprinted 1998
New edition published by Nicholson 2000

Researched and written by David Perrott and Jonathan Mosse.
Design by Bob Vickers.

The publishers gratefully acknowledge the assistance given by British Waterways and its staff in the
preparation of this guide.

Grateful thanks is also due to members of the Inland Waterways Association and
CAMRA representatives and branch members.

Photographs reproduced by kind permission of the following picture libraries:
British Waterways Photo Library pages 107; Bill Meadows Picture Library pages 93, 97, 127, 139;
Derek Pratt Photography pages 40, 51, 113, 122, 151.

Printed in Italy.

ISBN 0 7028 4162 5
ME10288
97/2/34

The publishers welcome comments from readers. Please address your letters to:
Nicholson Guides to the Waterways, HarperCollins Cartographic, HarperCollins Publishers,
Westerhill Road, Bishopbriggs, Glasgow, G64 2QT.

The canals and river navigations of Britain were built as a system of new trade routes, at a time when roads were virtually non-existent. After their desperately short boom period in the late 18th and early 19th centuries, they gracefully declined in the face of competition from the railways. A few canals disappeared completely, but thankfully most just decayed gently, carrying the odd working boat, and becoming havens for wildlife and the retreat of the waterways devotee.

It was two such enthusiasts, L.T.C. Rolt and Robert Aickman who, in 1946, formed the Inland Waterways Association, bringing together like-minded people from all walks of life to campaign for the preservation and restoration of the inland waterways. Their far-sightedness has at last seen its reward for, all over the country, an amazing transformation is taking place. British Waterways, the IWA, local councils, canal societies and volunteers have brought back to life great lengths of canal, and much of the dereliction which was once commonplace has been replaced with a network of 'linear parks'.

The canals provide something for everyone to enjoy: engineering feats such as aqueducts, tunnels and flights of locks; the brightly decorated narrow boats; a wealth of birds, animals and plants; the mellow unpretentious architecture of canalside buildings; friendly waterside pubs and the sheer beauty and quiet isolation that is a feature of so much of our inland waterways.

It is easy to enjoy this remarkable facet of our history, either on foot, often by bicycle, or on a boat. This book, with its splendid Ordnance Survey® mapping, is one of a series covering the waterways network, and gives you all the information you need.

▮ CONTENTS

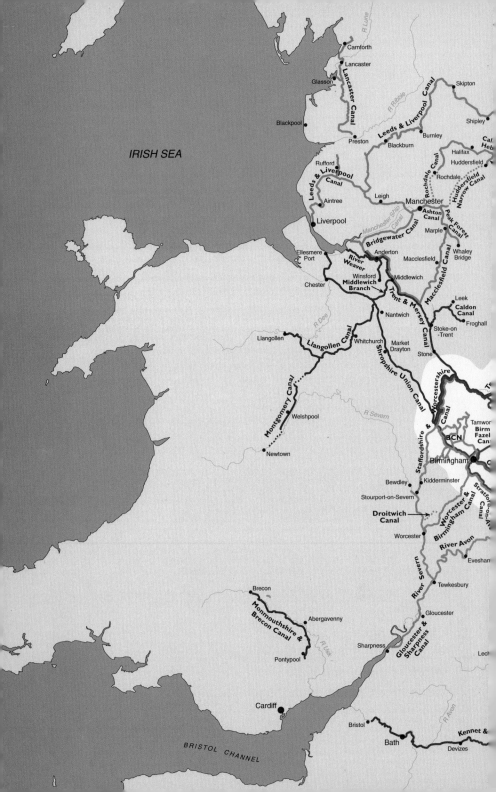

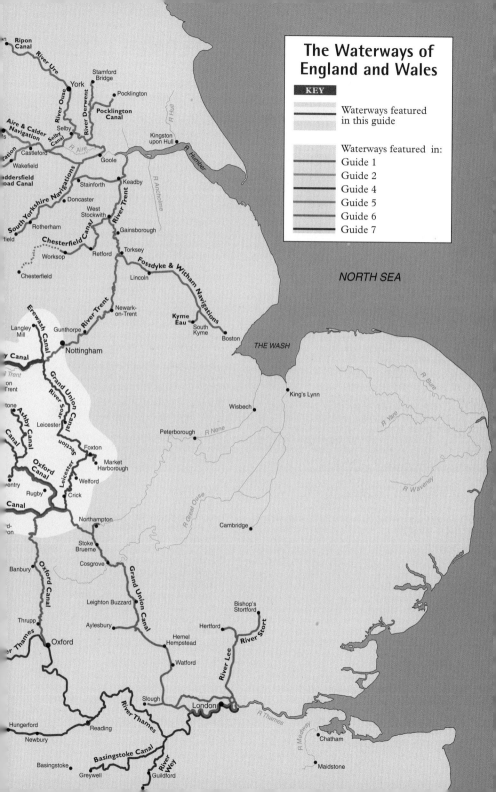

The Waterways of England and Wales

KEY

Waterways featured in this guide

Waterways featured in:
Guide 1
Guide 2
Guide 4
Guide 5
Guide 6
Guide 7

NORTH SEA

THE WASH

Ripon Canal
River Ure
York
Stamford Bridge
Pocklington
Pocklington Canal
River Ouse
River Derwent
Selby
Selby Canal
Aire & Calder Navigation
Kingston upon Hull
R Hull
R Aire
Castleford
Wakefield
Goole
Huddersfield Broad Canal
South Yorkshire Navigations
Stainforth
Keadby
Doncaster
West Stockwith
Rotherham
Chesterfield Canal
Gainsborough
Worksop
Retford
Torksey
Chesterfield
Lincoln
Fossdyke & Witham Navigations
Kyme Eau
South Kyme
Boston
R Ancholme
R Humber
R Trent
Newark-on-Trent
Langley Mill
Erewash Canal
Gunthorpe
River Trent
King's Lynn
Wisbech
Nottingham
Grand Union Canal
River Soar
Peterborough
R Nene
R Bure
R Yare
Trent
on Trent
Ashby Canal
Leicester
Leicester Section
Foxton
Market Harborough
Canal
Oxford Canal
Welford
Crick
R Waveney
ventry
Rugby
Canal
Northampton
Cambridge
R Great Ouse
d-on
Stoke Bruerne
Cosgrove
Banbury
Oxford Canal
Grand Union Canal
Leighton Buzzard
Bishop's Stortford
Thrupp
Aylesbury
Hertford
River Stort
r Thames
Oxford
Hemel Hempstead
River Lee
Watford
Slough
London
R Thames
Hungerford
River Thames
Reading
Chatham
Newbury
R Medway
Basingstoke Canal
River Wey
Basingstoke
Maidstone
Greywell
Guildford

GENERAL INFORMATION FOR CANAL USERS

The slogan Waterways For All was coined to take account of the wide diversity of people using the inland waterways for recreation.

Today boaters, walkers, fishermen, cyclists and gongoozlers (on-lookers) throng our canals and rivers, to share in the enjoyment of our quite amazing waterway heritage. British Waterways (BW), along with other navigation authorities, is empowered to develop, maintain and control this resource in order to maximise its potential: namely our enjoyment. It is to this end that a series of guides, codes, and regulations have come into existence over the years, evolving to match a burgeoning – and occasionally conflicting – demand. Set out below are the key points as they relate to everyone wishing to enjoy the waterways.

LICENSING – BOATS

The majority of the navigations covered in this book are controlled by BW and are managed on a day-to-day basis by local waterway offices. Waterway Managers are detailed in the introduction to each waterway. All craft using BW waterways must be licenced and charges are based on the length of the craft. This licence covers all navigable waterways under BW's control and in a few cases includes reciprocal agreements with other waterway authorities (as indicated in the text). As this edition goes to print, BW and the Environment Agency are preparing to go to consultation on an optional joint licence to cover both authorities' waterways. Permits for permanent mooring on the canals are also issued by BW. For further information contact BW Customer Services (see inside front cover). You can download licence fees and charges and an application form from the BW website (see inside front cover).

Since 1 January 1997, BW and the Environment Agency have introduced the Boat Safety Scheme, setting technical requirements for good and safe boat-building practice. A Boat Safety Certificate or, for new boats, a Declaration of Conformity, is necessary to obtain a craft licence. For powered boats proof of insurance for Third Party Liability for a minimum of £1,000,000 is also required. Further details from BW Customer Services. Other navigational authorities relevant to this book are mentioned where appropriate.

LICENSING – CYCLISTS

Not all towpaths are open to cyclists. This is because many stretches are too rough or narrow, or because cyclists cause too great a risk to other users. The maps on the BW website show which stretches of towpaths are open to cyclists. This information is also available from your local waterway office, which you should contact in any case to obtain the necessary permit to cycle on the towpath and a copy of the Waterways Code. When using the towpaths for cycling, you will encounter other

towpath users, such as fishermen, walkers and boaters. The Waterways Code gives advice on taking care and staying safe, considering others and helping to look after the waterways. A complete list of towpaths available for cycling is available in a National Cycle Pack, price £5.00 from BW Customer Services.

TOWPATHS

Few, if any, artificial cuts or canals in this country are without an intact towpath accessible to the walker at least. However, on river navigations towpaths have on occasion fallen into disuse or, sometimes, been lost to erosion. In today's leisure climate considerable efforts are being made to provide access to all towpaths with some available to the disabled. Notes on individual waterways in this book detail the supposed status of the path, but the indication of a towpath does not necessarily imply a public right of way or mean that a right to cycle along it exists. Maps on the BW website show all towpaths on the BW network, and whether they are open to cyclists. Motorcycling and horse riding are forbidden on all towpaths.

INDIVIDUAL WATERWAY GUIDES

No national guide can cover the minutiae of individual waterways and some Waterway Managers produce guides to specific navigations under their charge. Copies of individual guides (where they are available) can be obtained from the Waterway Office detailed in the introduction. Please note that times – such as operating times of bridges and locks – do change year by year and from winter to summer.

STOPPAGES

BW works hard to programme its major engineering works into the winter period when demand for cruising is low. It publishes a National Stoppage Programme and Winter Opening Hours leaflet which is sent out to all licence holders, boatyards and hire companies. Inevitably, emergencies occur necessitating the unexpected closure of a waterway, perhaps during the peak season. You can check for stoppages on individual waterways between specific dates on the BW website. Details are also announced on lockside noticeboards and on Canalphone (see inside front cover).

STARTING OUT

Extensive information and advice on booking a boating holiday is available on the BW website. Please book a waterway holiday from a licenced operator – only in this way can you be sure that you have proper insurance cover, service and support during your holiday. It is illegal for private boat owners to hire out their craft. If in doubt, please contact BW Customer Services. If you are hiring a canal boat for the first time, the boatyard will brief you thoroughly. Take notes, follow their instructions and *don't be afraid to ask* if there is anything you do not understand. BW have produced a short video giving basic information on using a boat safely. Copies of the video, and the Waterways Code for Boaters, are available free of charge from BW Customer Services.

GENERAL CRUISING NOTES

Most canals are saucer-shaped in section so are deepest at the middle. Few have more than 3–4ft of water and many have much less. Keep to the centre of the channel except on bends, where the deepest water is on the outside of the bend. When you meet another boat, keep to the right, slow down and aim to miss the approaching craft by a couple of yards: do not steer right over to the bank or you are likely to run aground. If you meet a loaded commercial boat keep right out of the way and be prepared to follow his instructions. Do not assume that you should pass on the right. If you meet a boat being towed from the bank, pass it on the outside. When overtaking, keep the other boat on your right side.

A large number of BW facilities in their north-east region – pump-outs, showers, electrical hook-ups and so on – are currently operated by smart cards, obtainable from BW Regional Office, Neptune Street, Leeds (0113 281 6800); local waterways offices (see introductions to individual navigations); lock keepers and some boatyards within the region. At the time of printing, a £6 card will purchase one pump-out, about 12 showers and electricity pro rata. Please note that if you are a week-end visitor, you should purchase cards *in advance.*

Speed

There is a general speed limit of 4 mph on most BW canals. This is not just an arbitrary limit: there is no need to go any faster and in many cases it is impossible to cruise even at this speed: if the wash is breaking against the bank or causing large waves, slow down.

Slow down also when passing moored craft, engineering works and anglers; when there is a lot of floating rubbish on the water (and try to drift over obvious obstructions in neutral); when approaching blind corners, narrow bridges and junctions.

Mooring

Generally speaking you may moor where you wish on BW property, as long as there is sufficient depth of water, and you are *not causing an obstruction.* Your boat should carry metal mooring stakes, and these should be driven firmly into the ground with a mallet if there are no mooring rings. Do not stretch mooring lines across the towpath. Always consider the security of your boat when there is no one aboard. On tideways and commercial waterways it is advisable to moor only at recognised sites, and allow for any rise or fall of the tide.

Bridges

On narrow canals slow down and aim to miss one side (usually the towpath side) by about 9 inches. *Keep everyone inboard when passing under bridges,* and take special care with moveable structures – the crew member operating the bridge should hold it steady as the boat passes through.

Tunnels

Make sure the tunnel is clear before you enter, and use your headlight. Follow any instructions given on notice boards by the entrance.

Fuel

Hire craft usually carry fuel sufficient for the rental period.

Water

It is advisable to top up every day.

Lavatories

Hire craft usually have pump-out toilets. Have these emptied *before* things become critical. Keep the receipt and your boatyard will usually reimburse you for this expense.

Boatyards

Hire fleets are usually turned around on a Saturday, making this a bad time to call in for services. Remember that moorings at popular destinations fill quickly during the summer months, so do not assume there will be room for your boat. Always ask.

LOCKS AND THEIR USE

A lock is a simple and ingenious device for transporting your craft from one water level to another.

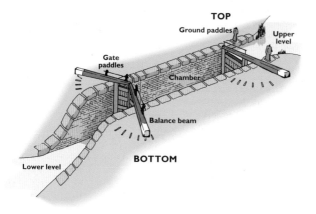

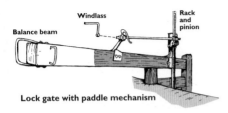

Lock gate with paddle mechanism

(labels: Windlass, Rack and pinion, Balance beam)

When both sets of gates are closed it may be filled or emptied using gate or ground paddles at the top or bottom of the lock. These are operated with a windlass.

General tips

- Make safety your prime concern. *Keep a close eye on young children.*
- Always take your time, and do not leap about.
- Never open the paddles at one end without ensuring those at the other are closed.
- Never drop the paddles – always wind them down.
- Keep to the landward side of the balance beam when opening and closing gates.
- Never leave your windlass slotted onto the paddle spindle – it will be dangerous should anything slip.
- Keep your boat away from the top and bottom gates to prevent it getting caught on the gate or the lock cill.
- Be wary of fierce *top gate* paddles, especially in wide locks. Operate them slowly, and close them if there is *any* adverse effect.
- Always follow the navigation authority's instructions, where these are given on notices or by their staff.

PLANNING A CRUISE

Many a canal holiday has been spoiled by trying to go too far too fast. Go slowly, don't be too ambitious, and enjoy the experience. Note that mileages indicated on the maps are for guidance only.

A *rough* calculation of time taken to cover the ground is the lock-miles system:

Add the number of *miles* to the number of *locks* on your proposed journey, and divide the resulting figure by three. This will give you a guide to the number of *hours* it will take. But don't forget your service stops (water, shopping, pump-out), and allow plenty of time to visit that special pub!

TIDAL WATERWAYS

The typical steel narrow boat found on the inland waterways system has the sea-going characteristics of a bathtub, which renders it totally unsuitable for all-weather cruising on tidal estuaries. However, the more adventurous will inevitably wish to add additional ring cruises to the more predictable circuits within the calm havens of inland Britain. Passage is possible in most estuaries if careful consideration is given to the key factors of weather conditions, crew experience, the condition of the boat and its equipment and, perhaps of overriding importance, the need to take expert advice. In many cases it will be prudent to employ the skilled services of a local pilot. Within the text, where inland navigations connect with a tidal waterway, details are given of sources of both advice and pilotage. This guide is to the inland waterways of Britain and therefore recognizes that tideways – and especially estuaries – require a different skill and approach. We therefore do not hesitate to draw the boater's attention to the appropriate source material.

GENERAL

Most inland navigations are managed by BW or the Environment Agency, but there are several other navigation authorities responsible for smaller stretches of canals and rivers. For details of these, contact the Association of Inland Navigation Authorities at www.cam.net.uk/home/aina or BW Customer Services. The boater, conditioned perhaps by the uniformity of our national road network, should be sensitive to the need to observe different codes and operating practices. Similarly it is important to be aware that some waterways are only available for navigation today solely because of the care and dedication of a particular restoration body, often using volunteer labour and usually taking several decades to complete the project. This is the reason that, in cruising the national waterways network, additional licence charges are sometimes incurred. The introduction to each waterway gives its background history, details of recent restoration (where relevant) and also lists the operating authority.

BW is a public corporation, responsible to the Department of the Environment, Transport and the Regions and, as subscribers to the Citizen's Charter, they are linked with an ombudsman. BW has a comprehensive complaints procedure and a free explanatory leaflet is available from Customer Services. Problems and complaints should be addressed to the local Waterway Manager in the first instance – the telephone number is listed in the introduction to individual waterways.

The Inland Waterways Association campaigns for the 'conservation, use, maintenance, restoration and development of the inland waterways', through branches all over the country. For more information contact them at PO Box 114, Rickmansworth, WD3 1ZY, telephone 01923 711114, fax 01923 897000, email iwa@waterways.org.uk or visit their website at www.waterways.org.uk/index.htm.

FREEPHONE CANALS

Emergency help is available from BW outside normal office hours on weekdays and throughout weekends via Freephone Canals (see inside front cover). You should give details of the problem and your location.

ASHBY CANAL

MAXIMUM DIMENSIONS
Length: 70'
Beam: 7'
Headroom: 6' 6"

MANAGER
(01283) 790236

MILEAGE
MARSTON JUNCTION (Coventry Canal) to
Burton Hastings: 3 miles

Hinckley Wharf: 6 miles
Stoke Golding Wharf: 8³/4 miles
Dadlington: 10 miles
Shenton Aqueduct: 13 miles
Market Bosworth Wharf: 15 miles
Congerstone: 17¹/4 miles
Shackerstone: 18¹/4 miles
Snarestone Tunnel: 21 miles

CANAL TERMINUS: 22 miles

No locks

Looking at this canal on a map it appears to be very much out on a limb. In fact the Ashby Canal was originally intended to be a through route from the River Trent at Burton to the Coventry Canal near Bedworth, but this plan was repeatedly shelved. In 1792, however, an Ashby Canal Company was formed and a Bill promoted, mostly by the owners of Leicestershire limeworks and the new coalfields near Ashby de la Zouch, who decided that an outlet southwards was required from their various works. The problem that soon arose was that, while the proposed canal could be built level for 30 miles (following the 300ft contour) from the junction with the Coventry Canal at Marston Jabbett, near Bedworth, to Moira, the section north of Moira would require expensive and complicated works, including locks, reservoirs, pumping engines and possibly a tunnel. Part of this cost was, in fact, avoided by building an extensive system of tramroads to and around the various coalmines and limeworks. However, while the canal was still being built (by a succession of engineers – Jessop, Outram, Whitworth senior and junior, and Thomas Newbold), the new coalmines near Ashby Wolds were found to be less productive than had been hoped. This, combined with the fact that the canal was never extended north to the Trent, was instrumental in preventing the Ashby Canal from making a profit for 20 years. However, a new coal mine sunk at Moira in 1804 eventually produced coal of such excellent quality that it became widely demanded in London and southern England. The canal flourished at last.

In 1845 the Midland Railway bought up the Ashby Canal – with the approval of all concerned except the Coventry and Oxford Canal companies, who stood to lose a lot in tolls if the coal traffic from Moira switched to rail carriage. These two companies managed to hamstring the Midland Railway so effectively over its management of the canal that, instead of switching to carriage by rail, the coal traffic from Moira continued along the canal at a substantial level through to the turn of the century. It is therefore hard to see what real benefit the railway company gained from buying the canal.

Subsidence from the coal mines near Measham (now stabilised with the completion of mining in the area) has caused great damage in this century to the canal that served them. This subsidence has brought about the abandonment of over 8 miles of the canal, so that the waterway now terminates just north of Snarestone, outside the coalfield. The last load to be carried along the canal was coal to Croxley (Herts), from Gopsall Wharf in 1970. Ambitious plans are in hand to re-open the waterway through to Moira, making use of the abandoned railway line in Measham.

Burton Hastings

At Marston Junction the Ashby Canal branches east off the Coventry Canal. Under the bridge there is a box containing guides to the waterway produced by the Ashby Canal Association. As soon as it leaves Marston, the canal changes completely and dramatically. The industry and housing estates that had accompanied the Coventry Canal through the Nuneaton-Bedworth conurbation suddenly vanish to be replaced by green fields, farms and trees. In this way the character of the Ashby Canal is established at once: also the first of the typical stone-arched bridges occurs which, together with the shallow and relatively clear water, suggests a rurality far from the industrial Midlands. Only the power lines that criss-cross this stretch are a memory of the other world to the west. A long wooded cutting leads the canal towards Burton Hastings, a typical farming village. Then the canal turns north, setting a course for Hinckley passing, to the east of bridge 13, Stretton Baskerville, a 'lost' village and scheduled ancient monument. The A5 (Watling Street) and the A47 cross near Hinckley. There is no navigation on the Hinckley Wharf Arm, which is used as a boat club mooring. Keeping west of the town, the canal continues through the fine rolling farmland that typifies the Ashby Canal.

NAVIGATIONAL NOTES

The canal is shallow throughout and progress is likely to be slow. Random mooring may be awkward due to shallow sides so use the wharfs and recognised moorings.

The towpath
The condition of the towpath is somewhat variable. As far as bridge 15 it is rutted and boggy in parts with erosion in bridge holes. Thereafter it improves as far as Snarestone.

● Burton Hastings

Warwicks. PO, tel. Quiet village set on a hill in open farmland. The pretty, well-placed church dedicated to St Botolph is a Grade II listed building, parts of its construction dating back to the 14thC. It has a decorated font of 1300.

● Hinckley

Leics. MD Mon, Fri & Sat. PO, tel, stores, garage, station. A hosiery manufacturing town that can boast having installed the first stocking machine in Leicestershire, in 1640. Buildings of interest include St Mary's church with the 'bleeding' tombstone in the churchyard; the Great Meeting Chapel (1722) and the museum. Only the bailey and part of the moat remain of the Norman castle. There is a greyhound stadium south of bridge 16 with *Wed & Sat* racing *commencing at 19.30.* Telephone (01455) 634006 for further details.

Concordia Theatre Stockwell Head, Hinckley (01455 615005). Small local theatre with performances *Sep–Jun.*

Hinckley and District Museum Framework Knitters Cottages, Lower Bond Street, Hinckley (01455 251218). Established in a row of restored 17th-C thatched cottages once used for framework knitting, the museum houses displays on the town and area from prehistoric to medieval times. Also depicted are the hosiery and boot and shoe making industries together with annually changing exhibitions reflecting different aspects of local history. *Open Easter Mon–Oct, Sat & B. Hol Mon 10.00–16.00, Sun 14.00–17.00.* Tea room and cottage garden. Small admission charge.

Snibston Discovery Park Ashby Road, Coalville (01530 510851). *24hr* information line (01530) 813256. See entry on page 17 for further details. It is feasible to access this all-weather attraction by bus from Hinckley. Stevenson's operate a service (route no 179) *Mon–Fri, five times daily,* terminating in Memorial Square, Coalville – approx 800yds from the site entrance. Further details from Busline (0116 251 1411).

Tourist Information Centre The Library, Lancaster Road, Hinckley (01455 635106).

Pubs and Restaurants

🍺 **Corner House Hotel** Bulkington Lane, Marston Jabbett (02476 386159). South of bridge 5 on B4112. Large friendly pub orientated around family eating. Food available *lunchtimes, evenings and all day Sunday* together with Marston's real ale. Vegetarian and children's menu. Patio.

🍺 **Lime Kilns Inn** Watling Street, Hinckley (01455 631158). Canalside at bridge 15. Marston's real ale in an old coaching house now refurbished with a downstairs boaters bar. A family pub serving bar food *lunchtimes and evenings, 7 days a week.* Children's menu and vegetarians catered for. Canalside seating, garden and children's play area. Darts and crib. *Open all day Fri & Sat.*

🍺 **Wharf Inn** Hinckley (01455 615830). East of bridge 17, near Hinckley Wharf. Marston's and Bateman real ales, and rolls served *lunchtime* in a pub dating back to the 1700s. Children's room and outdoor play area. Garden, darts, dominoes and crib. Quiz *Sun* and live entertainment on *alternate Sat.* There are a variety of services close by including a good general stores, butcher's shop, PO, Indian restaurant, take-away, newsagent and garage.

Stoke Golding

The canal now runs fairly directly to Stoke Golding where there is one of the finest churches in Leicestershire. There are no locks, but the typical Ashby accommodation bridges occur regularly. The Ashby Canal is remote and rural, an ironic contrast to its *raison d'être*, the Ashby coalfields. After Stoke Golding the contours cause the canal to meander carelessly, passing Dadlington, heading in a northerly direction towards the Bosworth Battlefield Centre near Shenton.

Pubs and Restaurants

⚑ ✕ **Oddfellows Arms** Higham on the Hill (01455 212322). Charles Wells real ales and food served *lunchtimes and evenings*. Children and vegetarians catered for. Patio seating and family room. Pub games.

⚑ **Fox Inn** Higham on the Hill (01455 212241). Bass and M&B real ales, with homemade bar snacks available *lunchtimes and early evenings in winter*. Beer garden.

⚑ **White Swan** Stoke Golding (01455 212313). Everards and guest real ales dispensed in a homely village local with friendly staff. Bar snacks available *lunchtimes and evenings, 7 days a week*. Twice monthly quiz, pub games and *summer* barbecues. Garden. Children welcome. *Open 12.00-14.00 & 18.00-23.00 (Fri, Sat & Sun 16.30-23.00)*.

⚑ **George & Dragon** Stoke Golding (01455 213268). Inexpensive, interesting and varied food available *lunchtimes and evenings, 7 days a week*. Tetley, Marston's and Bass real ales. Children and vegetarians catered for. Garden and children's play area. Book if eating *after 20.00*.

⚑ ✕ **Dog & Hedgehog** Dadlington (01455 212629). A most deceptive pub, tiny from the outside but able to seat upwards of 80 diners *(L & D, 7 days a week)* in its air-conditioned, ex-malthouse dining room and minstrels gallery.

Bass, Worthington and guest real ales. Children and vegetarians well catered for as are horses who have their own tethers and menu *outside*. No smoking dining room. Booking advisable *evenings and Sun lunchtimes*.

⚑ ✕ **Hercules Inn** Sutton Cheney, Nr Market Bosworth, Nuneaton (01455 292591). Theakston and guest real ales. Bar food and snacks *lunchtimes and evenings, 7 days a week* – booking advisable for *Sun lunch*. Children and vegetarians catered for. Patio. No food *Mon lunchtimes or Sun & Mon evenings*. Good value meal deals *Tue & Thu evenings*. Quiz *twice a month*; music *once a month*.

✕ ⚐ **Almshouse** Sutton Cheney, Nr Market Bosworth, Nuneaton (01455 291050). Lunches, afternoon teas and evening meals. Charming dining room, covered veranda and intimate garden seating. Barbecue area. Children and vegetarians catered for. B & B. Booking advisable.

⚑ ✕ **Royal Arms** Sutton Cheney, Nr Market Bosworth, Nuneaton (01455 290263). Marston's, Morland and four rotating guest real ales. Food (including six vegetarian dishes) is available *lunchtimes and evenings, 7 days a week*. Children welcome. B & B.

Boatyards

Ⓑ **The Barge** Hinckley Lane, Higham on the Hill, Nuneaton (01455 234213). Long-term mooring.

Ⓑ **Ashby Boat Company** The Canal Wharf, Stoke Golding, Nuneaton (01455 212671). 🚿 🚽 ⛽ D E Pump-out, narrow boat hire, gas, day hire craft, overnight mooring, long-term mooring, winter storage, chandlery, books, maps and gifts, boat building and fitting out, boat sales and repairs, engine sales and repairs, tea room, toilets, telephone. Emergency call-out.

Ⓑ **Ashby Canal Centre** Willow Park Marina, Stoke Golding, Nuneaton (01455 212636). ⛽ D Pump-out, short and long-term moorings, winter storage, crane, slipway, covered wet dock, boat brokerage, boat building and fitting-out, boat painting, engine sales, DIY facilities, boat and engine repairs, chandlery, solid fuel, boat surveys, books, maps, toilets. Emergency call-out.

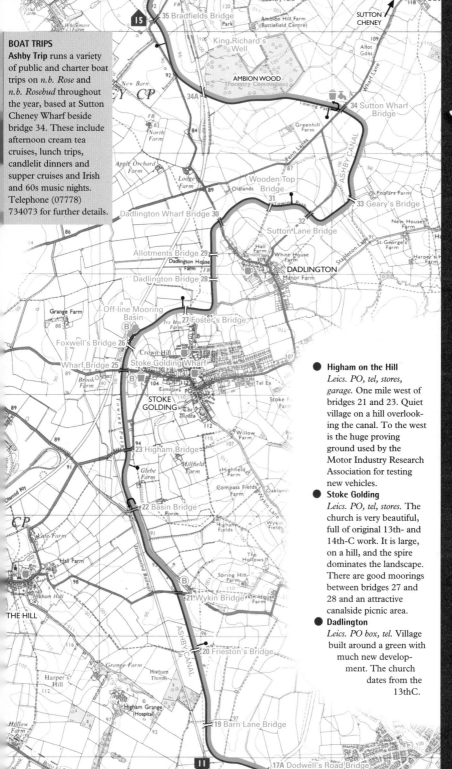

BOAT TRIPS
Ashby Trip runs a variety of public and charter boat trips on *n.b. Rose* and *n.b. Rosebud* throughout the year, based at Sutton Cheney Wharf beside bridge 34. These include afternoon cream tea cruises, lunch trips, candlelit dinners and supper cruises and Irish and 60s music nights. Telephone (07778) 734073 for further details.

35 Bradfields Bridge

34 Sutton Wharf Bridge

33 Geary's Bridge

32 Sutton Lane Bridge

31 Wooden Top Bridge

30 Dadlington Wharf Bridge

29 Allotments Bridge

28 Dadlington Bridge

27 Foster's Bridge

26 Foxwell's Bridge

25 Wharf Bridge

23 Higham Bridge

22 Basin Bridge

21 Wykin Bridge

20 Frieston's Bridge

19 Barn Lane Bridge

17A Dodwell's Road Bridge

Off-line Mooring Basin

Crown Hill

Stoke Golding Wharf

STOKE GOLDING

THE HILL

DADLINGTON

● **Higham on the Hill**
Leics. PO, tel, stores, garage. One mile west of bridges 21 and 23. Quiet village on a hill overlooking the canal. To the west is the huge proving ground used by the Motor Industry Research Association for testing new vehicles.

● **Stoke Golding**
Leics. PO, tel, stores. The church is very beautiful, full of original 13th- and 14th-C work. It is large, on a hill, and the spire dominates the landscape. There are good moorings between bridges 27 and 28 and an attractive canalside picnic area.

● **Dadlington**
Leics. PO box, tel. Village built around a green with much new development. The church dates from the 13thC.

Market Bosworth

Just before Shenton Aqueduct there are good moorings for the Battlefield Centre. Shenton Park is passed on an embankment, and then the aqueduct carries the canal over the road to Shenton village. It continues towards Congerstone, with Market Bosworth and Carlton away to the east. Beyond Congerstone the navigation crosses the River Sence.

● **Shenton**
Leics. Tel. Estate village clustered around the Hall, a house of 1629 much rebuilt in the 19thC.
Battle of Bosworth Field 22 August 1485 Ambion Hill, Sutton Cheney. The battlefield where Richard III, last of the Plantagenets, was killed by Henry Tudor who thus became Henry VII. ³/₄ mile walk from Shenton Embankment to the **Bosworth Battlefield Visitor Centre** Sutton Cheney, Market Bosworth (01455 290429). Award-winning interpretation of the battle. Cafeteria, shop. Toilets. Visitor Centre *open Apr–Oct, Mon–Fri 13.00–17.00, Sat, Sun & B. Hols 11.00–18.00; Jul & Aug opens 11.00, irregular winter opening, telephone for details.* Charge. Footpaths *open all year in daylight hours.* Disabled access to Visitor Centre and Battlefield Trails.
Whitemoors Antique and Craft Centre Main Street, Shenton, Market Bosworth (01455 212250). Craft and antique centre. Tearooms. *Open all year (except Xmas Eve & Xmas Day), daily 11.00–17.00.*

● **Market Bosworth**
Leics. MD Wed. PO, tel, stores, garage, chemist, bank. Almost a mile east of its wharf. Small market town remaining much as it was in the 18thC.
Battlefield Line Shackerstone Station, Shackerstone (01827 880754). Preserved railway line. A ride can be linked in with a visit to the Bosworth Battlefield Visitor Centre.
Bosworth Water Trust Market Bosworth (01455 291876). Just to the west of Bosworth Wharf bridge 42. Large leisure park with a 20-acre lake for

water pursuits. Wetsuits and craft for hire. Changing rooms, toilets, showers and snack bar *open during main season.* Site *open all year, daily 10.00–dusk.* Charge.
Cadeby Experience The Old Rectory, Cadeby, Nuneaton (01455 290462). South east of Market Bosworth. The museum houses the Boston Collection of model and miniature railways and agricultural road vehicles. *Open on some Sats, telephone to confirm.* Donations.
Snibston Discovery Park Ashby Road, Coalville (01530 510851). *24hr* information line (01530) 813256. See page 17 for further details. Feasible to access this all-weather attraction by bus from Market Bosworth. Route no 179 *Mon–Sat five times daily,* terminating in Memorial Square, Coalville. Further details from Busline (0116 251 1411).
Tourist Information Centre Bosworth Battlefield Visitor Centre, Sutton Cheney, Market Bosworth (01455 292841).

● **Congerstone**
Leics. Tel. Scattered village of small interest.

Pubs and Restaurants

🍺 ✕ **Black Horse** Market Place, Market Bosworth (01455 290278). Tetley, John Smith's, Marston's and guest real ales. Snacks and meals available *lunchtimes and evenings, 7 days a week* in bars and restaurant. There is always a vegetarian dish of the day. Children welcome. Patio area.
✕ **Victorian Tea Parlour** Wheatsheaf Courtyard, Market Bosworth (01827 880669). Off the Market Place. Coffees, teas and light lunches. Children and vegetarians catered for. *Open daily 10.00–17.00.*
🍺 **Dixie Arms** Market Bosworth (01455 290218). In the town centre. Burton Bridge and Bass real ales. Food available *lunchtimes and evenings (Mon–Sat) and Sunday lunches.* Vegetarians and children catered for.

🍺 **Ye Olde Red Lion Hotel** Market Bosworth (01455 291713). In town centre. Banks's, Marston's, Camerons, Theakston and guest real ales. Snacks and meals are available *lunchtimes, evenings and all day Sat and some Sun.* Children and vegetarians catered for. Open fires and pub games. Garden and camping. Open *all day Sat.* B & B.
🍺 **Gate Hangs Well** Carlton (01455 291845). Marston's, Mansfield and Greene King real ales. Bar snacks *lunchtimes and evenings 7 days a week.* Traditional Sun *lunches.* Children and vegetarians catered for. Conservatory, garden and children's play area.
🍺 ✕ **Horse & Jockey** Congerstone (01827

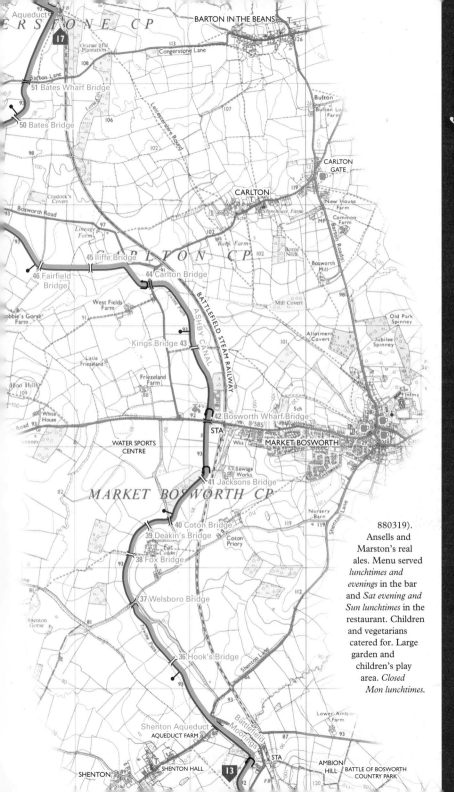

880319).
Ansells and
Marston's real
ales. Menu served
*lunchtimes and
evenings* in the bar
and *Sat evening and
Sun lunchtimes* in the
restaurant. Children
and vegetarians
catered for. Large
garden and
children's play
area. *Closed
Mon lunchtimes.*

Snarestone

After Gopsall Park the hills become more prominent, although the quality of the landscape does not change. There is an attractive picnic area beside Gopsall Wharf Bridge and a house selling duck eggs beside bridge 59. Snarestone sits on a ridge at right angles to the canal, which passes beneath the village through the tunnel, the only one on the canal. After the tunnel there are two more stone-arched bridges, and then the present terminus is reached. There is a winding hole, sanitary station, water point and picnic area. The Ashby Canal Association (01455 614816) provides a car park and slipway for its members. The canal once continued for another 8 miles to Moira, passing through Measham on the way; constant trouble from subsidence made it impossible to retain this last section. The present terminus means that the Ashby Canal is idyllic and rural throughout its length. There is no hint of the deep coal mines (now all closed) and heavy industry that prompted its creation. Ambitious plans are now well under way to re-open the canal through to its original terminus: the first part of the closed section to be re-watered will be at Moira, near the Furnace. In Measham a novel solution to re-routing the waterway through the town is to use the redundant railway line, passing through the abandoned station, which could become a museum. This revival of the Ashby Canal is seen as an integral part of the National Forest scheme for the area and would link in with the restored Moira Furnace and the Heart of the Forest Visitor Centre.

Pubs and Restaurants

Rising Sun Shackerstone (01827 880215). Marston's and guest real ales served in a wood-panelled bar in this old village pub. Food available *lunchtimes and evenings, 7 days a week.* Children and vegetarians catered for. Garden and *Fri* entertainment *in winter.* Pool.

Globe Inn Main Street, Snarestone, Swadlincote (01530 270272). Bass, Marston's, Worthington and Theakston real ales served in a relaxed and friendly atmosphere. Boaters are welcomed and reasonably priced meals and snacks are available in both the bar and restaurant *lunchtimes, evenings and all day Sat &Sun.* Vegetarians catered for and children's menu. Large garden and children's play area. Darts, dominoes and crib. Dogs welcome in the bar. B & B. *All day opening.*

● **Shackerstone**

Leics. Undeveloped and unchanged, Shackerstone is a farming village that reflects the pre-industrial feeling of the whole of the Ashby Canal. West of the village the canal flanks Gopsall Park; the house where Handel is reputed to have composed the *Messiah* was pulled down in 1951, and the park has since lost its original dignity and quality.

Battlefield Line Shackerstone Station, Shackerstone (01827 880754). Although the railway line that follows the Ashby Canal is now closed, the former Shackerstone Junction station (near canal bridge 52) has come to life again as a small railway museum (*open weekends 11.30–17.30*) and a depot for preserved steam locomotives which run 9-mile round trips to Shenton, via Market Bosworth, on *Sun (Mar–Nov) & Wed (Jul & Aug)*. Diesel trains operate services on *Sat (Apr–Oct), Wed (May, Jun & Sep), Fri (Jun–Aug)*. Victorian tearooms and on-train catering with bar. Souvenir shop. Charge. Can be linked in with a visit to the Bosworth Battlefield Centre.

● **Snarestone**

Leics. Tel. An 18th-C farming village built over the top of the canal, which passes underneath through the crooked tunnel (250yds). The Victorian Gothic water-works, 1/2 mile north, mark the end of the canal. The *nearest PO and shop* is now in Measham, a 20 minute walk away along the footpath following the line of the (currently) abandoned canal.

Measham Museum 56 High Street, Measham (01530 273956).

Follow the line of the old canal, from the present terminus at Snarestone, into Measham. Opposite St Lawrence's church. A uniquely personal history of a small community spanning 100 years as seen through the documents, artefacts and illustrations preserved by a former village doctor and his father. *Open Tue 10.00–12.00 & 14.00–17.00, Sat 10.00–12.00.* Donations appreciated.

Snibston Discovery Park Ashby Road, Coalville (01530 510851). *24hr* information line 01530 813256. A unique mixture of science, the environment and history together with brief glimpses into the future in an all-weather setting. Visitors can discover the wonders of technology through over 30 hands-on experiments and experience Leicestershire's rich industrial heritage. Four galleries embrace transport, engineering, extractives and textiles and fashion. Colliery tours, led by ex-miners, explore nearby mine buildings. The site includes 100 acres of landscaped grounds with nature reserve, fishing lakes, sculpture trail and picnic areas (indoor and outdoor). Site railway, coffee and gift shops. *Open daily Apr–Oct 10.00–18.00; Nov–Mar 10.00–17.00. Closed Xmas Day & Box. Day.* Charge. Whilst the Discovery Park is not adjacent to the canal it can make a very worthwhile (wet-weather) day out and is accessible by bus from Hinckley, Market Bosworth, Snarestone and Measham. From Snarestone and Measham Stevenson's Buses (route no 97) run *in the morning Mon–Sat,* terminating in Memorial Square, Coalville – approx 800yds from the site entrance. Contact Busline (0116 251 1411) for further details. Bus details from Hinckley and Market Bosworth appear on previous pages.

Tourist Information Centre Snibston Discovery Park, Ashby Road, Coalville (01530 813608). Opening hours as per the Discovery Park.

BIRMINGHAM CANAL NAVIGATIONS (BCN) – MAIN LINE

MAXIMUM DIMENSIONS
Length: 70'
Beam: 6' 10"
Headroom: 6' 6"

MANAGER
0121 506 1300

MILEAGES

Birmingham Canal new main line
BIRMINGHAM Gas Street to
SMETHWICK JUNCTION (old main line):
2⁷/8 miles
BROMFORD JUNCTION: 4⁷/8 miles
PUDDING GREEN JUNCTION
(Wednesbury Old Canal): 5⁵/8 miles
TIPTON FACTORY JUNCTION
(old main line): 8³/4 miles
DEEPFIELDS JUNCTION
(Wednesbury Oak loop): 10 miles
Bradley Workshops: 2¹/4 miles
HORSELEY FIELDS JUNCTION
(Wyrley & Essington Canal): 13 miles
Wolverhampton Top Lock: 13¹/2 miles
ALDERSLEY JUNCTION
(Staffordshire & Worcestershire Canal): 15¹/8
miles
Locks: 24

Birmingham Canal old main line
SMETHWICK JUNCTION to
SPON LANE JUNCTION: 1¹/2 miles
OLDBURY JUNCTION
(Titford Canal, 6 locks): 2¹/2 miles

BRADESHALL JUNCTION
(Gower Branch, 3 locks): 3¹/2 miles
Aqueduct over Netherton Tunnel Branch:
4³/8 miles
TIPTON JUNCTION (Dudley Canal):
5¹/2 miles
FACTORY JUNCTION (new main line):
6 miles
Locks: 9

Dudley No. 1 Canal
TIPTON JUNCTION to
Dudley Tunnel (north end): 3/8 miles
PARK HEAD JUNCTION: 2³/8 miles
Delph Bottom Lock (Stourbridge Canal):
4¹/2 miles
Locks: 12

Dudley No. 2 Canal
PARK HEAD JUNCTION to
WINDMILL END JUNCTION: 2⁵/8 miles
HAWNE BASIN: 5¹/2 miles
No locks

Netherton Tunnel Branch
WINDMILL END JUNCTION to
DUDLEY PORT JUNCTION: 2⁷/8 miles
No locks

Currently a British Waterways T–shaped anti-vandal key is needed for Wolverhampton locks. Other lock flights on the BCN are under review for similar treatment

The Birmingham Canal Company was authorised in 1768 to build a canal from Aldersley on the Staffordshire & Worcestershire Canal to Birmingham. With James Brindley as engineer the work proceeded quickly. The first section, from Birmingham to the Wednesbury collieries, was opened in November 1769, and the whole 22¹/2-mile route was completed in 1772. It was a winding, contour canal, with 12 locks taking it over Smethwick, and another 20 (later 21) taking it down through Wolverhampton to Aldersley Junction. As the route of the canal was through an area of mineral wealth and developing industry, its success was immediate. Pressure of traffic caused the summit level at Smethwick to be lowered in the 1790s (thus cutting out six locks – three on either side of the summit), and during the same period branches began to reach out towards Walsall via the Ryder's Green Locks, and towards Fazeley. Out of this very profitable and ambitious first main line there grew the Birmingham Canal Navigations, more commonly abbreviated to BCN.

As traffic continued to increase so did the wealth of the BCN. The pressures of trade made the main line at Smethwick very congested and brought grave problems of water supply. Steam pumping engines were installed in several places to recirculate the water, and the company appointed Thomas Telford to shorten Brindley's old main line. Between 1825 and 1838 he engineered a new main line between Deepfields and Birmingham, using massive cuttings and embankments to maintain a continuous level. These improvements not only increased the amount of available waterway (the old line remaining in use), but also shortened the route from Birmingham to Wolverhampton by 7 miles.

Railway control of the BCN meant an expansion of the use of the system, and a large number of interchange basins were built to promote outside trade by means of rail traffic. This was of course quite contrary to the usual effect of railway competition upon canals. Trade continued to grow in relation to industrial development and by the end of the 19thC it was topping $8^1/2$ million tons per annum. A large proportion of this trade was local, being dependent upon the needs and output of Black Country industry. After the turn of the century this reliance on local trade started the gradual decline of the system as deposits of raw materials became exhausted. Factories bought from further afield and developed along the railways and roads away from the canals. Yet as late as 1950 there were over a million tons of trade and the system continued in operation until the end of the coal trade in 1967 (although there was some further traffic for the Birmingham Salvage Department), a pattern quite different from canals as a whole. Nowadays there is no recognisable commercial traffic – a dramatic contrast to the roaring traffic on the newer Birmingham motorways.

As trade declined, so parts of the system fell out of use and were abandoned. In its heyday in 1865, the BCN comprised over 160 miles of canal. Today just over 100 miles remain. However, all the surviving canals of the BCN are of great interest; excellent for leisure cruising, walking and cycling, they represent a most vivid example of living history and will reward exploration – one of the most important monuments to the Industrial Revolution.

Much has been done in recent years in landscaping waste land (as at the south end of Dudley Tunnel), dredging old basins (such as at the top of the Wolverhampton 21) and restoring disused buildings (such as the Pump House at Smethwick). The Birmingham Canal Partnership (British Waterways, Birmingham City Council, Groundwork Birmingham and various other departments and partners including European funds) is implementing a programme of improvements, having recognised the unique recreational potential of the canal system and its value as an area of retreat for the harassed city dweller and as a new area of exploration for the canal traveller.

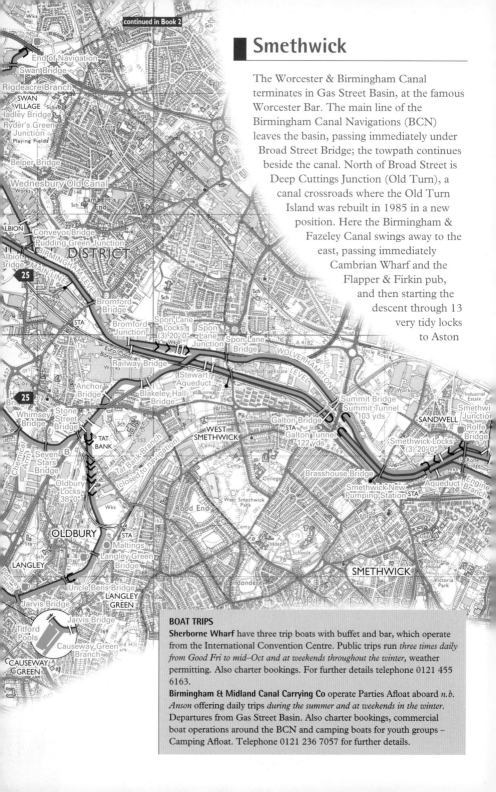

Smethwick

The Worcester & Birmingham Canal terminates in Gas Street Basin, at the famous Worcester Bar. The main line of the Birmingham Canal Navigations (BCN) leaves the basin, passing immediately under Broad Street Bridge; the towpath continues beside the canal. North of Broad Street is Deep Cuttings Junction (Old Turn), a canal crossroads where the Old Turn Island was rebuilt in 1985 in a new position. Here the Birmingham & Fazeley Canal swings away to the east, passing immediately Cambrian Wharf and the Flapper & Firkin pub, and then starting the descent through 13 very tidy locks to Aston

BOAT TRIPS

Sherborne Wharf have three trip boats with buffet and bar, which operate from the International Convention Centre. Public trips run *three times daily from Good Fri to mid–Oct and at weekends throughout the winter*, weather permitting. Also charter bookings. For further details telephone 0121 455 6163.

Birmingham & Midland Canal Carrying Co operate Parties Afloat aboard *n.b. Anson* offering daily trips *during the summer and at weekends in the winter*. Departures from Gas Street Basin. Also charter bookings, commercial boat operations around the BCN and camping boats for youth groups – Camping Afloat. Telephone 0121 236 7057 for further details.

Junction (see page 30). The main line turns west at Farmer's Bridge, while the short Oozell's Street loop goes to the south, quickly disappearing behind old warehouses. This loop, which now houses a boatyard and moorings, and the others further along, are surviving parts of Brindley's original contour canal, now known as the Birmingham Canal Old Main Line. The delays caused by this prompted the Birmingham Canal Company to commission Telford to build a straighter line, the Birmingham Canal New Main Line. This was constructed between 1823 and 1838, and when completed reduced Brindley's old $22\frac{1}{2}$-mile canal to 15 miles. The Oozell's Street loop reappears from the south, and then, after two bridges, the Icknield Port loop leaves to the south. This loop acts as a feeder from Rotton Park Reservoir and rejoins after $\frac{1}{4}$ mile at another canal crossroads – the Winson Green or Soho loop, which leaves the main line opposite the Icknield Port loop. This last loop is the longest of the three, running in a gentle arc for over a mile before rejoining the main line again. It is also the only loop to have a towpath throughout its length. At its eastern end is Hockley Port, formerly railway-owned but now used residential moorings. There are houseboats, a community hall, dry docks and workshops. The main line continues towards Smethwick Junction. Here there is a choice of routes: Brindley's old main line swings to the right, while Telford's new main line continues straight ahead – the old line is the more interesting of the two. The two routes run side by side, but the old line climbs to a higher level via the three Smethwick Locks. Here there were two flights of locks side by side. Beyond the junction, Telford's new line enters a steep-sided cutting. This 40ft-deep cutting enabled Telford to avoid the

NAVIGATIONAL NOTES

Since the Titford Canal is the highest level on the BCN, it is advisable to telephone the BW Waterway Office (0121 506 1300) to check that there is adequate water before you visit the canal.

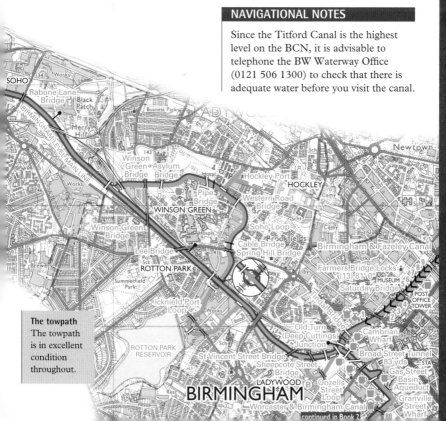

The towpath
The towpath is in excellent condition throughout.

changes in level of the old line and thus speed the flow of traffic. The two routes continue their parallel courses, the one overlooking the other, until the lower line passes under the Telford Aqueduct. This elegant single span cast iron structure carries the Engine Branch, a short feeder canal that leaves the old line, crosses the new line and then turns back to the south for a short distance. This arm is named after the first Boulton & Watt steam pumping engine to be bought by the Birmingham Canal Company. This continued to feed the old summit level for 120 years. It was then moved to Ocker Hill for preservation and demonstrations, until the 1950s, when it was finally retired. The sides of the cutting are richly covered with wild flowers and blackberry bushes, and the seclusion of the whole area has turned it into an unofficial nature reserve. The old pumping station at Brasshouse Lane has been restored after years of disuse as part of the new Galton Valley Canal Park development. A Tangyes Engine has been installed to replace the original. The New Main Line continues through natural wilderness to Galton Tunnel. Telford's Galton Bridge crosses the cutting in one magnificent 150ft cast iron span. This bridge is preserved as an ancient monument. The old and the new Birmingham canal lines continue their parallel course, and soon the pleasant semi-rural isolation of the cutting ends, to be replaced by a complex meeting of three types of transport system. The M5 motorway swings in from the east, carried high above the canal on slender concrete pillars; the railway stays close beside Telford's new line; and the canals enter a series of junctions that seem to anticipate modern motorway practice. The new line leaves the cutting and continues in a straight line through industrial surroundings. It passes under Stewart Aqueduct and then reaches Bromford Junction. Here a canal sliproad links the old and the new lines via the three Spon Lane Locks, joining the new at an angle from the east. Note the unusual split bridge at Spon Lane top lock, which was rebuilt in 1986. The old line swings south west following the 473ft contour parallel to the M5, crossing the new line on Stewart Aqueduct. Thus canal crosses canal on a flyover. Spon Lane Locks, the linking sliproad, survive unchanged from Brindley's day and are among the oldest in the country. The old and the new lines now follow separate courses. The old line continues below the motorway to Oldbury Locks Junction. Here the short Titford Canal climbs away to the south via the six Oldbury Locks; this canal serves as a feeder from Titford Pools to Rotton Park Reservoir. After the junction the old line swings round to the north west and continues on a parallel course to the new line once again, passing the old Les Allen boatbuilding yard. After Bromford Junction the new line continues its straight course towards Wolverhampton. At Pudding Green Junction the main line goes straight on; the Wednesbury Old Canal forks right to join the Walsall Canal, which in turn joins the Tame Valley Canal at Doebank Junction.

● The Titford Canal

Built in 1837 as part of the original Birmingham Canal scheme, acting as a feeder to Spon Lane, the Titford Canal served Causeway Green. This must have been a very busy canal in its heyday, with many branches, wharves and tramways connecting it to the surrounding mines and engineering works. Today it survives in shortened form and has the distinction of being the highest navigable part of the BCN, with a summit level above Oldbury Locks of 511ft. The locks are sometimes referred to as the Crow – a branch which left the canal above the third lock and served the alkali and phosphorus works of a local industrialist and benefactor Jim Crow. The last surviving recirculatory pumping station, now severely damaged by fire, can be seen by the top lock. It is hoped that BW, in partnership with the local Canal Society, can raise funds for its restoration. The waterway now terminates at the wide expanse of water of Titford Pools, scene of IWA Rallies in 1978 and 1982. It is well worth making the short diversion off the main line (see navigational note), and both walkers and cyclists will find the towpath in good condition and access easy. The canal leaves the Old Main Line at Oldbury Junction, under the M5 motorway. What is now a sterile place was once the base of Thomas Claytons of Oldbury, one of the last carriers to operate on the BCN, finally ending operations in 1966. Their boats carried mainly liquid cargoes of crude tar and gas water to the Springfield Tar Distillery, whose wharf can be seen to the left below the first lock. There is an attractive lock cottage, and the locks themselves are handsome, with wooden balance beams and traditional paddle gear. Locks 2 to 5 are enclosed by large side ponds.

Above the third lock the sealed off entrance to the Jim Crow Arm can be seen on the towpath side. The Tat Bank Branch, which leaves the main line above the top lock, was one of the last narrow canals to be built and now serves as a feeder to Rotton Park Reservoir. Beyond the next bridge are the old buildings of Langley Forge, where castings are still produced. A 1¹/₂

ton steam drop hammer, installed in 1900, is still in use here. After passing through Jarvis Bridge the canal splits into the Old Causeway Green and Portway Branches, connecting with Titford Pools. The M5 motorway passes high above, on stilts. At Uncle Bens Bridge there is a *PO, take-away and a useful selection of shops.* **Tourist Information Centre** see page 31.

Boatyards

Ⓑ **Sherborne Wharf** Sherborne Street Wharf, Birmingham (0121 455 6163). On the Oozell's Street Loop. 🚿 🚽 ♿ D E Pump-out, gas, day hire boats, overnight mooring, long-term mooring, wet docks, winter storage, chandlery, boat sales and repairs, engine sales and repairs, books, maps and gifts, boat fitting-out, DIY facilities, telephone, electrical hook-up, solid

fuel, toilets, showers, groceries. *24hr* emergency call-out.
Ⓑ **Oldbury Boat Services** Oldbury Wharf, Stone Street Bridge, Oldbury (0121 544 1795). D Gas, long-term mooring, winter storage, boat and engine repairs, chandlery, boat fitting-out, maps, solid fuel. Emergency call-out.

Pubs and Restaurants

In a large city such as Birmingham there are many fine pubs and restaurants. As a result of the recent development of the area adjoining the canal, between Gas Street Basin and Cambrian Wharf, there are now approaching two dozen eating and drinking establishments. This choice is further expanded by walking south along Broad Street, from Broad Street Bridge, at Gas Street Basin. However beyond the canalside the enterprising boater (walker and cyclist) might like to seek out some of the City's more diverse hostelries:
🍺 **Flapper & Firkin** Cambrian Wharf, Kingston Row (0121 236 2421). Firkin real ales in a student type pub. Food *lunchtimes and evenings,* with vegetarian choices. Children welcome, and there is table football, Giant Jenga and Connect-4. Outside terrace seating by the basin. *Open all day.* Light music most evenings.
🍺 **Figure of Eight** 236-239 Broad Street (0121 633 0917). Sensibly priced Banks's, Courage, Theakston, Younger and guest real ales in a pub handy for Gas Street Basin. Food *lunchtimes and evenings,* outside seating and no smoking area. Disabled access. *Open all day.*
🍺 **Anchor** 308 Bradford Street (0121 622 4516). Food available *lunchtimes and evenings* together with Ansells, Tetley and guest real ales in a Victorian pub tucked away behind the Digbeth coach station. Also an excellent range of bottled beers from far and wide. Outside seating. *Open all day.*
🍺 **Old Contemptibles** 176 Edmund Street (0121 236 5264). Bass, M & B, Hook Norton and Highgate real ales in popular

drinkers pub. Food *Mon-Fri evenings until 20.00 and Sat lunchtimes. Open all day Mon– Sat, closed Sun.*
🍺 **Gunmaker's Arms** Bath Street (0121 236 1201). Bass and M & B real ales. Food *lunchtimes and evenings.* Outside seating and pub games. *Open all day Mon-Fri. Closed Sun evenings.*
🍺 **White Swan** 57 Grosvenor Street, Five Ways (0121 643 6064). Near Tesco's. Traditional two-roomed city pub, with a wide ranging clientele, dispensing Ansells, HP&D, Marston's and Tetley real ales together with food *lunchtimes and evenings.* Pub games and no machines.
🍺 **Black Eagle** 16 Factory Road, Hockley (0121 523 4008). North of Hockley Port. Ansells, Marston's and guest real ales. Food available *lunchtimes and evenings.* Outside seating. Booking advisable for meals.
🍺 **Olde Windmill** 84 Dudley Road, Winson Green (0121 455 6907). East of Lee Bridge, opposite the hospital. M & B and guest real ales in a compact, traditional old pub. *Lunchtime* food, beer garden and pub games. *Open all day.*
🍺 **Finings & Firkin** 91 Station Road, Langley (0121 544 6467). A range of Firkin real ales brewed and dispensed in the old HP&D brewery tap. Friendly, welcoming atmosphere; pub games and *lunchtime* bar snacks. *Open all day.*
🍺 **New Navigation** Jarvis Bridge, Langley. Ansells real ale in a canalside brewery pub. *Lunchtime* food.
🍺 **Whiteheath Tavern** 400 Birchfield Lane, Whiteheath (0121 552 3603). Just west of Titford Pools, near M5 junction 2. Ansells and Banks's real ales. Traditional pub games.

Dudley

At Bradeshall Junction the Gower Branch links the two lines, descending to the lower level of the new line through three locks. To the south west of Tipton Junction is the branch leading to the Black Country Museum and the Dudley Tunnel. This branch connects with the Dudley Canal, the Stourbridge Canal, and thus with the Staffordshire & Worcestershire Canal. The old line turns north at the junction, rejoining the new line at Factory Junction. At Albion Junction the Gower Branch turns south to join the old line at Bradeshall. At Dudley Port Junction the Netherton Tunnel Branch joins the main line. The Netherton Tunnel Branch goes through the tunnel to Windmill End Junction; from here boats can either turn south down the old Dudley Canal to Hawne Basin, or west towards the Stourbridge Canal, and thus to the Staffordshire & Worcestershire Canal. North of Dudley Port the new line crosses a main road on the Ryland Aqueduct. Continuing its elevated course the new line reaches Tipton, where there are moorings with shops close by, and a small basin. The new line climbs the three Factory Locks and immediately reaches Factory Junction, where the old line comes in from the south. There are good moorings at Coseley Stop. Beyond, the canal continues straight to Deepfields Junction. Here the old canal swings away to the east on the Wednesbury Oak Loop.

Pubs and Restaurants

Old Court House Lower Church Lane (0121 520 2865). North east of Dudley Port Station. Bar meals *lunchtimes and evenings Mon–Sat.*

Bottle & Glass Inn Black Country Living Museum, Tipton Road, Dudley (0121 557 9643). Holden's real ale in a wonderful old pub, moved to the site. Sandwiches available *all day. Open 10.00–17.00.* More substantial refreshment available in the adjoining Stables Restaurant and 1930s fish & chip shop.

Port 'N' Ale 178 Horsley Heath, Tipton (0121 557 7249). One of the rare, genuine free houses left dispensing Enville, Highgate, RCH and at least three more guest real ales. Perry is often available also. Children's room, outside seating and traditional pub games.

Rising Sun 116 Horsley Road, Tipton (0121 530 9780). North of Dudley Port railway station. *Evening* food *(except Sun)*; Banks's, Marston's and guest real ales and a friendly welcome make this pub worth the walk. Also real cider. Open fires in winter and traditional pub games. Camping.

Barge & Barrel Factory Road, Tipton (0121 520 6962). A recently refurbished pub in a wine bar setting, serving Banks's and Camerons real ale, and inexpensive *lunchtime* bar meals, with vegetarian and children's menus.

Boat Inn Coseley (01902 492993). Banks's, Bass and guest real ales served in a friendly, canalside pub. Snacks and basket meals available *lunchtimes and evenings.* Children welcome. Garden seating and traditional pub games. Karaoke *Wed & Sat evenings.* Barbecue facilities available for patrons use.

Boatyards

Ⓑ **Oldbury Boat Services**
Oldbury Wharf, Stone Street
Bridge, Oldbury (0121 544
1795). See page 23.
Ⓑ **Malthouse Chandlery**
Malthouse Stables, Hurst
Lane, Tipton (01527 510930).
Chandlery, books, maps, gifts.

BOAT TRIPS
The *Aaron Manby* operates
trips from outside the
Malthouse Chandlery.
Telephone 0121 520 7861
for further details.

● **Black
Country Museum**
Tipton Road, Dudley (0121
557 9643). A superb outdoor
museum built around a reconstructed
canalside village, with a pub, shops and an
inland port. See demonstrations of sweet-
making, glass-cutting and metal-working, ride on a
tram or trolly bus, take a boat trip into Dudley Tunnel
or a coalmine tour. And if you have time, participate in an
old-time school lesson, ride on the fairground, watch an old
film and meet the horses and ponies. *Open Mar–Oct, daily
10.00–17.00 & Nov–Feb, Wed–Sun 10.00–16.00.* Charge.

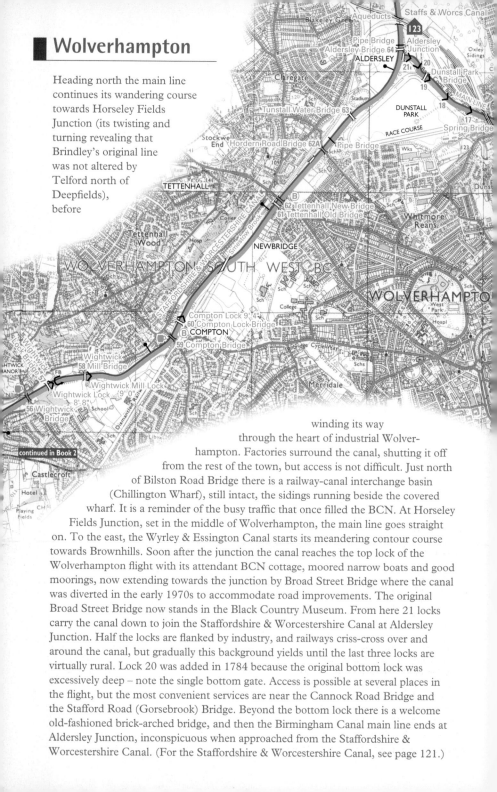

Wolverhampton

Heading north the main line continues its wandering course towards Horseley Fields Junction (its twisting and turning revealing that Brindley's original line was not altered by Telford north of Deepfields), before

winding its way through the heart of industrial Wolverhampton. Factories surround the canal, shutting it off from the rest of the town, but access is not difficult. Just north of Bilston Road Bridge there is a railway-canal interchange basin (Chillington Wharf), still intact, the sidings running beside the covered wharf. It is a reminder of the busy traffic that once filled the BCN. At Horseley Fields Junction, set in the middle of Wolverhampton, the main line goes straight on. To the east, the Wyrley & Essington Canal starts its meandering contour course towards Brownhills. Soon after the junction the canal reaches the top lock of the Wolverhampton flight with its attendant BCN cottage, moored narrow boats and good moorings, now extending towards the junction by Broad Street Bridge where the canal was diverted in the early 1970s to accommodate road improvements. The original Broad Street Bridge now stands in the Black Country Museum. From here 21 locks carry the canal down to join the Staffordshire & Worcestershire Canal at Aldersley Junction. Half the locks are flanked by industry, and railways criss-cross over and around the canal, but gradually this background yields until the last three locks are virtually rural. Lock 20 was added in 1784 because the original bottom lock was excessively deep – note the single bottom gate. Access is possible at several places in the flight, but the most convenient services are near the Cannock Road Bridge and the Stafford Road (Gorsebrook) Bridge. Beyond the bottom lock there is a welcome old-fashioned brick-arched bridge, and then the Birmingham Canal main line ends at Aldersley Junction, inconspicuous when approached from the Staffordshire & Worcestershire Canal. (For the Staffordshire & Worcestershire Canal, see page 121.)

continued in Book 2

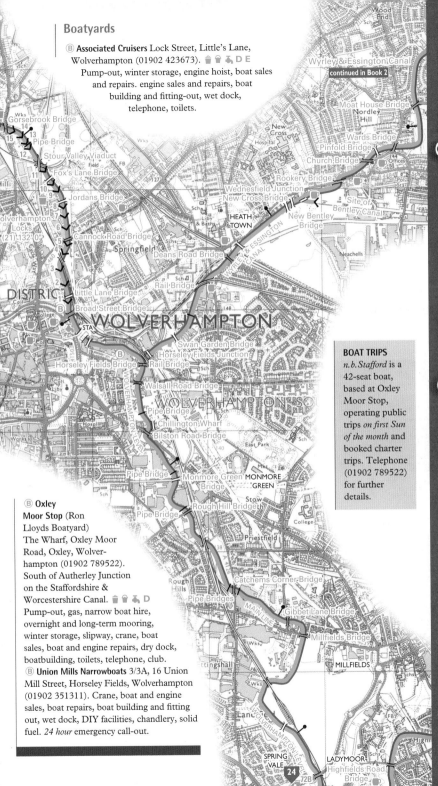

Boatyards

Ⓑ **Associated Cruisers** Lock Street, Little's Lane, Wolverhampton (01902 423673). 🛒🚿⚓ D E
Pump-out, winter storage, engine hoist, boat sales and repairs. engine sales and repairs, boat building and fitting-out, wet dock, telephone, toilets.

Ⓑ **Oxley Moor Stop** (Ron Lloyds Boatyard) The Wharf, Oxley Moor Road, Oxley, Wolverhampton (01902 789522). South of Autherley Junction on the Staffordshire & Worcestershire Canal. 🛒🚿⚓ D
Pump-out, gas, narrow boat hire, overnight and long-term mooring, winter storage, slipway, crane, boat sales, boat and engine repairs, dry dock, boatbuilding, toilets, telephone, club.

Ⓑ **Union Mills Narrowboats** 3/3A, 16 Union Mill Street, Horseley Fields, Wolverhampton (01902 351311). Crane, boat and engine sales, boat repairs, boat building and fitting out, wet dock, DIY facilities, chandlery, solid fuel. *24 hour* emergency call-out.

BOAT TRIPS
n.b. Stafford is a 42-seat boat, based at Oxley Moor Stop, operating public trips *on first Sun of the month* and booked charter trips. Telephone (01902 789522) for further details.

continued in Book 2

Pubs and Restaurants

In a town such as Wolverhampton there are many pubs to choose from. Below are a selection for the enterprising to seek out:

Feathers Molineux Street, Wolverhampton (01902 426924). By the football ground. Banks's real ale in a small friendly local renowned for its garden. *Lunchtime food Mon–Fri.* Pub games. *Open all day Mon-Sat.*

Clarendon Chapel Ash, Wolverhampton (01902 420587). A41, just to the west of the town centre. Refurbished, somewhat to its detriment, this pub offers Banks's and Camerons real ale and *lunchtime and evening food (not Sat & Sun evenings). Also breakfast available from 08.00.* Children's room. *Open all day.*

Kearney's Chapel Ash, Wolverhampton (01902 421880). Banks's and guest real ales served in a terraced house look-alike: both cosy and intimate. Open fires and garden. *Lunchtime* food. Children welcome, disabled access.

Great Western Sun Street, Wolverhampton (01902 351090. Batham and Holden's real ales, railway memorabilia and good local cooking *lunchtimes only (not Sun).* Garden and traditional pub games. Children over 12 years old welcomed.

Lewisham Arms 69 Prosser Street, Wolverhampton (01902 53505). Off the Cannock Road. Archetypal Victorian alehouse complete with etched glass and iron balconies. Banks's real ale and traditional pub games. *Open all day Sat.*

Queen's Arms 13 Graisley Row, Wolverhampton (01902 426589). Off the Stafford Road. Small, welcoming establishment tucked away on an industrial estate serving Burtonwood and Forshaw's real ales. Food available *lunchtimes and evenings Mon–Sat.* Garden and pub games.

The Dog & Doublet pub, Bodymoor Heath (see page 33)

BIRMINGHAM & FAZELEY CANAL

MAXIMUM DIMENSIONS
Length: 70'
Beam: 7'
Headroom: 7' 6"

MILEAGE
FARMER'S BRIDGE JUNCTION
(Birmingham Canal) to ASTON JUNCTION
(Digbeth Branch): 1^1/$_2$ miles
SALFORD JUNCTION (Tame Valley
Canal): 3^1/$_4$ miles
Minworth Top Lock: 6^1/$_4$ miles
Curdworth Tunnel: 8^1/$_2$ miles
Bodymoor Heath Bridge: 11^1/$_2$ miles

FAZELEY JUNCTION (Coventry Canal):
15 miles
Hopwas: 17^3/$_4$ miles
Whittington Brook: 20^1/$_2$ miles

Locks: 38

MANAGER
(01283) 790236

The Birmingham & Fazeley Canal was authorised in 1784, after a great deal of opposition from the well-established Birmingham Canal Company (who very soon merged with it), as a link between Birmingham and the south east. Until then, London-bound goods from Birmingham had to go right round by the River Severn. Naturally, the canal was useless until the Coventry Canal had at least reached Fazeley, but the new Birmingham & Fazeley Company ensured – even before its enabling Act was passed – that the other canals important to its success were completed. Thus at Coleshill in 1782 the Oxford Canal Company agreed to finish its line to Oxford and the Thames; the Coventry Canal Company agreed to extend its line from Atherstone to Fazeley; the new Birmingham & Fazeley Company agreed to build its proposed line and continue it along the defaulting Coventry route from Fazeley to Whittington Brook; and the Trent & Mersey Company pledged to finish the Coventry's line from Whittington Brook to Fradley Junction on the Trent & Mersey Canal.

This rare example of cooperation among canal companies paid off when, in 1790, the great joint programme was finished and traffic immediately began to flow along the system. The Birmingham & Fazeley Company employed John Smeaton to build their canal: he completed it in 1789. The flights of narrow locks at Farmer's Bridge and Aston became very congested, especially after the Warwick canals had joined up with the Birmingham & Fazeley Canal at Digbeth; two new canals were built to bypass this permanent obstacle, one on each side. The Tame Valley Canal and the Birmingham & Warwick Junction Canal were opened in 1844, and traffic flowed more smoothly. After this the Birmingham & Fazeley Canal became more attractive to carriers and it continued to be an important link route. It still provides this link, but is now worthy of exploration in its own right.

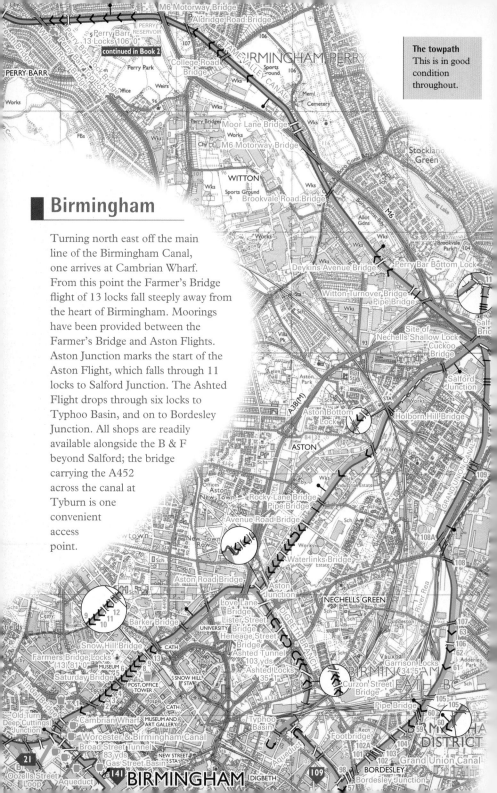

Birmingham

Turning north east off the main line of the Birmingham Canal, one arrives at Cambrian Wharf. From this point the Farmer's Bridge flight of 13 locks fall steeply away from the heart of Birmingham. Moorings have been provided between the Farmer's Bridge and Aston Flights. Aston Junction marks the start of the Aston Flight, which falls through 11 locks to Salford Junction. The Ashted Flight drops through six locks to Typhoo Basin, and on to Bordesley Junction. All shops are readily available alongside the B & F beyond Salford; the bridge carrying the A452 across the canal at Tyburn is one convenient access point.

The Digbeth Branch This leaves the Birmingham & Fazeley main line at Aston Junction, and descends through six locks to Typhoo Basin, where it meets the former Warwick & Birmingham Canal, which became part of the Grand Union Canal when the GUC Company was formed in 1929. There was a stop lock – called Warwick Bar – at the junction by Bordesley Basin. One of the lesser-known tunnels on the canal system is on this branch – Ashted Tunnel. There is a narrow towpath through it, protected by railings and with a corrugated surface for the towing horses to get a good grip on.

Tourist Information Centre Birmingham Convention and Visitor Bureau, City Arcade (0121 643 2514).

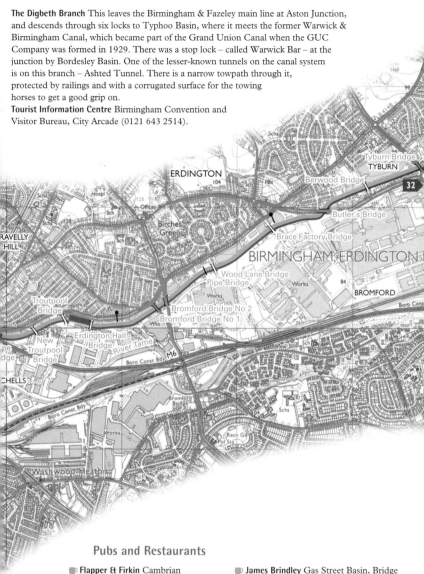

Pubs and Restaurants

Flapper & Firkin Cambrian Wharf, Kingston Row (0121 236 2421). Firkin real ales in a student type pub. Food *lunchtimes and evenings,* with vegetarian choices. Children welcome, and there is table football, Giant Jenga and Connect-4. Outside terrace seating by the basin. *Open all day.* Light music most evenings.

The Malt House Overlooking Deep Cuttings Junction (0121 633 4171). Greenalls real ale and food *12.00–19.00 every day.* Children welcome.

James Brindley Gas Street Basin, Bridge Street (0121 616 7941). Bass and guest real ales and bar meals *lunchtimes and evenings (not Sat evenings).* Vegetarian options. Children welcome *at meal times.* There is a jazz session each *Sun lunchtime.*

Reservoir Cuckoo Bridge, Lichfield Road (0121 327 3336). A friendly pub serving bar meals *lunchtimes and evenings,* with vegetarian choices. Children welcome if eating. Disco each *Sat,* and a monthly quiz.

Curdworth

Most of the factories on this section ignore the canal, although the Cincinnati works are a laudable exception: landscaped lawns and gardens run down from the buildings to the water's edge. Minworth Locks start the descent towards Fazeley, and gradually the canal loses the industry that has accompanied it from Birmingham. Curdworth is passed in a tree-lined cutting: the church tower here has been visible for some time. The cutting continues beyond Curdworth Bridge, and enters a short tunnel (57yds), with the towpath alongside. From now until Fazeley the canal makes its passage in complete isolation through the empty fields, only the 11 locks falling down to Fazeley Junction breaking its journey. The lack of hedges in this area is very noticeable and only those by the towpath seem to have survived. As the canal swings north, hedges and trees thankfully reappear, and after Bodymoor Heath trees line the canal on both sides for two miles. By the bottom lock there is a swing bridge (kept open) which contributes to what is a pretty canal scene. Flooded gravel pits, and the bird life they attract, enliven the surroundings.

● **Tyburn**
Warwicks. PO, tel, stores. A mixture of factories and houses.

● **Minworth**
Warwicks. PO, tel, stores. A mainly residential area on the city outskirts, totally dominated by roads. There is a handy transport café close to Hansons Bridge.

● **Curdworth**
Warwicks. PO, tel, stores, garage. Now set in the shadow of the motorway, and not far from the sewage works, Curdworth still manages to cling to a village identity. The squat church is partly Norman, circa 1170; note the finely carved Norman font, with images of standing men, a monster and a lamb.

● **Bodymoor Heath**
Warwicks. Tel. A scattered village beyond which gravel pits, many flooded, break up the fields. Yet, amidst this broken landscape

there are occasional 18th-C buildings, surviving as a memory of the pre-industrial Midlands. The pub, the Dog & Doublet, is one such example.

Kingsbury Water Park Bodymoor Heath (01827 872660). A 600-acre landscaped park containing 30 lakes and pools, created from gravel pits worked over the last 50 years. Walks, nature trails, fishing, horse riding, sailing, power-boating and windsurfing. There is also a rare breeds farm at Broomey Croft (01827 873844 – charge). Visitor centre and coffee shop. Excellent programme of events *Apr–Sep* (modest charge per event).

Pubs and Restaurants

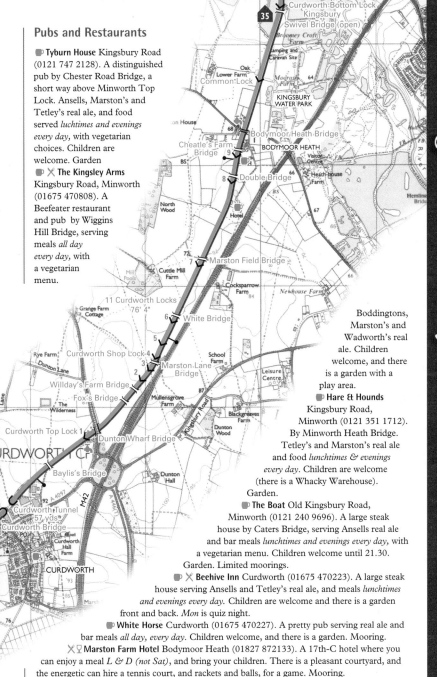

Tyburn House Kingsbury Road (0121 747 2128). A distinguished pub by Chester Road Bridge, a short way above Minworth Top Lock. Ansells, Marston's and Tetley's real ale, and food served *luchtimes and evenings every day*, with vegetarian choices. Children are welcome. Garden

The Kingsley Arms Kingsbury Road, Minworth (01675 470808). A Beefeater restaurant and pub by Wiggins Hill Bridge, serving meals *all day every day*, with a vegetarian menu.

Boddingtons, Marston's and Wadworth's real ale. Children welcome, and there is a garden with a play area.

Hare & Hounds Kingsbury Road, Minworth (0121 351 1712). By Minworth Heath Bridge. Tetley's and Marston's real ale and food *lunchtimes & evenings every day*. Children are welcome (there is a Whacky Warehouse). Garden.

The Boat Old Kingsbury Road, Minworth (0121 240 9696). A large steak house by Caters Bridge, serving Ansells real ale and bar meals *lunchtimes and evenings every day*, with a vegetarian menu. Children welcome until 21.30. Garden. Limited moorings.

Beehive Inn Curdworth (01675 470223). A large steak house serving Ansells and Tetley's real ale, and meals *lunchtimes and evenings every day*. Children are welcome and there is a garden front and back. *Mon* is quiz night.

White Horse Curdworth (01675 470227). A pretty pub serving real ale and bar meals *all day, every day*. Children welcome, and there is a garden. Mooring.

Marston Farm Hotel Bodymoor Heath (01827 872133). A 17th-C hotel where you can enjoy a meal *L & D (not Sat)*, and bring your children. There is a pleasant courtyard, and the energetic can hire a tennis court, and rackets and balls, for a game. Mooring.

Dog & Doublet Dog Lane, Bodymoor Heath (01827 872374). A smart and handsome red-brick canalside pub by Cheatles Farm Bridge, serving Bass, Highgate and guest real ales. Bar meals *lunchtimes and evenings*, with vegetarian options. Canalside garden with good views. Children welcome. A venue well worthy of its popularity. Mooring. B & B.

Fazeley

Continuing north, the canal runs through quiet and attractive open farmland, flanked on both sides by oak trees, their roots often projecting into the water. The isolation of the canal ends at Drayton Bassett where the A4091 swings in to run parallel as far as Fazeley. By Drayton Bassett is a curious footbridge, a marvellous folly, and immediately after it a second swing bridge. These features make the Birmingham & Fazeley Canal pleasantly eccentric, allowing it to end with an unexpected flourish. The countryside then gives way to the outskirts of Fazeley, which are quickly followed by the junction with the Coventry Canal.

● **Drayton Bassett**
Staffs. PO, tel, stores, fish & chips. The village is set 1/2 mile to the west of the canal. The best feature is the charming and totally unexpected Gothic-style footbridge over the canal. Its twin battlemented towers would look quite commanding but for their ridiculously small size. This bridge is unique, and there seems to be no explanation for its eccentricity, thus greatly increasing its attraction.
Drayton Manor Family Theme Park Alongside the canal, off the A4091 at Drayton Manor Bridge. 24 hr recorded information for general enquiries on (01827) 287979. Formerly the site of the house of Sir Robert Peel's father, built 1820–35. The now extinct house was designed by Sir Robert Smirke and the garden, 15 acres of wood and parkland, was originally laid out by William Gilpin. It now has an extensive series of exciting rides, including Storm Force Ten, and amusements. *Open late Mar–Oct, 10.00–late afternoon.* Charge.
● **Fazeley**
Staffs. PO, tel, stores, garage. Its importance as a road and canal junction determines the character of Fazeley; it is a small, industrial centre that has grown up around the communication network. From the canal the town appears more attractive than it really is. Useful as a supply centre.
● **Fazeley Junction**
Staffs. The Birmingham & Fazeley Canal joins the Coventry Canal here. Originally the Coventry Canal was to continue westwards to

meet the Trent & Mersey Canal at Fradley; however, the Coventry company ran out of money at Fazeley, and so the Birmingham & Fazeley Canal continued on to Whittington (this section is covered within the Coventry Canal, for continuity). The Trent & Mersey Company then built a linking arm from Fradley to Whittington, which was later bought by the Coventry Company, thus becoming a detached section of their canal. The junction has been tastefully restored, with good moorings and a canalside seat made from a balance beam, overlooked by a fine navigation office. It was at Fazeley, in the 1790s, that Robert Peel, father of the prime minister, in partnership with Joseph Wilkes, transformed the area, building mills and wharves, chapels and watercourses, and making it a centre of industry that was to last until the depression of the mid-19thC. Just to the south of the canal junction is the Bourne Brook Cut, which has its source in reservoirs to the north of Watling Street and originally supplied the bleach and dye works here. A little further south of the junction, by the Birmingham & Fazeley Canal, is Fazeley Mill, built in 1886 as a tape mill and which has continued as such largely unaltered. Just beyond the next bridge, on the opposite side of the canal, is one of the best surviving mills of the Richard Arkwright pattern, built in 1791 with three storeys and 19 bays. In Coleshill Street a fine terrace of 20 workers' houses can still be seen.

Boatyards

Ⓑ **Fazeley Mill Marina** Coleshill Road, Fazeley (01827 261138). ⚓ D Pump-out, gas, overnight and long-term mooring, solid fuel, DIY facilities.
Ⓑ **Debbies Day Boats** Canal Wharf, Coleshill Road, Fazeley (01827 262042). ⚓ ⚓ Gas, day

hire boats, overnight and long-term mooring, slipway, boat and engine sales and repairs, boat-building, telephone, toilets, chandlery, solid fuel, DIY facilities, emergency call-out.
Ⓑ **BW Fazeley** Peel's Wharf, Fazeley (01827 252000). 200yds west of the junction. ⚓ ⚓ ⚓

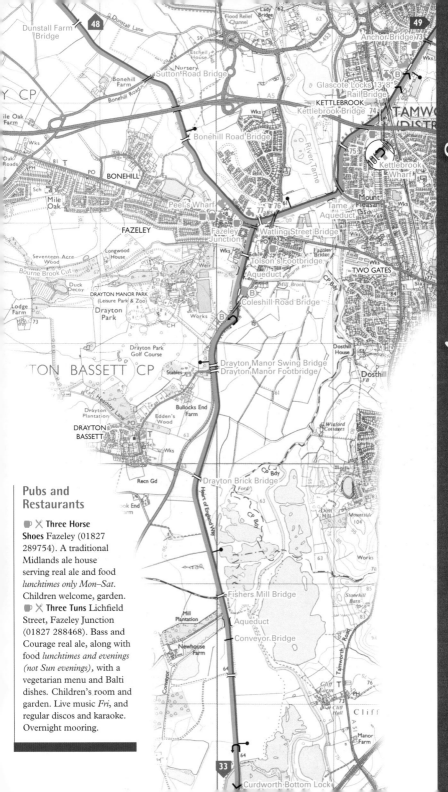

Pubs and Restaurants

▣ ✕ **Three Horse Shoes** Fazeley (01827 289754). A traditional Midlands ale house serving real ale and food *lunchtimes only Mon–Sat*. Children welcome, garden.

▣ ✕ **Three Tuns** Lichfield Street, Fazeley Junction (01827 288468). Bass and Courage real ale, along with food *lunchtimes and evenings (not Sun evenings)*, with a vegetarian menu and Balti dishes. Children's room and garden. Live music *Fri*, and regular discos and karaoke. Overnight mooring.

Coventry Canal, near Hartshill (see page 44)

COVENTRY CANAL

MAXIMUM DIMENSIONS	Hartshill: 14 miles
Length: 70'	Atherstone Top Lock: 16½ miles
Beam: 7'	Polesworth: 21½ miles
Headroom: 6' 6"	Alvecote Priory: 23¼ miles
	Glascote Bottom Lock: 25½ miles
MANAGER	*FAZELEY JUNCTION* (Birmingham &
(01283) 790236	Fazeley Canal): 27 miles
	Hopwas: 29¾ miles
MILEAGE	Whittington Brook: 32½ miles
COVENTRY BASIN to	Huddlesford Junction: 34 miles
HAWKESBURY JUNCTION (Oxford Canal):	*FRADLEY JUNCTION* (Trent & Mersey
5½ miles	Canal): 38 miles
MARSTON JUNCTION (Ashby Canal): 8¼ miles	
Boot Wharf, Nuneaton: 10½ miles	Locks: 13

The Coventry Canal, whose enabling Act of Parliament was passed in 1768, was promoted by pit owners such as the Parrotts of Hawkesbury and the Newdigates of Arbury with two main objectives: to connect the fast-growing town of Coventry with the new trade route called the Grand Trunk, now the Trent & Mersey Canal; and to provide Coventry with cheap coal from Bedworth coalfield, 10 miles to the north. The first, long-term objective was not achieved for some years until the company had overcome financial difficulties, but – wisely – the stretch between Coventry and Bedworth was completed early on, so that the profitable carriage of local coal was quickly established along the canal, in 1769.

By the time the canal reached Atherstone in 1771, all the authorised capital had been spent and James Brindley, the original engineer of the canal, had been sacked. For these reasons – and because of the interminable wrangle with the Oxford Canal Company, whose scheme to link Coventry with southern England had followed hard upon the original Coventry scheme – the Coventry Canal did not reach Fazeley, nearly 12 miles short of its intended terminus at Fradley, until 1790.

By this time, the Birmingham & Fazeley Canal had been built, extending along the Coventry Canal's original proposed line to Whittington Brook, from where the Grand Trunk Canal Company carried it north to Fradley. The Coventry Company later bought this section back, which explains the fact that there is now a detached portion of the Coventry Canal from Whittington Brook to Fradley Junction.

In 1790 also, the Oxford Canal was completed through to Oxford and thus to London by the Thames. The profits of the Coventry Canal rose quickly, and rose even higher when the Grand Junction Canal was completed in 1799, shortening the route to London by 60 miles. Other adjoining canals contributed to the Coventry Canal's prosperity: the Ashby, the Wyrley & Essington and the Trent & Mersey. The extension of the Grand Junction Canal via Warwick to Birmingham naturally dismayed the Coventry, but the numerous locks – and high tolls on the stretch of the Oxford Canal between Braunston and Napton Junctions – ensured that a lot of traffic to and from Birmingham still used the slightly longer route via the Coventry and Birmingham & Fazeley Canals, especially after the Oxford Canal was shortened by 14 miles between Braunston and Longford. The continuous financial success of the Coventry Canal could be attributed both to its being part of so many long distance routes and to the continued prosperity of the coal mines along its way. It was certainly one of the most persistently profitable canals ever built in Britain, paying a dividend until 1947.

Coventry

The Coventry Canal begins at the large Bishop Street Basin, opened in 1769, near the town centre. It is an interesting situation on the side of a hill, overlooked by tall new buildings and attractive old wooden canal warehouses; the warehouses date from 1914, although there were, of course, earlier such buildings on the site. They once stored grain, food and cement, and were well restored in 1984. The old Weighbridge Office is now a shop and information centre, looking out over the basin towards the Vaults, which were used to store coal. The canal leaves the terminus through bridge number 1, a tiny structure designed to be easily closed with a wooden beam each evening: indeed at one time no boats were allowed to stay in the basin overnight (it is now an excellent mooring). At one time there was a toll house here. To the west of this bridge is Canal House, built for the local trader Alderman Clarke. The canal company purchased the house in 1809 and it was used for successive canal managers until 1947, when the last manager of the Coventry Canal, John Kaye, purchased it upon his retirement. It is now owned by the City Council. The canal now begins to wind through what were busy industrial areas towards Hawkesbury: it is in places quite narrow, and often flanked by buildings. Just beyond bridge number 2 are 'Cash's Hundred Houses', an elegant row of weavers houses, where the living accommodation was on the lower two floors, with the top storey being occupied by looms, driven by a single shaft from a steam engine. There never were 100 houses: only 48 were built, and of these only 37 remain. The canal then, after various contortions, continues towards Hawkesbury, passing through the outskirts of Coventry. Before it ducks under the motorway, just beyond bridge number 10, you will notice the canal is wider: this was the site of the original junction between the Oxford and Coventry Canals. It was known as Longford Junction. Hawkesbury Junction, their present meeting, contains all the elements expected of such a notable place: plenty of traditional boats, interesting buildings including a fine engine house, a splendid pub and useful facilities for boaters. To the east of the junction is Hawkesbury Hall (private), at one time the home of mine owner and sponsor of the Coventry Canal, Richard Parrott. The towpath between Coventry and Hawkesbury is decorated with some excellent sculptures, as the Canal Art Trail (watch the lights come on at bridge 6!).

● **Coventry**
West Midlands. MD Wed, Fri, Sat. PO, tel, stores, garage, station, cinema, theatre. Recorded as Couentrev in the Domesday Book, Coventry's modern history begins with the foundation of a Benedictine priory by Leofric and his wife Godgyfu in 1043, but its fame came with Lady Godiva, who in legend rode naked through the streets, to divert Leofric's anger from the town. This episode is first recorded in the *Flores Historiarum* of 1235. Following the Norman invasion, the town became second in commercial importance to London. Largely destroyed during World War II, it is today a modern and well-planned city, although a restored row of medieval buildings can be visited in Spon Street, in the west of the city centre. The origin of the popular phrase to send to Coventry, meaning to cold shoulder or ignore, is uncertain, but there is no reason to connect it with the present population, who seem generally warm and friendly.
Herbert Art Gallery & Museum Jordan Well (02476 832381). Graham Sutherland sketches for the design of the Coventry Cathedral tapestry.

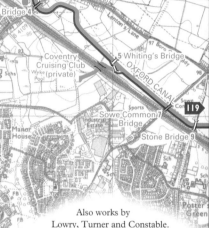

Also works by
Lowry, Turner and Constable.
*Open Mon–Sat 10.00–17.00, Sun
12.00–17.00.* Free. Tea room.
Coventry Cathedral (02476 227597).
Designed by Sir Basil Spence, building
began on the new cathedral in 1954 and was
completed in 1962. The modern stained glass
windows all reflect their light towards the altar,
behind which is a tapestry by Graham Sutherland. The font, a boulder from a hillside near
Bethlehem, stands in front of the Baptistry
window by John Piper. The whole is topped by a
bronze flèche (a slender spire with windows),
dropped into place by a helicopter and known
locally as Radio Coventry. The visitor centre, gift
shop and tearoom are run by volunteers. Cathedral
*open daily 09.30–17.30, visitor centre open April–Oct
10.00–18.00.* Tea room *open summer only.* Venture
to the top of the spire on *Sat 10.00–18.00 (summer)
and 10.00–17.00 (winter).* Free, but donations are
appreciated.
Cathedral Church of St Michael Only the ruins of the
old Cathedral, destroyed by the Luftwaffe in 1940, still
remain. Some of the original stained glass windows
survived. Many interesting artefacts are on display within
the ruins. *Gates open same times as the new cathedral.* **Museum
of British Road Transport** Hales Street (02476 832425). Walk
south from the canal basin. Reputedly the largest display of
British-made transport in the world, with over 150 cars, 75 motor-
bikes and 200 cycles on view. There are also period street scenes, royal
vehicles, the blitz experience and an audio-visual run in Thrust 2, at 633 mph,
to enjoy. *Open daily 10.00–17.00.* Free. Café on site.

Tourist Information Centre Bayley Lane, Coventry, near the Cathedral and University (02476 832303).

● **Longford Bridge**
West Midlands. PO, tel, stores, off-licence, chandlery. It was here, between 1769 and 1865, that members of the nearby Salem Baptist Chapel were baptised in the canal.

● **Hawkesbury Junction**
Hawkesbury Junction is also known as Sutton's Stop, after the name of the toll clerks here. It was always a busy canal centre, and remains so today, with plenty of narrow boats permanently moored at the junction. There are also other things to see: a fine canal pub, a stop lock and a disused engine house. The latter used to pump water up into the canal from a well. Its engine was installed in 1821, having been previously employed for nearly 100 years at Griff Colliery, a few miles up the canal towards Nuneaton. This Newcomen-type atmospheric steam engine, called Lady Godiva, is now in Dartmouth Museum. It ceased work in 1913. Sephtons House and Boatyard once faced the junction: it was here, in 1924, that n.b. *Friendship* was built. This boat can now be seen at the Boat Museum, Ellesmere Port.

The Chandlery 16 Sutton Stop (02476 360355). General supplies including groceries, Calor gas, maps and books, coal and gifts.

Boatyards

Ⓑ **Club Line Cruisers** Swan Lane Wharf, Swan Lane, Stoke Heath, Coventry (02476 258864). 🚿 🚿 ♿ D Pump-out, gas, narrow boat hire, overnight and long-term mooring, slipway, groceries, chandlery, boat building, engine sales, boat and engine repairs, toilets.

The towpath
This is in good condition for walkers throughout, and the stretch between Coventry and Hawkesbury is now enlivened as the Canal Art Trail. Cyclists will find parts of the towpath bumpy.

A. K. A. SUTTON'S STOP

Hawkesbury Junction was more commonly known to the boat people as Sutton's Stop. It took this name from a family called Sutton who, during the 1800s, were the toll clerks here. The Greyhound overlooks the junction now as it did then. Corn, oats and maize used to be stored around the back of the pub, as feed for the towing horses. It was often the children's job to bag this up for a trip, lowering the sacks down using a small hand crane.

Pubs and Restaurants

✕ **Buckinghams Tea Rooms** Canal Basin, Coventry (02476 633477). Excellent cooked breakfasts, light meals, coffee and tea. *Open daily 10.00-17.00 (open 11.00 Sun).* Outside seating.

● **Admiral Codrington** St Columba's Close, Coventry. By the canal basin. Garden.

● ✕ **Royal Hotel** (02476 686152). Near bridge 7. *Lunchtime* snacks. Children's room and garden, quiz on *Mon evenings.*

● ✕ **The Longford Engine** 270 Bedworth Road, Coventry (02476 365556). A comfortable canalside pub by bridge 10, with large public bar and a pleasant lounge and conservatory. Bass real ale is served, and food is available *all day, every day.* Terrace by the waterway. Mooring.

● ✕ **Greyhound** Hawkesbury Junction (02476 363046). A fascinating pub beside the junction, decorated with canal and rugby memorabilia, together with an immense collection of Toby jugs, warmed by log fires in winter. An imaginative selection of food, especially pies and salads, is served in the bar or restaurant *lunchtimes and evenings every day,* with a vegetarian menu, and a choice of real ales is available. Canalside garden and safe children's play area. Folk music on *third Thu each month.*

● **Boat Inn** Black Horse Road, Longford (02476 361438). A fine friendly pub with unspoilt rooms and a cosy lounge, all decorated with antiques, just a three minute walk northwest of the junction. Ansells, Greene King and Tetley's real ales, and also real draught cider. *Lunchtime* bar snacks. Children welcome. Garden for the summer and a real fire for the winter.

BOAT TRIPS
nb. *Coventrian* is a 38-seater boat, making trips from Coventry Basin *Easter-Sep, Sun & B Hols 15.15 & 17.15.* Also private charter. Details from (02476) 258864.

Coventry Canal Basin

Nuneaton

Leaving Hawkesbury Junction, the canal passes through Bedworth in a long cutting: the town seems to be composed mainly of vast housing estates, but these make little impression upon the canal. At Marston Junction the Ashby Canal (see page 10) branches to the east through pleasant countryside, while the Coventry Canal bends due west for a short way before resuming its course towards Nuneaton to the north. There is a pleasant short stretch of open fields, giving a welcome breathing space, before the canal once again enters the suburbs, this time of Nuneaton. There are good moorings and easy access to the town by Boot Bridge (20). The canal takes a route around the town, marked by a succession of housing estates and allotments.

● **Nuneaton**
Warwicks. MD Sat. PO, tel, stores, garage, station, cinema. A rather typical Midlands town with much industrial development. On the site of the Griff Colliery canal arm are the hollows said to be the origin of the Red Deeps of the *Mill on the Floss* by George Eliot, who was born here in 1819.
Nuneaton Museum & Art Gallery Riversley Park (02476 376158). Archaeological specimens of Nuneaton from prehistoric to medieval times, and also items from the local earthenware industry. Geological and mining relics, ethnography from Africa, Asia, America and Oceania. Paintings, prints and watercolours. Personalia collection of the novelist George Eliot. *Open Tue–Sat 10.30–16.30, Sun 14.00–16.30. Closed Mon except B. Hols.* Free. Tea room on site.
Arbury Hall (02476 382804). Two miles south west of the canal off B4102. Originally an

Elizabethan house, it was gothicised by Sir Roger Newdigate in 1750–1800 under the direction of Sanderson Miller, Henry Keene and Couchman of Warwick. Fine pictures, furniture, china and glass. The Hall is in a beautiful park setting. *Open Easter–last Sun in Sep, Sun & B. Hol Mons only; house 14.00–17.000, gardens 14.00–18.00.* Charge.
Tourist Information Centre Nuneaton Library, Church Street, Nineaton (02476 384027).
● **Chilvers Coton**
Warwicks. PO, tel, stores. A suburb of Nuneaton. Its church dates from 1946 and was designed by H. N. Jepson and built by German prisoners of war.
● **Bedworth**
Warwicks. MD Tue, Fri, Sat. PO, tel, stores. The most impressive parts of this town are its church by Bodley and Garner, 1888–90, and the almshouses built in 1840. Good shops.

Pubs and Restaurants

⬤ ✕ **Navigation Inn** Bulkington Road, Nuneaton (02476 311990). Canalside at bridge 14. Large pub with a comfortable lounge and a pleasant garden with swings. Bass real ale and bar meals *lunchtimes Tue-Fri & Sun, and evenings every day.* Mooring.
⬤ **Boot Inn** Boot Wharf, Bridge Street, Chilvers Coton (02476 385635). M & B real ale in a pub with a large bar and quiet lounge. The enclosed garden has swings for the children and barbecues are held *in summer.* Bar meals available *lunchtimes and evenings except Sun evenings,* with a vegetarian menu. Post box outside. Live music *Tue,* with a cheap guest beer.

⬤ **Fleur de Lys** Coventry Road, Chilvers Coton (02476 382366). Two minutes' walk down the hill from bridge 19a. There is a large bar and pleasant lounge where M & B real ale may be enjoyed and children are welcome. Garden. Regular *weekend* entertainment and games nights.
⬤ **King William** Coton Road, Chilvers Coton (02476 348308). About ¼ mile north east from bridge 19a. Bass, Boddington's and Flower's real ales are served. There is a pets corner in the garden.

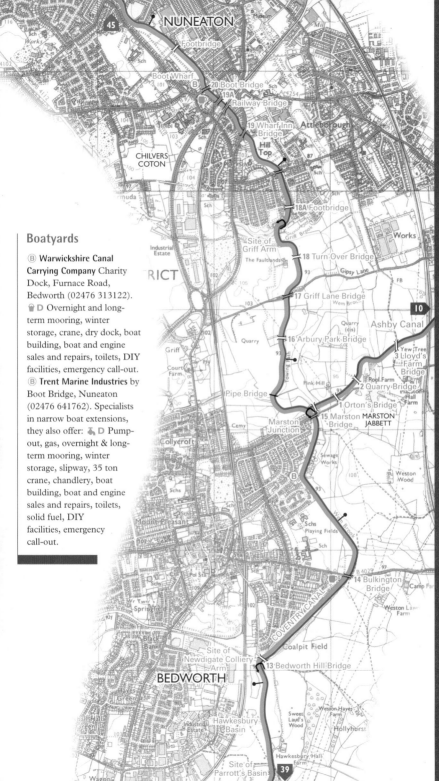

Boatyards

Ⓑ **Warwickshire Canal Carrying Company** Charity Dock, Furnace Road, Bedworth (02476 313122). 🛒 D Overnight and long-term mooring, winter storage, crane, dry dock, boat building, boat and engine sales and repairs, toilets, DIY facilities, emergency call-out.

Ⓑ **Trent Marine Industries** by Boot Bridge, Nuneaton (02476 641762). Specialists in narrow boat extensions, they also offer: 🛢 D Pump-out, gas, overnight & long-term mooring, winter storage, slipway, 35 ton crane, chandlery, boat building, boat and engine sales and repairs, toilets, solid fuel, DIY facilities, emergency call-out.

Hartshill

There is a fish & chip shop, and a Chinese take-away by bridge 21. Continuing north west out of Nuneaton, the canal winds along the side of a hill into a landscape which is curiously exciting. What were once quarries and spoil heaps are now landscaped, with many transformed into nature reserves. The largest mountain of waste, built with spoil from the old Judkins Quarry, is known as Mount Judd. This distinctly man-made landscape is broken up with unexpected stretches of open countryside, with fine views away to the north across the Anker valley. The earth here has given the canal water a distinct rust colour. The canal passes below the town of Hartshill; the attractive buildings in the British Waterways yard are crowned by a splendid clock tower, and those travelling on the canal will want to slow right down to enjoy the mellow architecture and old dock. The canal then continues towards Mancetter, leaving the quarry belt and moving into open rolling country backed by thick woods to the west. The railway closes from the east as the canal approaches Atherstone.

Hartshill

Warwicks. PO, tel, stores, garage. Once a mining community, Hartshill has now been swallowed up by Nuneaton, and as such its interest lies mainly in its past. The Romans recognised its strategic importance, and evidence of their occupation has been recovered. Hugh de Hardreshull chose it as a site for his castle in 1125, the view from the ridge enabling him to see as far as the distant peaks of Derbyshire on a clear day. Below, on the plains, can be counted the towers and steeples of 40 churches. There is evidence too of the Romans having settled here, as both kilns and fragments of pottery have been unearthed. Hartshill's most famous claim is that it was the birthplace of the poet Drayton in 1563, a friend of both Ben Johnson and Shakespeare. Drayton's greatest work was *Polyolbion*, a survey of the country with a song for each county. He died in 1631 and was buried in Westminster. There are fine walks over Hartshill Green to Oldbury Camp, a bronze age hillfort covering

7 acres. Hartshill's shops are a 15-minute walk from the canal.

Hartshill Yard Part of the yard contains a 19th-C carpenters workshop and blacksmiths' forge. Visits are by appointment *for groups only* – telephone (01283) 790236 for details.

Mancetter

Warwicks. PO, tel, stores, garage. About ¹/2 mile east of bridge 36. The church dates from the 13thC, but its best feature is the large collection of 18th-C slate tombstones displaying all the elegance of Georgian incised lettering. There are some almshouses of 1728 in the churchyard, and across the road another row with pretty Victorian Gothic details. The manor, south of the church, is rather over-restored. It was from this house, in 1555, that Robert Glover was led when the Bishop of Lichfield ordered his arrest. A victim of the reign of Mary Tudor, he was seized and taken to the stake, where he was executed alongside a poor cap-maker from Coventry.

Pubs and Restaurants

🍺 **Cock & Bear** Queens Road (02476 385875). A large pub ¼ mile east of bridge 21, serving M & B real ale. Garden.

🍺 **Stag & Pheasant** (02476 393173) About a ½-mile walk up the lane behind Hartshill Yard, this village green pub has outside seating and a family room, serving Flowers real ale and food *all day*.

🍺 **Anchor Inn** Mancetter Road, Hartshill (02476 398839). Popular and friendly brick-built canalside pub by bridge 29, with a large garden and play area with a fine array of imaginative playthings. Look for the milestone painted on the wall. Everards and a guest real ale are served, along with good food *lunchtimes and evenings every day (all day Sat & Sun),* with a vegetarian menu. Open fire *for winter* and barbecues *in summer.* Children welcome.

Boatyards

Ⓑ **Valley Cruises** Springwood Haven, Mancetter Road, Nuneaton (02476 393333). 🚽 🔧 D Pump-out, gas, narrow boat hire, overnight and long-term mooring, narrowboat slipway, boat and engine sales and repairs, boat building, telephone, toilets, showers, DIY facilities, emergency call-out. Café, chandlery, solid fuel and laundrette planned for 2001.

BW Hartshill Yard Clock Hill, Hartshill (02476 392489). 🔧

Ⓑ **Chris Bradbury** 6 Slacks Avenue, Autherley (01827 718136). Fenders, ropes, woodwork and boat-fitting.

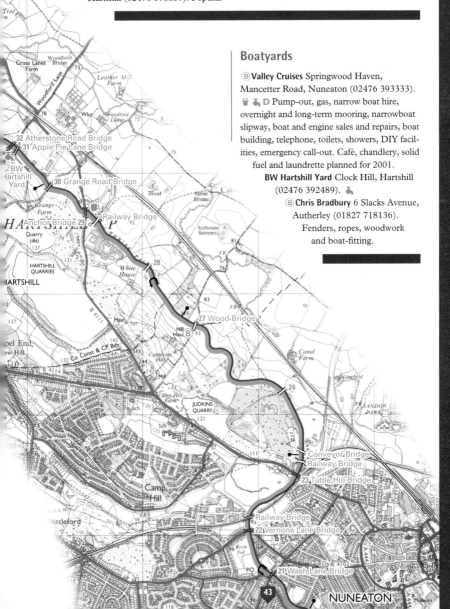

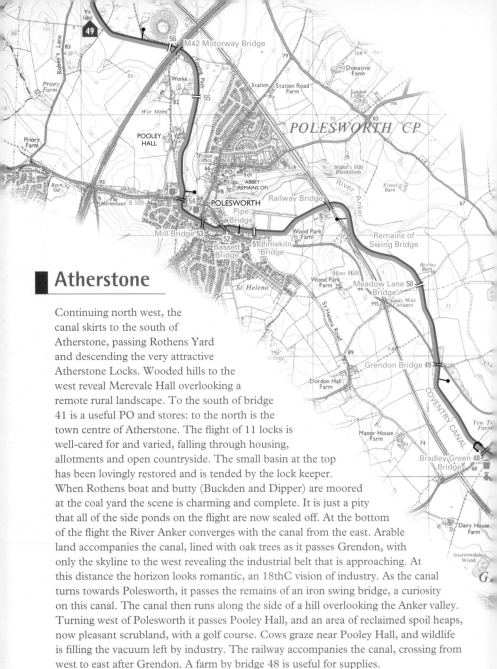

Atherstone

Continuing north west, the
canal skirts to the south of
Atherstone, passing Rothens Yard
and descending the very attractive
Atherstone Locks. Wooded hills to the
west reveal Merevale Hall overlooking a
remote rural landscape. To the south of bridge
41 is a useful PO and stores: to the north is the
town centre of Atherstone. The flight of 11 locks is
well-cared for and varied, falling through housing,
allotments and open countryside. The small basin at the top
has been lovingly restored and is tended by the lock keeper.
When Rothens boat and butty (Buckden and Dipper) are moored
at the coal yard the scene is charming and complete. It is just a pity
that all of the side ponds on the flight are now sealed off. At the bottom
of the flight the River Anker converges with the canal from the east. Arable
land accompanies the canal, lined with oak trees as it passes Grendon, with
only the skyline to the west revealing the industrial belt that is approaching. At
this distance the horizon looks romantic, an 18thC vision of industry. As the canal
turns towards Polesworth, it passes the remains of an iron swing bridge, a curiosity
on this canal. The canal then runs along the side of a hill overlooking the Anker valley.
Turning west of Polesworth it passes Pooley Hall, and an area of reclaimed spoil heaps,
now pleasant scrubland, with a golf course. Cows graze near Pooley Hall, and wildlife
is filling the vacuum left by industry. The railway accompanies the canal, crossing from
west to east after Grendon. A farm by bridge 48 is useful for supplies.

Boatyards

Ⓑ **A G & R A Rothen** Top Lock Wharf, Atherstone (01827 717884). **D** Coal and gas. Canal carrying.

Atherstone

Warwicks. MD Tue, Fri. PO, tel, stores, garage, station, cinema. A pleasant town, with a strong 18th-C feeling, especially in the open market place in front of the church. Beside the canal is Wilson & Staffard's Hat Mill – the shop here is *open Mon–Fri 10.00–16.00.*

Merevale A large battlemented house; high to the west is Merevale Hall, an early 19th-C mock Tudor mansion. To the west are the remains of the 12th-C abbey and the very pretty 13th-C church which contains fine stained glass, monuments and brasses.

Grendon

Warwicks. 1/2 mile north east of bridge 48. Grendon is just a small church set in beautiful parkland. The woods and rolling fields are a last refuge before the industrial landscape that precedes Tamworth.

Polesworth

Warwicks. MD Thu. PO, tel, stores, garage, fish & chips, station. The splendid gatehouse and the clerestory are all that remain of the 10th-C abbey, where Egbert, first Saxon King of England, built a nunnery.

Pubs and Restaurants

Barge & Bridge (01827 711774) Just south of bridge 41, on the far side of Rothens yard. Mansfield real ale. Meals *lunchtimes & evenings every day,* with vegetarian choices. Children are welcome, and there is a large garden.

Old Red Lion Hotel Long Street, Atherstone (01827 713156). Friendly residential hotel. Bar snacks *lunchtimes and evenings every day.* Restaurant meals *D only,* with a vegetarian menu available. Children welcome. B & B.

Kings Head Grendon (01827 717945). Canalside by the A5 bridge. Davenports and Bass real ale, along with bar and à la carte meals *lunchtimes and evenings every day,* with vegetarian options. Children allowed in *at meal times.* Outside seating, mooring.

✕ **Black Swan** Watling Street, Grendon (01827 713640). Meals *lunchtimes* and *evenings* every day, with a vegetarian menu. Marston's and John Smith's real ale and Harry Hedgehog's Fun Factory – a soft toy activity centre for children. Outside seating, mooring.

Bulls Head Tamworth Road, Polesworth (01827 893022). West of bridge 54. M & B, Bass and guest real ales. Bar meals *lunchtimes and evenings.* Vegetarian menu. Children welcome, and seats outside.

Fosters Yard Hotel & Balti Restaurant Market Street, Polesworth (01827 899313). South of bridge 53. Banks's real ale and meals *every day* in a listed building. Vegetarian menu. Moorings 100 yards away at the bridge. Children welcome. B & B.

Royal Oak Grendon Road, Polesworth (01827 892462). South of bridge 52. M & B and Bass real ale. Outside seating, children welcome and regular quiz nights.

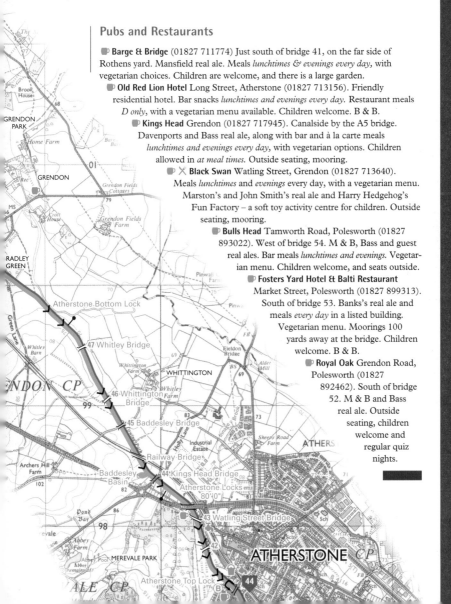

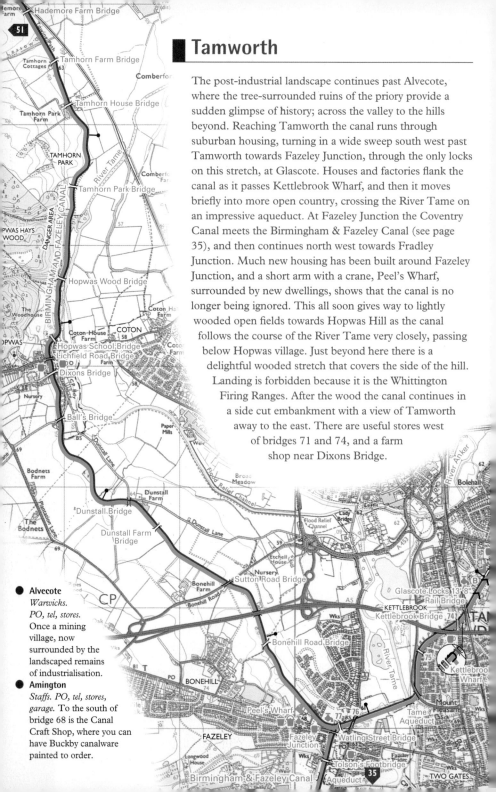

Tamworth

The post-industrial landscape continues past Alvecote, where the tree-surrounded ruins of the priory provide a sudden glimpse of history; across the valley to the hills beyond. Reaching Tamworth the canal runs through suburban housing, turning in a wide sweep south west past Tamworth towards Fazeley Junction, through the only locks on this stretch, at Glascote. Houses and factories flank the canal as it passes Kettlebrook Wharf, and then it moves briefly into more open country, crossing the River Tame on an impressive aqueduct. At Fazeley Junction the Coventry Canal meets the Birmingham & Fazeley Canal (see page 35), and then continues north west towards Fradley Junction. Much new housing has been built around Fazeley Junction, and a short arm with a crane, Peel's Wharf, surrounded by new dwellings, shows that the canal is no longer being ignored. This all soon gives way to lightly wooded open fields towards Hopwas Hill as the canal follows the course of the River Tame very closely, passing below Hopwas village. Just beyond here there is a delightful wooded stretch that covers the side of the hill. Landing is forbidden because it is the Whittington Firing Ranges. After the wood the canal continues in a side cut embankment with a view of Tamworth away to the east. There are useful stores west of bridges 71 and 74, and a farm shop near Dixons Bridge.

- **Alvecote**
  Warwicks. PO, tel, stores. Once a mining village, now surrounded by the landscaped remains of industrialisation.
- **Amington**
  Staffs. PO, tel, stores, garage. To the south of bridge 68 is the Canal Craft Shop, where you can have Buckby canalware painted to order.

● **Tamworth**
Staffs. MD Sat. PO, tel, stores, garage, station, cinema. Tamworth was originally a Saxon settlement, although only earthworks survive from this period.
Castle Museum Holloway, set in castle pleasure grounds (01827 63563). *Open Mon–Sat 10.00–17.30, Sun 14.00–17.30, last admission 16.30.* Charge. Gift shop.
Tourist Information Centre 29 Market Street, Tamworth (01827 709581).

● **Fazeley Junction**
Staffs. PO and stores in Fazeley. The Coventry Canal joins the Birmingham & Fazeley Canal here.
● **Hopwas**
Staffs. PO, tel, stores. A pretty and tidy village with a green, built on the side of a hill. Anyone walking should look out for the danger flags for Whittington Firing Ranges.

Boatyards

ⓑ **Narrowcraft** The Boatyard, Robey's Lane, Alvecote (01827 898585). Pump-out, gas, day hire craft, overnight and long-term mooring, slipway, winter storage, dry dock, boat building, boat and engine sales and repairs, telephone, toilets, showers, chandlery, solid fuel, DIY facilities. Club house, bar and restaurant.

ⓑ **S M Hudson** Glascote Basin Boatyard, Basin Lane, Glascote (01827 311317). Pump-out, gas, long-term mooring, slipway, dry dock, engine sales and repairs, boat repairs, boat building, DIY facilities. *Closed Sun.*
ⓑ **BW Fazeley Office** Peel's Wharf, Fazeley (01827 252000). 200yds west of the junction.

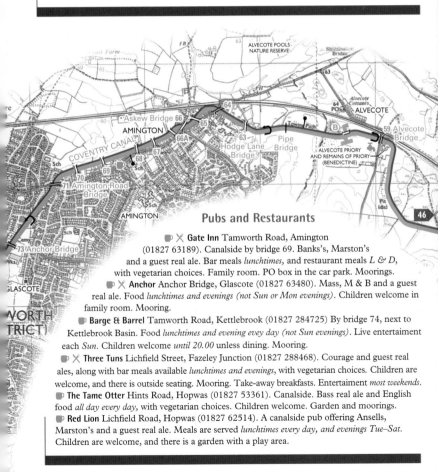

Pubs and Restaurants

Gate Inn Tamworth Road, Amington (01827 63189). Canalside by bridge 69. Banks's, Marston's and a guest real ale. Bar meals *lunchtimes,* and restaurant meals *L & D,* with vegetarian choices. Family room. PO box in the car park. Moorings.

Anchor Anchor Bridge, Glascote (01827 63480). Mass, M & B and a guest real ale. Food *lunchtimes and evenings (not Sun or Mon evenings).* Children welcome in family room. Mooring.

Barge & Barrel Tamworth Road, Kettlebrook (01827 284725) By bridge 74, next to Kettlebrook Basin. Food *lunchtimes and evening evey day (not Sun evenings).* Live entertainment each *Sun.* Children welcome *until 20.00* unless dining. Mooring.

Three Tuns Lichfield Street, Fazeley Junction (01827 288468). Courage and guest real ales, along with bar meals available *lunchtimes and evenings,* with vegetarian choices. Children are welcome, and there is outside seating. Mooring. Take-away breakfasts. Entertainment *most weekends.*

The Tame Otter Hints Road, Hopwas (01827 53361). Canalside. Bass real ale and English food *all day every day,* with vegetarian choices. Children welcome. Garden and moorings.

Red Lion Lichfield Road, Hopwas (01827 62514). A canalside pub offering Ansells, Marston's and a guest real ale. Meals are served *lunchtimes every day, and evenings Tue–Sat.* Children are welcome, and there is a garden with a play area.

Whittington and Fradley Junction

As the canal reaches Whittington and bridge 78, it changes back from being the Birmingham & Fazeley Canal to the Coventry Canal (see Introduction). A stone marks the actual point. At Huddlesford the remains of the eastern end of the Wyrley & Essington Canal, now used only for moorings, branches to the south west. The Coventry Canal then runs northwards through flat, open country towards Fradley Junction. There are no locks, but a swing bridge announces your arrival at Fradley Junction. Here the Coventry Canal meets the Trent & Mersey Canal.

- **Fisherwick**
  Staffs. Tel. A small hamlet overlooking the canal.
- **Whittington**
  Staffs. PO, tel, stores, garage, chemist, Chinese take-away, off-licence. The village centre is to the west of Whittington Bridge.
- **Lichfield**
  Staffs. PO, tel, stores, garage, cinema, station. Two miles south west along the A38. Although not on the canal, Lichfield is well worth a visit.
  Art Gallery The Friary, Lichfield Library (01543 510700). *Open Mon, Wed & Fri 09.30–17.00, Tue & Thu 09.30–19.00 and Sat 09.00–13.00. Closed Sun.* Admission free.
  Tourist Information Centre Donegal House, Bore Street, Lichfield (01543 252109).
- **Huddlesford**
  Staffs. PO box. At Huddlesford Junction the

Wyrley & Essington Canal used to join the Coventry, but this end has long been abandoned: the first 1/4 mile is used for moorings.
- **Fradley**
  Staffs. PO, tel, stores. A small village set to the east of the canal, and well away from the junction. It owed its prosperity to the airfield which is not used as such any more.
- **Fradley Junction**
  Staffs. PO box, tel, garage. A long-established canal centre where the Coventry Canal joins the Trent & Mersey Canal. There is a boatyard, a British Waterways office and maintenance yard, BW moorings, a boat club and a popular pub – all in the middle of a five-lock flight.

Boatyards

Ⓑ **Streethay Wharf** Streethay Basin, Streethay, Lichfield (01543 414808). 🛥 🛢 🔧 D Pump-out, gas, day hire craft, overnight and long-term mooring, winter storage, wet dock, slip-way, crane, boat and engine sales and repairs, boat building, telephone, toilets, showers, chandlery, solid fuel, laundrette, DIY facilities, emergency call-out.

Ⓑ **BW Waterways Office** Fradley Junction (01283 790236). 🛥 🛢 🔧 Overnight mooring, long-term mooring, toilets.
Ⓑ **Swan Line Cruisers** Fradley Junction (01283 790332). 🔧 D Pump-out (*not weekends*), gas, narrow boat hire, overnight mooring, dry dock, groceries, chandlery, books and maps, boat building, boat sales, engine sales and repairs.

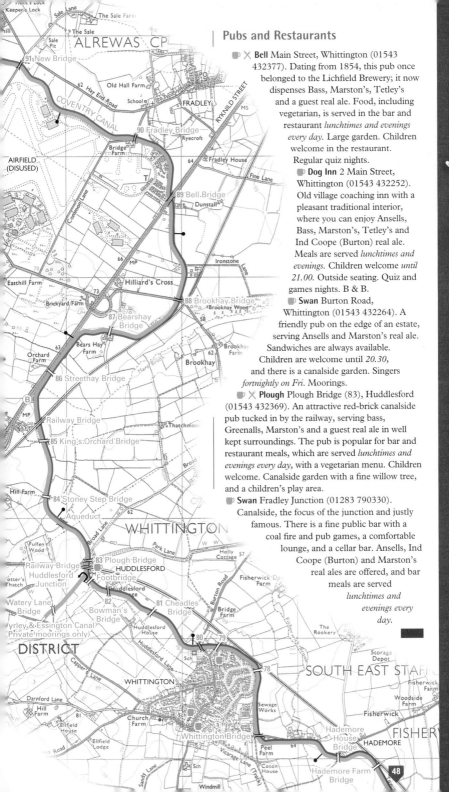

Pubs and Restaurants

Bell Main Street, Whittington (01543 432377). Dating from 1854, this pub once belonged to the Lichfield Brewery; it now dispenses Bass, Marston's, Tetley's and a guest real ale. Food, including vegetarian, is served in the bar and restaurant *lunchtimes and evenings every day*. Large garden. Children welcome in the restaurant. Regular quiz nights.

Dog Inn 2 Main Street, Whittington (01543 432252). Old village coaching inn with a pleasant traditional interior, where you can enjoy Ansells, Bass, Marston's, Tetley's and Ind Coope (Burton) real ale. Meals are served *lunchtimes and evenings*. Children welcome *until 21.00.* Outside seating. Quiz and games nights. B & B.

Swan Burton Road, Whittington (01543 432264). A friendly pub on the edge of an estate, serving Ansells and Marston's real ale. Sandwiches are always available. Children are welcome until *20.30,* and there is a canalside garden. Singers *fortnightly on Fri*. Moorings.

Plough Plough Bridge (83), Huddlesford (01543 432369). An attractive red-brick canalside pub tucked in by the railway, serving bass, Greenalls, Marston's and a guest real ale in well kept surroundings. The pub is popular for bar and restaurant meals, which are served *lunchtimes and evenings every day,* with a vegetarian menu. Children welcome. Canalside garden with a fine willow tree, and a children's play area.

Swan Fradley Junction (01283 790330). Canalside, the focus of the junction and justly famous. There is a fine public bar with a coal fire and pub games, a comfortable lounge, and a cellar bar. Ansells, Ind Coope (Burton) and Marston's real ales are offered, and bar meals are served *lunchtimes and evenings every day.*

Coventry Canal

Whittington and Fradley Junction

EREWASH CANAL

MAXIMUM DIMENSIONS
Length: 72' 0"
Beam: 10' 6"
Draught: 2' 6"
Headroom: '7' 4"

MILEAGE
TRENT LOCK to
Sandiacre Lock: 3¹/₄ miles
Hallam Fields Lock: 5¹/₂ miles
LANGLEY MILL: 11³/₄ miles
Locks: 15

MANAGER
(0115) 946 1017

The Erewash Canal is one of five canals built towards the end of the 18thC to carry coal from the pits of the Nottinghamshire/Derbyshire coalfield to the towns of the East Midlands. The construction of the canal was supported by local merchants and landowners who were keen to profit from the coal deposits of the Erewash Valley, as were the local colliery owners who could see the financial benefits of widening their markets. Completed in 1779 at a cost of £21,000 by the engineer John Varley, the canal involved the construction of 14 locks which took the navigation up 109 feet from Trent Lock to Langley Mill. Begun in 1778, its 11³/4 mile course was open to navigation by the following summer. As £23,000 had been raised in £100 shares in order to finance the project, the capital outlay was low. Abundant trade from local collieries, brickworks and ironworks made the canal one of the most prosperous in the country. The monopoly that the company had over transport in the area along with the high demand for coal meant that the £100 shares had risen to an incredible £1300. The enormous success of the Erewash Canal encouraged the promotion and construction, during the following decade, of the Cromford, Nottingham, Derby and Nutbrook Canals. However, by 1834 the Canal Company was in trouble. High tolls plus the competition presented by the railways were taking trade away from the navigation. The Company reduced their tolls in an attempt to regain trade but the railway system was expanding rapidly in the area and the Canal Company was unable to compete. The surrounding canals were bought up by the railway companies which further added to the problems of the Erewash Canal. The railway companies were happy to see these neighbouring waterways fall into disuse, thus putting an end to through traffic. By 1932 the Erewash Canal Company admitted defeat and was bought up by the Grand Union Canal Company. Having also bought the Loughborough and Leicester Navigations it was their intention to revitalise the network by creating a through navigation from the coalfields of Derbyshire to London. Sadly their attempts failed. Nationalisation of the canals in 1947 brought the Erewash Canal under the administration of the British Transport Commission and in 1962 this body closed to navigation the upper section from Gallows Inn to Langley Mill. The need to supply water to the lower section for navigation and industry, however, meant that the upper section had still to be maintained and boats were allowed to navigate it upon application to the Commission and subsequently to its successor, the British Waterways Board. With the cessation of narrow boat carrying in 1963, such boats had been few, but the growing interest in pleasure boating resulted in more and more craft venturing up the canal from the popular River Trent. With increased use the canal gradually improved and the news that the major portion of it was to be designated a remainder waterway in the impending 1968 Transport Act was received locally with dismay. A public meeting led to the formation of the Erewash Canal Preservation and Development Association (ECPDA), a body consisting of representatives of boating and fishing interests, residents and local authorities. The need to convince local authorities of the value of the canal as an amenity was recognised at a very early stage and the association's efforts eventually met with success when, in 1972, Derbyshire and Nottinghamshire County Councils agreed to share the cost, with the British Waterways Board, of the restoration of the canal to cruising waterway standards. This ambition was achieved in February 1983 when the canal was upgraded and boaters can now enjoy the entire course of the waterway. Further improvements are already afoot due to the continued involvement of the Erewash Initiative, a joint project involving British Waterways, Erewash Borough Council and Groundwork Erewash.

Trent Lock (see page 54)

Long Eaton

The Erewash Canal leaves the Trent Navigation at Trent Lock. There is a useful supermarket just above Dockholme Lock, on the offside. North of the big concrete bridge carrying the A52 at Sandiacre is a delightfully landscaped free overnight mooring.

NAVIGATIONAL NOTES

Trent Lock should always be left *full,* with the top gates open, except when there is much traffic about. This will ensure that any flotsam coming down the canal is able to escape over the bottom gates.

● **Trent Lock**
An important waterway junction and a long-established boating centre. Boats navigating the Trent in this rather complicated area should beware of straying too near Thrumpton Weir.

● **Long Eaton**
Derbs. MD Wed, Fri, Sat. Flea market Tue. All services.
Long Eaton Leisure Centre Wilsthorpe Road, Long Eaton (0115 946 1400). Open *daily until 20.00.* Charge.

Lock Cottage Sandiacre. The last remaining toll house on the Erewash Canal. Open *14.30–17.00 on Sunday afternoons throughout the summer and on B. Hols.*

● **Derby Canal**
The closure of the Derby Canal ended Derby's link with the navigable waterways which dated back to the time when the Danes sailed up the River Derwent to found the settlement of Deoraby.

BOAT TRIPS
Thompson Boat Company 336 Bennett Street, Long Eaton (0115 972 5373). Day boat hire and 31 passenger *n.b. Destiny* for charter *throughout the year.* Operates from Trent Lock.

Boatyards

ⓑ ✕ **Sawley Bridge Marina** Long Eaton, Nottingham (01159 734278). 🚽 🛢 ⚓ P D Pump-out, gas, extensive moorings both overnight and long-term, slipway, crane, boat and engine sales and repairs, telephone, toilets, showers, chandlery, coffee shop, solid fuel, laundrette.

ⓑ **n.b. Jackal and Butty Hereford** C & J Deuchar, School of Agriculture, Sutton Bonington, Loughborough (07860 828723). Moored outside BW Waterway office. Windlasses, solid fuel, canalware, books, gifts, fenders, BW sanitary station and handcuff lock keys available out of hours, decorative

boat painting. Sometimes cruising during summer months so telephone before visiting.
ⓑ **Trent Lock Marine Services** Trent Lock, Lock Lane, Sawley, Long Eaton (01159 727936). Boat and engine repairs, boat building, fitting out, dry and wet docks, DIY facilities.
ⓑ **Mills Dockyard** Trent Lock, Lock Lane, Long Eaton (0115 973 2595). Overnight and long-term mooring, winter storage, engine repairs, dry dock, wooden boat restoration and repairs, general boat maintenance, fitting out and repairs, houseboat construction.
ⓑ **Wyvern Marine** Wyvern Avenue, Long Eaton (0115 946 1752). Long-term moorings.

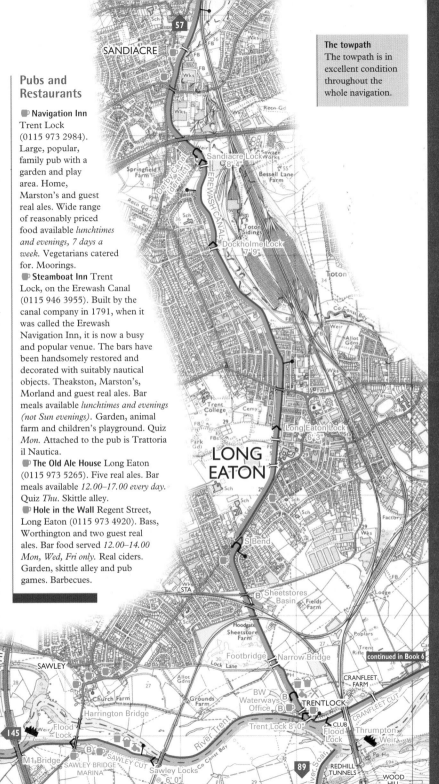

Pubs and Restaurants

🍺 **Navigation Inn** Trent Lock (0115 973 2984). Large, popular, family pub with a garden and play area. Home, Marston's and guest real ales. Wide range of reasonably priced food available *lunchtimes and evenings, 7 days a week*. Vegetarians catered for. Moorings.

🍺 **Steamboat Inn** Trent Lock, on the Erewash Canal (0115 946 3955). Built by the canal company in 1791, when it was called the Erewash Navigation Inn, it is now a busy and popular venue. The bars have been handsomely restored and decorated with suitably nautical objects. Theakston, Marston's, Morland and guest real ales. Bar meals available *lunchtimes and evenings (not Sun evenings)*. Garden, animal farm and children's playground. Quiz *Mon.* Attached to the pub is Trattoria il Nautica.

🍺 **The Old Ale House** Long Eaton (0115 973 5265). Five real ales. Bar meals available *12.00–17.00 every day*. Quiz *Thu.* Skittle alley.

🍺 **Hole in the Wall** Regent Street, Long Eaton (0115 973 4920). Bass, Worthington and two guest real ales. Bar food served *12.00–14.00 Mon, Wed, Fri only*. Real ciders. Garden, skittle alley and pub games. Barbecues.

The towpath
The towpath is in excellent condition throughout the whole navigation.

Ilkeston

At Stanton Gate the M1 motorway looms up and then crosses the canal on its way to Sheffield. The outskirts of Ilkeston appear on the left side while, across the shallow Erewash valley, the course of the disused Nottingham Canal appears from the east, twisting along the contours of the hillside. Like the Erewash Canal, its course is generally northerly, but the two waterways do not meet until Langley Mill. Meanwhile the Erewash Canal passes extensive low-lying playing fields before reaching the pub at Gallows Inn Lock with *PO, stores, take-aways, laundrette and garages to the west of the navigation.* North of Gallows Inn Lock, the canal passes housing estates on one side and water meadows and a main line railway on the other. The town of Ilkeston is on the hillside on the west side of the canal. In spite of its proximity to these built-up areas, the canal is relatively unspoiled and surprisingly rural.

● **Sandiacre**
Derbs. PO, tel, stores, butcher, take-away, garage, bank. Services are all conveniently near the canal, but there is not much of interest in these outskirts, apart from the handsome Springfield Mill by the canal and the church, which is set on a rise called Stoney Clouds (clearly visible from the canal at Pasture Lock). The mill was built by Ernest Terah Hooley of Risley Hall in 1888. It houses four separate spiral staircase towers, each catering for an individual lace company. The canal was used for the transportation of the raw materials needed by the lace industry and for the finished articles. There are fine views over the industrial valley from the church which features some original Norman work inside, including carvings. Outside is an old tombstone bearing a skull and crossbones. The font is 600 years old.

● **Ilkeston**
Derbs. MD Thu, Sat. All services. Cinema. A market and textile town, with a compact main square. Pedestrianised areas make this a pleasant place to stroll. The parish church of St Mary dates from 1150 and has an unusual 14th-C stone screen. The annual three-day funfair is held in the Market Place in *Oct.*
Erewash Museum High Street, off East Street, Ilkeston (0115 944 0440). Set in a late 18th-C house, the museum tells the story of the local and social history of the Erewash area as well as housing permanent displays of an Edwardian period kitchen and wash house and an exhibition

of children's toys. *Open Tue, Thu–Sat & B. Hols 10.00–16.00. Closed Jan, Xmas Day & New Year.* Free.

● **Cossall**
Notts. Tel. Cossall is a refreshing contrast to Ilkeston, an attractive village built on top of a hill, spreading gently down to the Nottingham Canal. D.H. Lawrence used it as his background for Cossethay in *The Rainbow.* A narrow street winds among the houses, all of which seem to be surrounded by pretty gardens. The little church contains an oak screen made by village crafts-men: in the churchyard is a memorial to a soldier killed at Waterloo. Next to the church is Church Cottage, once the home of Louie Burrows to whom Lawrence was engaged. She was the model for the character of Ursula Brangwen.

● **Nutbrook Canal**
This little branch off the Erewash Canal used to lead for 4¹/2 miles almost parallel to the Erewash Canal and slightly west of it. It still flows into the Erewash Canal upstream from Stanton Lock and parts of it are in water. The canal opened in 1795 at a cost of £22,800. Colliery owners Edward Miller-Mundy and Sir Henry Hunloke employed Benjamin Outram as engineer. It was in fact mining subsidence which caused much of the canal to be derelict by 1895 when it fell into disuse. Two of the three reservoirs which supplied the canal with water are still in evidence at Shipley. The short section that used to pass through the old Stanton Ironworks was filled in in 1962 and is now quite untraceable.

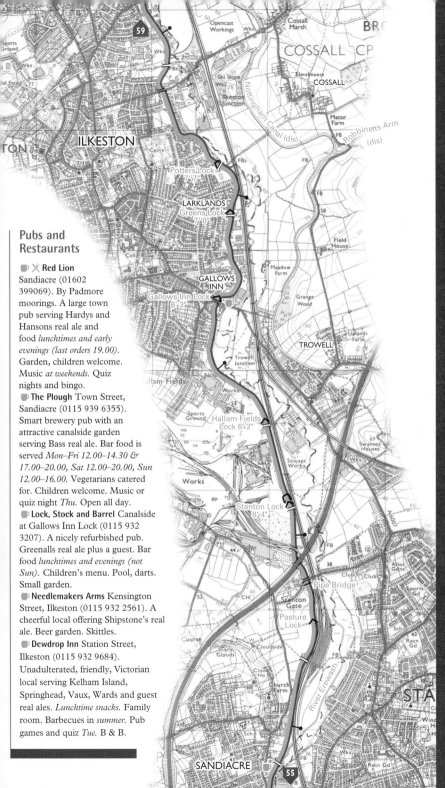

Pubs and Restaurants

🍺 ✕ **Red Lion** Sandiacre (01602 399069). By Padmore moorings. A large town pub serving Hardys and Hansons real ale and food *lunchtimes and early evenings (last orders 19.00)*. Garden, children welcome. Music *at weekends*. Quiz nights and bingo.

🍺 **The Plough** Town Street, Sandiacre (0115 939 6355). Smart brewery pub with an attractive canalside garden serving Bass real ale. Bar food is served *Mon–Fri 12.00–14.30 & 17.00–20.00, Sat 12.00–20.00, Sun 12.00–16.00*. Vegetarians catered for. Children welcome. Music or quiz night *Thu*. Open all day.

🍺 **Lock, Stock and Barrel** Canalside at Gallows Inn Lock (0115 932 3207). A nicely refurbished pub. Greenalls real ale plus a guest. Bar food *lunchtimes and evenings (not Sun)*. Children's menu. Pool, darts. Small garden.

🍺 **Needlemakers Arms** Kensington Street, Ilkeston (0115 932 2561). A cheerful local offering Shipstone's real ale. Beer garden. Skittles.

🍺 **Dewdrop Inn** Station Street, Ilkeston (0115 932 9684). Unadulterated, friendly, Victorian local serving Kelham Island, Springhead, Vaux, Wards and guest real ales. *Lunchtime snacks*. Family room. Barbecues in *summer*. Pub games and quiz *Tue*. B & B.

Langley Mill

The northernmost section of the Erewash Canal is more isolated than the rest, and is definitely more rural and attractive. There are two splendid old canal buildings beside Shipley Lock – one was a stable and the other a slaughterhouse for worn-out canal horses. Just above the lock, the River Erewash creeps under the canal, which is carried above it on a very small aqueduct. Beyond the next pleasant rural stretch is Langley Mill, where the canal terminates at the Great Northern Basin beyond the final lock. Boatmen who have navigated the whole of the Erewash to this point are invited to call at *n.b. Ambergate* or Langley Mill Boat Company in order to obtain a head of navigation plaque or a certificate. See notice in the basin for further details.

● **Great Northern Basin**
This restored basin, officially reopened in 1973, once formed the junction of the Erewash, Cromford and Nottingham canals. A feeder enters here from Moorgreen Reservoir. Since it passed through a coalfield on its way to the basin, it brought down a lot of coal silt – which over the years filled up the Great Northern Basin. Now the Erewash Canal Preservation & Development Association has restored the basin and lock, so that boats may reach a good mooring site with an enjoyable pub beside it. The Nottingham and Cromford canals can never be restored here, for their closure was necessitated by mining subsidence – although substantial lengths of both canals are still in water, away from Langley Mill. The Cromford Canal was engineered by William Jessop and Benjamin Outram, its 14 1/2 mile length being completed in 1793. One of its chief instigators had been Richard Arkwright who had come to Cromford in 1771 and built the world's first successful water-powered cotton spinning mill. The canal was used for transporting raw cotton and textile yarn as well as coal, iron, lead and building stone. Jessop was joined by James Green in engineering the Nottingham Canal. Running from Langley Mill to the River Trent at Nottingham it involved 20 locks including a flight of 14 at Wollaton. The stretch from Langley Mill to Lenton had to be abandoned in 1937 but the remaining section through to the River Trent is still in use. Both canals pass through an interesting mixture of heavily industrial surroundings and quiet open countryside. The northern 5 miles of the Cromford Canal, from Ambergate to Cromford (a length still in water) is strongly recommended to all walkers, country lovers and especially industrial archaeologists. Explorers will find all kinds of exciting things, including two aqueducts and a fine old pumping station regularly in steam.

● **Langley Mill**
Derbs. PO, tel, stores, take-away, station. Near the head of the Erewash Canal, with the little Erewash river going past it.

● **Eastwood**
Notts. PO, tel, stores, garage, bank. Up on the hill east of the Great Northern Basin, this mining town is best known as the childhood home of D.H.

Lawrence. He was born at 8a Victoria Street, and the early part of *Sons and Lovers* is set in the town. The cemetery contains the Lawrence family graves. Lawrence's own headstone was brought from Vence in France and is now on display in the local library. A meeting at the Sun Inn in 1843, between local coal owners and iron masters, led to the construction of the Midland Railway. There are many mill shops in this area.

D.H. Lawrence Birthplace Museum 8a Victoria Street, Eastwood (01773 763312). Birthplace of the novelist, poet and playwright, David Herbert Lawrence. The house has been restored to reflect the lifestyle of a working class Victorian family. There is also a video presentation of the author's Eastwood days. Also available from the museum is a leaflet entitled *The Blue Line Trail* which guides you around Eastwood's Lawrentian connections. *Open Sun & B. Hols, Apr–Oct 10.00–17.00; Nov–Mar 10.00–16.00.* Charge.

Eastwood Library Wellington Place, Nottingham Road, Eastwood (01773 712209). The library houses a display of letters, books and first editions connected with D.H. Lawrence. Open *Mon, Tue, Thu 09.30–19.00, Fri 09.30–18.00, Sat 09.30–13.00.* Free.

American Adventure Theme Park Shipley (01773 769931). 1 1/4 miles south west of the canal. Leave the canal at Shipley Lock and after crossing the railway by the footbridge, follow the footpath to the A6007. Turn right towards Shipley and then follow the signs. Two hundred acres of parkland offering fun for the whole family. A chance to test your courage on some of the rides or unwind with a game of golf. *Open daily 10.00–17.00 during season with varying times out of season.* Telephone (0345) 617617 for further details. Charge.

Tourist Information Centre Market Place, Ripley (01773 841488). *Open Mon–Fri 09.30–17.30, Sat 09.00–16.00.* This office produces an excellent guide to the Cromford Canal featuring both a complete walk along its 15 mile course, from the Great Northern Basin to its terminus at Cromford and shorter circular walks taking in specific highlights. There is much of interest to visit in the Amber valley, to the north west of Langley Mill, all of which is very accessible by bus or train. So before navigating the waterway contact the TIC for their comprehensive information pack.

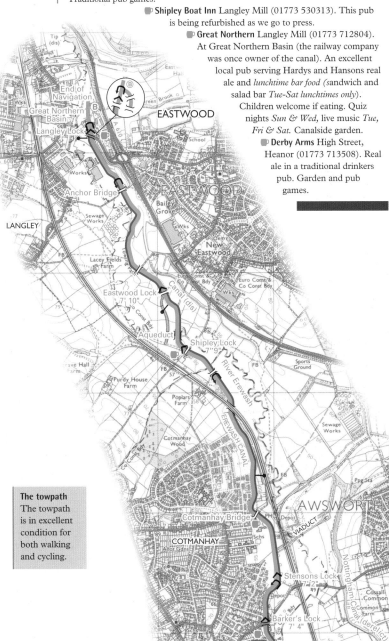

Pubs and Restaurants

Bridge Inn Awsworth Road, Ilkeston (0115 932 9903). Canalside pub with a large garden and adventure playground. Popular in season. Burton real ale and meals *12.00–14.00 every day (Sun 12.00–15.00)*. Moorings below Barker's Lock.

Bridge Inn Bridge Street, Cotmanhay (0115 932 2589). Small canalside local offering Hardys and Hansons real ale, and sandwiches. Garden with swings. Traditional pub games.

Shipley Boat Inn Langley Mill (01773 530313). This pub is being refurbished as we go to press.

Great Northern Langley Mill (01773 712804). At Great Northern Basin (the railway company was once owner of the canal). An excellent local pub serving Hardys and Hansons real ale and *lunchtime bar food (s*andwich and salad bar *Tue-Sat lunchtimes only)*. Children welcome if eating. Quiz nights *Sun & Wed*, live music *Tue, Fri & Sat*. Canalside garden.

Derby Arms High Street, Heanor (01773 713508). Real ale in a traditional drinkers pub. Garden and pub games.

The towpath
The towpath is in excellent condition for both walking and cycling.

Boatyards

Ⓑ **Langley Mill Boat Co** Great Northern Basin, Langley Mill (01773 760758). ▮ ▮ ▮ D
Pump-out, gas, overnight mooring, long-term mooring (by arrangement), winter storage, boat repairs, engine repairs, boat building and

fitting out, dry dock, DIY facilities, solid fuel, toilets.
Ⓑ **ECPDA** 73 Sudbury Avenue, Larklands, Ilkeston (0115 932 8042). Moorings in Great Northern Basin.

GERMANS COTTON ON

Before the arrival of Richard Arkwright and his partners in August 1771, the area around Cromford was a scattered community of families who earned their livings in the lead mines. By Christmas of that year Arkwright was already utilising the waters of a local lead mine drain, the Cromford Sough, and of the Bonsall Brook, to power what was soon to become the world's first successful water-powered cotton spinning mill. By 1777 there were two mills in Cromford and further developments were soon to take place in Derby and Matlock Bath. New housing built to accommodate the workers in Cromford featured an additional upper storey which acted as a workroom. Visiting industrialists from New England were entertained in the new Greyhound Hotel. So impressed were they with the developments in Cromford that they returned to America and used Sir Richard's mills as a model for their own. By 1783 continental Europe was catching up with the rest of the world when its first water-powered cotton spinning mill was erected near Ratingen, Germany. Johann Gottfried Brägelmann created his very own cotton new town and named it Cromford in recognition of Arkwright's innovation.

Foxton Locks (see page 68)

GRAND UNION CANAL – LEICESTER SECTION AND THE RIVER SOAR

MAXIMUM DIMENSIONS

Norton Junction to Foxton Junction
Length: 72'
Beam: 7'
Headroom: 7' 6"

Market Harborough to Leicester
Length: 72'
Beam: 13'
Headroom: 7'

Leicester West Bridge to River Trent
Length: 72'
Beam: 14' 4"
Headroom: 7' 6"

MANAGER

Norton to Foxton (including the Welford Arm):
01788 890666
Foxton to the Trent (including the Market Harborough Arm): 0115 946 1017

MILEAGE

NORTON JUNCTION to
Crick: 5 miles
Welford Arm: $15^1/2$ miles
Market Harborough Arm: $23^1/4$ miles
Blaby: 36 miles
Leicester West Bridge: $41^1/4$ miles
Cossington Lock: 49 miles
Barrow upon Soar: $53^1/4$ miles
Loughborough Basin: $57^1/4$ miles
Zouch Lock: $60^1/2$ miles
RIVER TRENT: $66^1/4$ miles

Locks: 59

The River Soar is a tributary of the River Trent and is approximately 40 miles long. It runs mainly through Leicestershire, rising at Smockington Hollow on the Warwickshire border. For most of the way from Aylestone (just south of Leicester) to the Trent, the Soar forms the Leicester section of the Grand Union Canal.

In 1634 Thomas Skipworth of Cotes attempted to make the River 'portable for barges and boats up to the town of Leicester' by means of a grant from King Charles I in return for 10 per cent of the profits. This scheme was a failure. But, after several other attempts, prominent citizens of Loughborough secured an Act of Parliament in 1776, and the River Soar Navigation (Loughborough Canal) was opened two years later, bringing great prosperity to the town. The continuation of the navigation up to Leicester (the Leicester Canal) was built under an Act passed in 1791. Its opening was marked by the arrival in Leicester of two boats loaded with provisions from Gainsborough on 21 February 1794. The engineers concerned with construction of the River Soar Navigation were John Smith and John May (Loughborough Canal) and William Jessop (Leicester Canal). With the completion of the Grand Junction Canal between Brentford and Braunston, a connection was soon established between this and the River Soar Navigation, built to the narrow gauge, thwarting the Grand Junction's scheme for a system of wide canals.

The Loughborough Navigation was one of the most prosperous canals in England, by virtue of its position in relation to the Nottinghamshire/Derbyshire coalfield and the Erewash Canal. However, railway competition took its usual toll, and although trade revived when the Grand Union Canal purchased the Loughborough and Leicester Navigations in 1931, the improvement proved temporary. It remains a pretty, rural river and is much enjoyed by those on pleasure craft.

Norton Junction

Leaving Norton Junction there is a quiet, meandering mile through light woods and rolling fields before the motorway and railway take over; the canal passes the back door of the Watford Gap service area. The noise and bustle of the motorway and main railway line intrude, accentuating the sedate pace of those using the original of the three transport systems. The Watford Gap motorway service station (south of bridge 6) is by no means inaccessible from the towpath and could provide the boater with *24hr* sustenance and provisions. Otherwise the Leicester Section of the Grand Union Canal is very attractive, quiet and in no hurry to reach Foxton. It wanders through rolling, hilly country, riverlike with constant changes of direction that guide it gently north eastwards. It avoids villages and civilisation generally; only the old wharves serve as a reminder of the canal's function. The slow course of the canal, its relative emptiness and its original plan combine to make it very narrow in places; reeds, overhanging trees and shallow banks quite often do not allow two boats to pass. After negotiating Watford Locks and reaching the summit level of 412ft there is nothing strenuous to look forward to, as this level continues for the next 20^1/2 miles. Four of these locks form a staircase – adopt a 'one up, one down' procedure, and use both ground and side paddles when going either up or down. At Watford the canal swings east away from the M1 for good. The locks and Crick Tunnel with its wooded approaches offer canal excitement to contrast with the quiet of the landscape.

NAVIGATIONAL NOTES

1. Please consult the lock keeper before using Watford Locks which are *open daily: summer Mon-Thu 08.00-17.00, Fri-Sun 08.00-18.00; winter 08.00-15.30.*
2. Local branches of the IWA have produced a guide to the Leicester Arm obtainable from various lockside positions (using a BW key) or from 30 Lutterworth Road, Leicester, LE2 8PF.

● **Welton**
Northants. Tel. The village climbs up the side of a steep, winding hill, which makes it compact and attractive, especially around the church.

● **Watford**
Northants. PO, tel, stores. Set in the middle of wooded parkland, Watford gives the impression of being a private village. The church and Watford Court dominate, and luckily the M1 has made no impact. The 13th-C church contains some interesting monuments. The Court is partly 17th-C, although there are Victorian additions. The rich brown stone used throughout the village adds to the feeling of unity.

● **Crick Tunnel**
1528yds long, the tunnel was opened in 1814. All tunnels built in this area suffered great problems in construction. Quicksands caused the route of the tunnel to be changed and greatly affected work. Stephenson found similar difficulties when building the nearby Kilsby Tunnel for the London to Birmingham railway.

Pubs and Restaurants

▣ ✕ **New Inn** Long Buckby Wharf (01327 842540). Canalside, at Buckby Top Lock. Cosy alcoved free house, serving Marston's and Bass real ale and a range of inexpensive meals and snacks *all day, every day*. Children and vegetarians catered for. Canalside seating and patio. Moorings. Darts, dominoes and skittles. Music *Sun. Open all day.*

▣ ✕ **Stag's Head** Watford Gap (01327 703621). Award-winning restaurant with a lovely canalside rose garden. An extensive menu – ranging from bar snacks to table d'hôte and a wide à la carte selection – is available *L & D, 7 days a week.* The cuisine encompasses English, French and Portuguese dishes. Very much a family establishment with prices to match. Everards real ale. Occasional Portuguese food theme *evenings in winter.* Moorings.

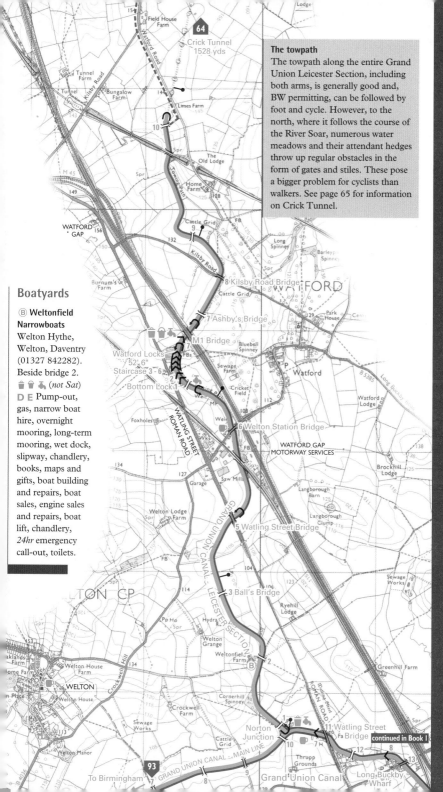

The towpath

The towpath along the entire Grand Union Leicester Section, including both arms, is generally good and, BW permitting, can be followed by foot and cycle. However, to the north, where it follows the course of the River Soar, numerous water meadows and their attendant hedges throw up regular obstacles in the form of gates and stiles. These pose a bigger problem for cyclists than walkers. See page 65 for information on Crick Tunnel.

Boatyards

Ⓑ **Weltonfield Narrowboats**
Welton Hythe, Welton, Daventry (01327 842282). Beside bridge 2.
🚿 🚿 🛠 (*not Sat*)
D E Pump-out, gas, narrow boat hire, overnight mooring, long-term mooring, wet dock, slipway, chandlery, books, maps and gifts, boat building and repairs, boat sales, engine sales and repairs, boat lift, chandlery, *24hr* emergency call-out, toilets.

continued in Book 1

Yelvertoft

Leaving Crick Tunnel the navigation bypasses the village and is soon alongside a smart, newly constructed marina. After skirting Crack's Hill, a curious tree-topped mound, the canal wanders to the east in a series of loops which cause it to miss both Yelvertoft and Winwick, the only villages in the section. Hills surround the course of the canal, encouraging its meandering. At one point it passes under the same road three times in under a mile. Occasional woods add to the pleasure of the isolation.

Boatyards

Ⓑ **ABNB** Crick Wharf, West Haddon Road, Crick (01788 822115/07721 378653). Boat sales.

Ⓑ **Crick Wharf** West Haddon Road, Crick (01788 824034). 🚰 Overnight mooring, long-term mooring, boat building and fitting-out.

Ⓑ **Crick Marina** West Haddon Road, Crick (01788 824056). 🚿 🚽 🚰 D E (by arrangement) Pump-out, gas, solid fuel, overnight mooring, dry dock, boat repairs, long-term mooring, toilets, laundrette, telephone.

Ⓑ **Paul Mudie Marine Services** Hakuna Matata, Crick Wharf, West Haddon Road, Crick (01788 822384/07961 809739). Boat and engine repairs, slipway, drydock, CORGI registered gas fitter. *24 hour* emergency call-out.

After Winwick, a vague north east course is resumed, passing the long abandoned village of Elkington. There are no locks, but a regular procession of brick- arched bridges serves as a reminder that it is still a canal.

● Crick

Northants. PO, tel, stores. A large village built around the junction of two roads. There are several attractive stone houses, and the large church has managed to escape restoration. It contains much decorative stonework and a circular Norman font. There is an intriguing second hand shop *open Wed, Fri & Sat 14.00–18.00* that could well warrant a visit.

● Yelvertoft

Northants. PO, tel, stores, garage. Set back from the canal, the village is built round a wide main street, terminated in the east by the church. Sadly, many of the original thatched roofs have been replaced.

● Winwick

Northants. Tel. One mile south east bridge 23. The 16th-C Manor House, built of richly decorated brick and with an ornamental Tudor gateway, is the major building in this neat, sleepy, village.

The towpath

Walkers and cyclists bypassing Crick Tunnel need to take the short track on the right of the tunnel mouth and, on joining the minor road, turn left. Follow this into the village and turn right down Boathorse Lane. When the road bends sharply to the left walkers may follow the footpath straight ahead (signposted to West Haddon), cross a field along the hedgerow (still following the waymarking to West Haddon) and, having negotiated the stile, bear left diagonally, downhill across the next field following the line of the drainage pits to the sign in the hedge, which is immediately above the northern tunnel cutting. Cyclists are advised to follow the road through the village, bearing right and rejoining the canal at bridge 12.

Pubs and Restaurants

✕♀ **Edwards of Crick** Crick (01788 822517). Beside bridge 12. Restaurant and coffee house offering a wide ranging menu from inexpensive *lunchtime* snacks through to a mouth-watering à la carte selection, *available at any time of the day.* Good value *Sunday lunch,* children half price. Everything home-made, including the bread. Excellent wine list and Hook Norton real ale. *Closed Sun evenings and Mon.*

🍺 **Red Lion** Main Street, Crick (01788 822342). Morland, Marston's, Theakston and Webster's real ale dispensed in a cosy, unadulterated pub with low ceilings and coal fires. Excellent home-cooked meals served with fresh vegetables *lunchtimes and evenings (not Sun).* Vegetarians catered for. Children *lunchtimes only.*

🍺 **Wheatsheaf** Main Street, Crick (01788 822284). Refurbished pub dispensing

Mansfield real ale. Food available *lunchtimes, evenings and all day Sun.* Children and vegetarians catered for. Pool. Garden. *Open all day.*

🍺 **Royal Oak** Church Street, Crick (01788 822340). Marston's, Theakston and guest real ales in an attractive old village local, with an unusual triangular, raised, wood-panelled bar area. Traditional pub games and *monthly* Sat night singing.

🍺 **Knightly Arms** Yelvertoft (01788 822401). Popular village local serving Greene King and guest real ales. Home cooked food available *lunchtimes (except Mon & Tue) and evenings (not Sun-Tue).* Traditional *Sunday lunches.* Children allowed in bar only if eating. Conservatory and large patio area. Garden. Table skittles, darts, dominoes and crib. *Closed Mon & Tue lunchtimes.*

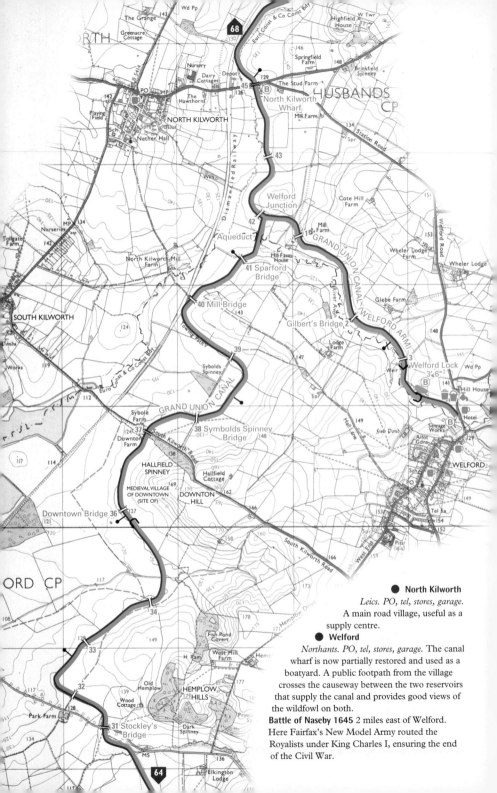

North Kilworth
Leics. PO, tel, stores, garage.
A main road village, useful as a
supply centre.

Welford
Northants. PO, tel, stores, garage. The canal
wharf is now partially restored and used as a
boatyard. A public footpath from the village
crosses the causeway between the two reservoirs
that supply the canal and provides good views of
the wildfowl on both.
Battle of Naseby 1645 2 miles east of Welford.
Here Fairfax's New Model Army routed the
Royalists under King Charles I, ensuring the end
of the Civil War.

Welford

Continuing north east the canal wanders on through open fields, backed by wood-ed hills to the east. To the west there are splendid views over the Avon valley. The river passes under the canal before the Welford Arm. Beyond the valley the spires of South and North Kilworth churches can be seen for several miles. The Welford Arm, which was completed in 1814, branches away to the south east for 1^1/2 miles, linking the canal with the Welford and Sulby Reservoirs, and reaches its terminus in a small basin; there is one shallow lock on the arm. Otherwise it is quiet and tree-lined, following closely the path of the Avon, whose source is just east of Welford. The arm was reopened to navigation in 1969, having been derelict for some years. The main line continues, entering the wooded cutting that announces Husbands Bosworth Tunnel. There are no locks, but many of the bridges are original, fine faded red brick, echoing the seclusion of the canal.

Stanford Hall Lutterworth (01788 860250). Two miles west of bridge 31. A William and Mary brick mansion (the south elevation is in stone), built in 1697–1700, with a Georgian stable block. Furniture, paintings, costume, motorcycle museum and a replica of the experimental flying machine built by Percy Pilcher in 1898. Walled rose garden and nature trail. Teas, shop and craft centre. *Open Easter–Sep, Sat, Sun, B. Hol. Mon & following Tue 14.30–17.00 (Craft centre open Sun & B. Hols).* Charge.

Boatyards

B **Welford Marina** Canal Wharf, Welford (01858 575995). ⬛ ⬛ ⬛ D Gas, day hire craft, overnight mooring, long-term mooring, boat and engine repairs, boat fitting-out, wet dock, dry dock, DIY facilities, solid fuel, toilets.

B **Coronet Canal Carrying Company** Kilworth Marina, North Kilworth (01788 510410). Narrow boat hire including rebuilt working boat with accommodation under insulated canvas. Canal carriers between Norton Junction and Welford.

B **Anglo Welsh Waterway Holidays** Kilworth Marina, North Kilworth (01858 880484). By bridge 45. Narrow boat hire.

B **North Kilworth Narrowboats** Kilworth Marina, North Kilworth (01858 880484). By bridge 45. ⬛ ⬛ ⬛ D E Pump-out, gas, day hire boats, overnight mooring, long-term mooring (up to 26ft only), winter storage, slipway, wet dock, chandlery, boat sales and repairs, engine sales and repairs, DIY facilities, *24hr* emergency call-out, books, maps and gifts, toilets, groceries, off-licence.

Pubs and Restaurants

⬛ ✕ **Wharf Inn** Canal Wharf, Welford (01858 575075). Marston's and guest real ales. Bar snacks and restaurant menu available *lunchtimes and evenings. Sunday lunchtime* carvery. Children and vegetarians catered for. Large canalside garden.

⬛ **Shoulder of Mutton** High Street, Welford (01858 575375). Up the hill, towards the top of the village. Home-made food *lunchtimes and evenings (not Thu)* and well kept Worthington, Bass and guest real ales dispensed in a heavily-beamed, 17th-C hostelry. Family room. Darts, skittles, dominoes. Large garden.

⬛ ✕ **Elizabethan** High Street, Welford (01858 575311). At the top of the hill, beyond the Shoulder of Mutton. Bass real ale and food available *L & D (no food on Sun & Mon L & D & Tue D).* Fri & Sat dinner dances to 50s and 60s disco music plus *monthly Fri* theme evenings.

⬛ ✕ **White Lion** Lutterworth Road, North Kilworth (01858 880260). Marston's and guest real ales and food *lunchtimes and evenings (except Mon evenings).* Garden and pub games. Disabled access.

⬛ ✕ **Swan Inn** Lutterworth Road, North Kilworth (01858 880957). Tetley's, Ansells and guest real ales. Bar food and à la carte meals available *L & D Tue-Sat and Sun L.* Children and vegetarians catered for. Games room and patio.

Husbands Bosworth

Continuing north east, the canal enters a remote, but attractive stretch. There are no villages on the canal here, Husbands Bosworth being hidden by the tunnel. The A50 crosses over the tunnel and meets the A427 in Husbands Bosworth. The canal runs north east through fields to the top of Foxton Locks. It then falls 75ft to join the former Leicester & Northampton Union Canal. At the bottom of the locks the 5³/₄ mile Market Harborough Arm branches off to the east.

NAVIGATIONAL NOTES

Foxton Locks are *open daily as per Watford Locks on page 62.*

● **Husbands Bosworth**
Leics. PO, tel, stores, garage. Access from canal: walk up the lane from bridge 46.
Husbands Bosworth Tunnel 1166yds long, opened in 1813.
Foxton Locks The Foxton staircase was opened in 1812. There are two staircases of five locks each with a passing pound in the middle. Check each flight of five is clear before you enter.
Foxton Inclined Plane In 1900 an inclined plane was opened to bypass Foxton Locks. Two caissons carrying either two narrow boats or one barge moving sideways on rails up and down the plane. A steam-driven winch pulling an endless cable was used to start the caissons moving. The journey time was reduced from 70 to 12 minutes. Mechanical problems and high running costs, plus the fact that the planned widening of the Watford flight never took place, soon made the plane a white elephant. The cut leading to the bottom of the plane is still navigable, and the plane itself can still be traced, running at right angles to the east of the locks. Exploratory trail and museum *open Easter–Oct, daily 11.00–17.00; Nov–Easter, weekends 10.00–16.00 (opening times subject to staff availability).* Charge. Restoration is in the hands of **Foxton Inclined Plane Trust** Middle Lock, Foxton Locks, Foxton, Market Harborough (0116 279 2657). There is a picnic site, car park and toilets (including disabled) at bridge 60, beside the Gumley road. Charge.

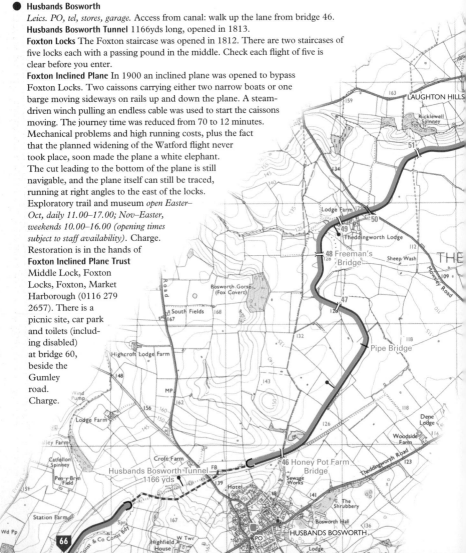

Boatyards

Ⓑ **Foxton Boat Services** Bottom Lock, Foxton, Market Harborough (0116 279 2285). 🚿 🚻 ⚓ D Pump-out, gas, narrow boat hire, day hire craft, overnight mooring, long-term mooring, winter storage, slipway, crane (20 tons), boat fitting-out, chandlery, boat sales and repairs, engine sales and repairs, wet dock, DIY facilities, telephone, toilets, showers, groceries, café and pub, laundrette, books, maps and gifts. Commercial boat hire. *24 hour* emergency call-out.

The towpath

Walkers and cyclists confronted with Husbands Bosworth Tunnel should take the track climbing up to the left of the tunnel mouth and follow it over the hill to the road on the outskirts of the village (A50). Cross this road and follow the track over the disused railway line, down a tree-lined glade, rejoining the waterway at the eastern tunnel portal.

Pubs and Restaurants

✗ ⚑ **Fernie Lodge** Berridges Lane, Husbands Bosworth (01858 880551). Hotel and restaurant. *L & D table d'hôte menus available 7 days a week.* Children's portions.

🍺 ✗ **Bell Inn** Kilworth Road, Husbands Bosworth (01858 880246). Greene King real ale. Meals *lunchtimes and evenings, 7 days a week.* Family room and garden. Pub games.

🍺 **Bridge 61** In the midst of Foxton Boat Services (0116 279 2476). Adnams and Everards real ale and home-made bar food

lunchtimes and evenings, 7 days a week. Children and dogs welcome. Canalside seating.

🍺 **Bell** Gumley (0116 279 2476). Bass, Boddingtons, Ridleys, Wadworth and guest real ales dispensed in a friendly, old village local. Food available *lunchtimes and evenings (not Sun or Mon evenings)* and vegetarians and children (over 5) catered for. No smoking restaurant, garden and traditional pub games (no machines). Real cider and real fires in winter.

BOAT TRIPS

Vagabond & Vixen Horse-drawn and motorised canal trips for casual visitors *on summer Sunday afternoons and B. Hols* from Foxton bottom lock; available for charter by parties any other day (minimum 20 passengers, maximum 51). Telephone 0116 279 2285 for details.

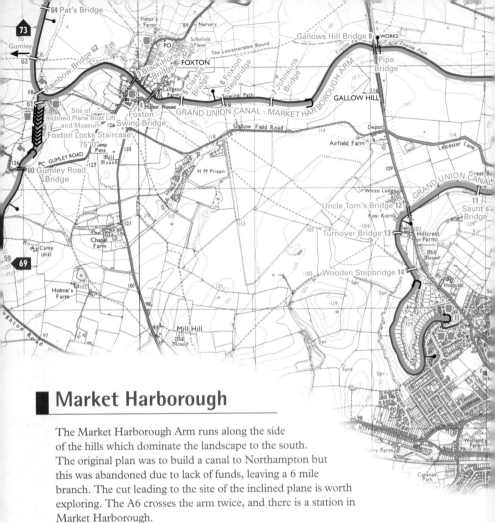

Market Harborough

The Market Harborough Arm runs along the side
of the hills which dominate the landscape to the south.
The original plan was to build a canal to Northampton but
this was abandoned due to lack of funds, leaving a 6 mile
branch. The cut leading to the site of the inclined plane is worth
exploring. The A6 crosses the arm twice, and there is a station in
Market Harborough.

● **Foxton**
Leics. Tel. A village built on the side of a hill,
either side of the canal, in pretty countryside.
There is an excellent information leaflet and
village trail available from Foxton Boat Services
and Market Harborough Tourist Information
Centre.

● **Market Harborough**
*Leics. MD Tue, Fri, Sat. PO, tel, stores, garage,
banks, station.* Established as a market town by
1203, Market Harborough still retains much of
its rural elegance and local importance.
There is an antique and collectors market *every
Sunday* in the market hall (01604 882399).
Busline (0116 251 1411). For full details on bus
travel to local (and not so local) attractions.

Frank Haynes Gallery 50 Station Road, Great
Bowden, Market Harborough (01858 464862).
3/4 mile north of the station. Two galleries with
paintings and pottery from the region. Cards,
etc. *Open Thu–Sun 10.00–17.00.* Free.
Harborough Leisure Centre Northampton Road,
Market Harborough (01858 410115). The usual
mix of swimming pool, child-enticing water
features, fitness room, etc. Also bar, bistro and
crèche.
Harborough Museum Council Offices, Adam and
Eve Street, Market Harborough (01858
4432468). Contains the Civic Society's own
collection and illustrates local life from the
earliest times. Relics of the Battle of Naseby, a
reconstructed bootmakers workshop and the

Symington Collection of corsetry. *Open Mon–Sat 10.00–16.30 & Sun 14.00–17.00. Closed G. Fri, Xmas Day & Box. Day.* Free. Disabled access via council offices so contact staff in advance *on Sat, Sun & B. Hols.*

Harborough Theatre Church Square, Market Harborough (01858 463673).

Market Harborough Canal Basin Significant as the site of the first Inland Waterways Association campaigning rally held in 1950 which, arguably, laid the foundations for a resurgence in canal interest that could easily be taken for granted by the contemporary pleasure boater. The canal basin has recently been extended and the surrounding area developed with apartments and facilities for craft units. There are new BW moorings together with a shower block, DIY pump-out, toilets, etc. (See Navigational Notes on page 75).

Parish Church of St Dionysius High Street. Built in the 14thC by Scropes and enlarged a century later. The broach spire and west tower are notable.

Old Grammar School High Street. Founded by Robert Smyth. It stands on wooden carved pillars, and behind the arches was held the ancient butter market. The building was used as the grammar school until 1892 and is now a meeting hall.

Tourist Information Centre Council Offices, Adam and Eve Street, Market Harborough (01858 821010). *Open Mon-Fri 08.45-17.00, Sat 09.30-12.00.*

Pubs and Restaurants

Black Horse Main Street, Foxton (01858 545250). Marston's and guest real ales. An excellent selection of home-made food is available *lunchtimes and evenings, 7 days a week.* (Bookings advisable *summer evenings and Sun lunchtimes*). Vegetarian and children's menu. No smoking, conservatory dining area. Garden with animals for children. Jazz *Wed.* Crib, darts and skittle alley.

Shoulder of Mutton Main Street, Foxton (01858 545666). Tetley and two guest real ales. Food served *lunchtimes and evenings, 7 days a week.* Children and vegetarians catered for. Large garden and children's play area. Non-smoking room. Pub games and live music *Sat.* B & B.

The Union Leicester Road, Market Harborough (01858 463690). Courage real ale and bar food available *lunchtimes.* Pool and darts. Disco *Fri & Sat.*

Angel Hotel High Street, Market Harborough (01858 462702). Full à la carte restaurant menu through to bar meals, *served L & D, 7 days a week.* Patio. B & B.

Three Swans Hotel High Street, Market Harborough. Ruddles and Courage real ales and a comprehensive range of food, *L & D 7 days a week.* The restaurant (*closed Sun evenings*) offers both table d'hôte and à la carte menus whilst meals are available in the bar *every lunchtime and evening.* Vegetarians and children catered for. B & B.

Red Cow 58–59 High Street, Market Harborough (01858 463637). Marston's real ales.

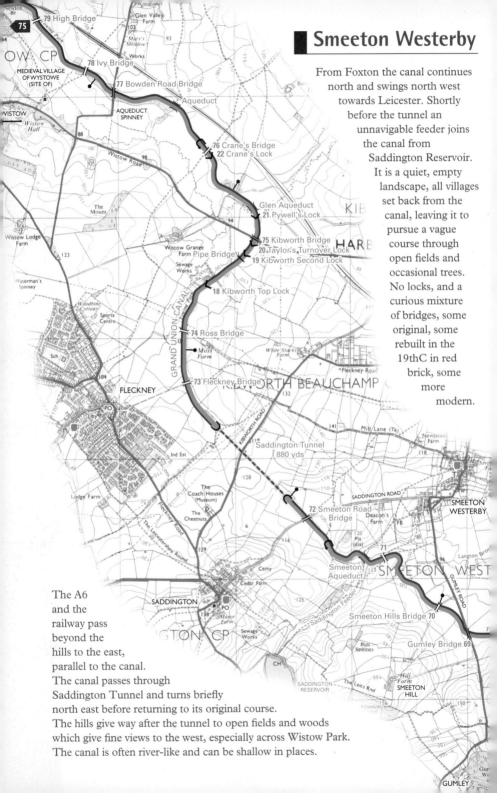

Smeeton Westerby

From Foxton the canal continues north and swings north west towards Leicester. Shortly before the tunnel an unnavigable feeder joins the canal from Saddington Reservoir. It is a quiet, empty landscape, all villages set back from the canal, leaving it to pursue a vague course through open fields and occasional trees. No locks, and a curious mixture of bridges, some original, some rebuilt in the 19thC in red brick, some more modern.

The A6 and the railway pass beyond the hills to the east, parallel to the canal.
The canal passes through Saddington Tunnel and turns briefly north east before returning to its original course.
The hills give way after the tunnel to open fields and woods which give fine views to the west, especially across Wistow Park.
The canal is often river-like and can be shallow in places.

Map labels:
Newton Br
79 High Bridge
Glen Valley Farm
Mary's Meadow
Works
78 Ivy Bridge
MEDIEVAL VILLAGE OF WYSTOWE (SITE OF)
77 Bowden Road Bridge
Aqueduct
AQUEDUCT SPINNEY
WISTOW
Wistow Hall
Wistow Road
76 Crane's Bridge
22 Crane's Lock
The Mount
Glen Aqueduct
21 Pywell's Lock
KIB
Wistow Lodge Farm
Wistow Grange Farm Pipe Bridge
75 Kibworth Bridge
20 Taylor's Turnover Lock
19 Kibworth Second Lock
HARB
Sewage Works
Waterman's Spinney
18 Kibworth Top Lock
Woodbine Cottage
Sports Centre
74 Ross Bridge
Moss Farm
White Stocks Farm
Fleckney Road
Sch
73 Fleckney Bridge
KIBWORTH BEAUCHAMP
FLECKNEY
Lib
PO
GRAND UNION CANAL
Ind Est
Saddington Tunnel 880 yds
Mill Lane (Tk)
Newstead Farm
Lodge Farm
The Coach Houses (Museum)
The Chestnuts
SADDINGTON ROAD
72 Smeeton Road Bridge
Deacon's Farm
FB
SMEETON WESTERBY
71
Langton Brook
SADDINGTON
PO
Manor Farm
Cemy
Cedar Farm
Smeeton Aqueduct
SMEETON WEST
GUMLEY ROAD
Sewage Works
Bull Spinney
Smeeton Hills Bridge 70
Gumley Bridge 69
CH
SADDINGTON RESERVOIR
The Leics Rnd
Hill Farm
SMEETON HILL
GUMLEY

Gumley
Leics. PO box, tel. 1/2 mile west bridge 63. Small village scattered among trees, set on a hillside high above the canal. The Italianate tower of Gumley Hall rises above the trees, overlooking the valley.

Saddington
Leics. PO, tel. Small village set back from the canal, with only the church tower breaking the skyline.

Smeeton Westerby
Leics. Tel. The village undulates over the hills to the east of the canal, built along the sides of the main street. The church is Victorian, by Woodyer.
Saddington Tunnel 880yds long, the tunnel was completed in 1797, after great difficulties owing to its being built crooked. Naturalists enthuse about the bats that nowadays live in the tunnel.

Fleckney
Leics. PO, tel, stores. An industrial village just 10 minutes' walk from the canal. Very useful for its supermarket, fish & chip shop and Chinese take-away.

Wistow
Leics. For a while the canal runs through woods and parkland to the west adjoining Wistow Park. Wistow itself has a church and a Hall, the church with Norman work but mostly 18th-C, including fine monuments. The Hall is Jacobean in principle but was largely rebuilt in the 19th-C.

Pubs and Restaurants

Queens Head Main Street, Saddington (0116 240 2536). A village centre pub with attractive gardens and a cosy restaurant, set in a tasteful extension with superb views over Saddington Reservoir. A wide range of food from a full à la carte menu to tasty snacks and an extensive range of bar meals *L & D (no food Sun evenings)*. Vegetarians catered for and children over five welcome. Everards, Adnams and guest real ales. Live music *Sun.* Booking advisable *especially at weekends.*

Kings Head Smeeton Westerby (0116 279 2676). Unadulterated, village local offering a friendly welcome and Ansells, Marston's and Tetley real ale. Inexpensive food available *lunchtimes and evenings except Mon & Tue evenings* (special *evening* meal deals). Vegetarians catered for, outside seating. Darts, dominoes, crib.

Old Crown Fleckney (0116 240 2223). West of bridge 73. Wide range of appetising snacks and nourishing main meals in this friendly, welcoming village pub. Food is available *lunchtimes, evenings and all day Fri and Sat.* Everards, Adnams and guest real ales. Children and vegetarians catered for. Patio, darts, dominoes and pool. Several of the walls are lined with a colourful array of books: bring a book and you are welcome to exchange it.

Boatyards

Ⓑ **Debdale Wharf Marina** Kibworth (0116 279 3034). Pump-out, gas, narrow boat hire, overnight mooring, long-term mooring, winter storage, crane (25 tons), slipway, dry dock, wet dock, chandlery, boat lengthening, boat sales and repairs, engine sales and repairs, boat building & boat fitting-out, DIY facilities, books, maps solid fuel, general fabrication. Emergency call-out.

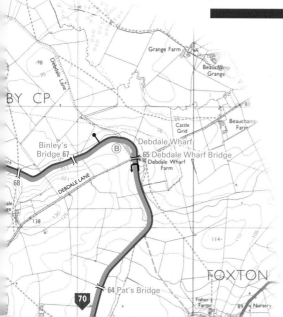

Wigston

Newton Harcourt breaks the unwritten rule of this navigation by being right beside it (other villages keep their distance). The tunnel, the bridges and the locks which begin the descent to Leicester provide plenty of canal interest although the amount of rubbish in the waterway begins to increase. The A6 and the main railway slowly encroach on the canal to the east. The navigation follows the north-westerly course of the River Sence, bounded by low hills to east and west and still remote, until Kilby Bridge where indications of the town of Leicester begin with distant views of housing estates and factories. By Ervin's Lock at South Wigston the town seems to take over. The locks continue the steady fall, giving the stretch its individuality. The A50 crosses at Kilby Bridge, where there are good moorings, showers and a pump-out (card operated – see page 7), and the railway keeps the canal company to the east. Immediately to the north west of Leicester Road Bridge 98 is the original site of Pickfords Canal Carriers, established when they transferred their activities from horse and cart to the newly burgeoning canals. A little further west, before the navigation swings north, are the disused clay pits and derelict brickyard, once owned by the Union Canal Company, to produce the materials used to construct its locks and bridges.

Boatyards

BW Kilby Bridge Yard Kilby Bridge (0115 946 1017). Pump-out, moorings, showers.

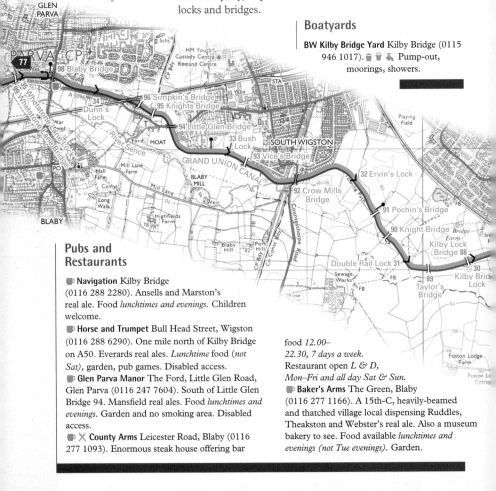

Pubs and Restaurants

Navigation Kilby Bridge (0116 288 2280). Ansells and Marston's real ale. Food *lunchtimes and evenings*. Children welcome.

Horse and Trumpet Bull Head Street, Wigston (0116 288 6290). One mile north of Kilby Bridge on A50. Everards real ales. *Lunchtime* food (*not Sat*), garden, pub games. Disabled access.

Glen Parva Manor The Ford, Little Glen Road, Glen Parva (0116 247 7604). South of Little Glen Bridge 94. Mansfield real ales. Food *lunchtimes and evenings*. Garden and no smoking area. Disabled access.

County Arms Leicester Road, Blaby (0116 277 1093). Enormous steak house offering bar

food *12.00–22.30, 7 days a week*. Restaurant open *L & D, Mon–Fri and all day Sat & Sun*.

Baker's Arms The Green, Blaby (0116 277 1166). A 15th-C, heavily-beamed and thatched village local dispensing Ruddles, Theakston and Webster's real ale. Also a museum bakery to see. Food available *lunchtimes and evenings (not Tue evenings)*. Garden.

Newton Harcourt

Leics. Scattered village bisected by the railway in a cutting. The Hall is 17th-C, with later rebuilding; it has a fine gateway. Newton Harcourt is a well-known Leicester beauty spot, popular on *Sunday afternoons.*
Busline (0116 251 1411). For full details on bus travel to local (and not so local) attractions.
David Smithust Gallery Wistow Garden Centre (0116 259 3287). See entry below for access details, etc. Wide range of furniture, paintings, gifts and a gallery.
Wistan Le Dale Model Village Wistow Garden Centre, Wistow, Nr Great Glen (0116 259 2009). Take footpath south from Ivy Bridge 78 to the church. Acclaimed model village (setting for the children's storybook *Tales from Old Wistan*), 1/18th scale, mid-Victorian period. Village railway. Also craft shop, artists studios, teashop *serving lunches, teas and coffee,* garden centre and village store. *Open daily except Tue.* Donations to Rainbow a children's hospice charity.

Kilby Bridge
Leics. PO, tel, garage.

South Wigston
Leics. PO, tel, stores, garage. Wigston is now a part of Leicester, but traces of its earlier independence can still be found. Much of the handsome church dates from the 14thC, especially the interior, while the cottages in Spa Lane with their long strips of upper window indicate an old Leicester industry, stocking making. At Wigston Parva there is a tiny Norman church and a monument to the Roman town of Veronae. Unfortunately,

only housing estates and a school can be seen from the canal, but exploration is worthwhile. **Leicestershire Record Office** Long Street, Wigston Magna, Leicester (0116 257 1080). Manuscripts, photographs, registers, archive film, newspapers, sound recordings, etc dating back to 1881, all of which may be studied. *Open Mon, Tue & Thu 09.15–17.00, Wed 09.15–19.30, Fri 09.15–16.45, Sat 09.15–12.15. Closed Public Hols. & Sat proceeding B. Hols.* Free. Disabled access.
Wigston Framework Knitters Museum 42/44 Bushloe End, Wigston (0116 288 3396). About 1/2 mile north of Kilby Bridge 87. Heritage award-winning 18th-C knitters house and workshop. Demonstrations. Refreshments. *Open every Sun, first Sat of month & B. Hol Mon (except Xmas & New Year) 14.00–17.00.* Charge.

Blaby
Leics. PO, tel, stores, garage. The church is partly 14th-C, with a fine 18th-C gallery unsuited to the Blaby of today. The County Arms, a monumental 1930s roadhouse beside Bridge 98, is more in keeping.

NAVIGATIONAL NOTES

1 A handcuff key (as used on the Erewash Canal) is needed to operate the water saving gear between Ervin's Lock and Aylestone Mill. Keys are obtainable from boatyards and the Navigation pub at Kilby bridge.

2 BW owned shower blocks and DIY pump-outs are now card operated and cards are available from the same outlets as above.

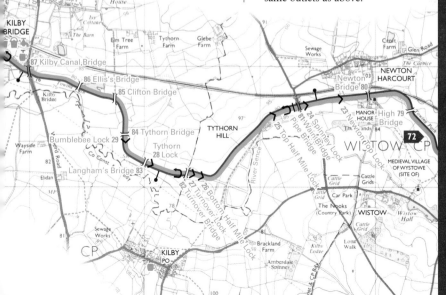

Aylestone

Following the River Sence to its junction with the Soar, the canal makes a wide swing around Glen Parva and then flows north into Leicester along the Soar valley. After Glen Parva the buildings suddenly cease, and there follows a mile of pleasant rural canal, lightly wooded to the east, and the extensive water meadows of the Soar to the west. The river and canal flow side by side separated only by the towpath; inevitably in winter this can cause flooding, *and anyone intending to navigate this stretch after heavy rainfall should check the state of the water before proceeding.* Only the pylons and the distant views of Braunston and Aylestone reveal the closeness of Leicester. The canal and the Soar meet by the old gasworks where there is a huge weir; care is needed during times of flood. The canal enters Leicester along a pleasant cutting. A variety of buildings line the banks and there is a fine canalside walk under the ornamental bridges that lead straight into the town centre by West Bridge. These factors combine to make the canal entry to Leicester outstanding among large towns. The A46 and A426 run parallel to the canal, but the railway which follows it, the old Great Central line, is now closed.

NAVIGATIONAL NOTES

The canal and the River Soar meet just above Freeman's Meadow Lock, where there is an enormous unprotected weir. Care is needed, especially in time of flood. KEEP WELL OVER TO THE TOWPATH SIDE.

● **Glen Parva**
Leics. PO, tel, stores, garage. Suburb of Leicester inseparable now from the main town. Curiously enough there was a Saxon cemetery in the town from which 6th-C grave ornaments have been excavated.

● **Aylestone**
Leics. PO, tel, stores, take-aways, chemist, bank, garage. A Leicester suburb coming down to the east bank of the canal. The church contains an interesting stained glass window of 1930. To the west of the canal the Soar is crossed by an old stone packhorse bridge of eight low arches, perhaps dating from the 15thC. This area still retains the feel of a country village, at least in the area sandwiched between the main Rugby road and the navigation. Narrow streets, bordered by pretty brick cottages, isolate the walker from the bustle of what is otherwise a busy suburb of Leicester. Aylestone Hall and its surrounding gardens and recreational park is a particular haven of peace. On the west of the waterway Aylestone Meadows is now a nature reserve stretching for a mile and half along the canal and Great Central Way (once the route of the Great Central Railway and now a cycle route and footpath). There are waymarked circular walks along a network of paths together with excellent illustrated interpretation boards. The nature reserve is operated by Leicester City Council (0116 252 7297) who employ rangers who patrol the riverside on motorcycles and can provide advice and assistance. Access for shops and the Union Inn is east from Freestone Bridge 106. There is also a useful farm shop between Packhorse Bridge 105 and the railway bridge.

Busline (0116 251 1411). For full details on bus travel to local (and not so local) attractions.

Gas Museum British Gas, Aylestone Road, Leicester (0116 253 5506). Situated in the Victorian gatehouse of one of the city's gas works: the first museum to tell the story of the impact of gas on our lives from 19th-C lighting to a gas hairdryer and radio. *Open Tue–Fri 12.30–16.30. Closed G. Fri, Xmas Day & Tue following B. Hols.* Free. Disabled access to ground floor.

Raw Dykes Ancient Monument Aylestone Road, Leicester (0116 247 3021). A large earthwork near to the canal and River Soar; presumed to be a Romano-British aqueduct. Viewing area *open at all times.* Disabled access.

Grand Union Canal – Leicester Section — Aylestone

TO DYE – THE DEATH

For nearly two decades the appearance of the combined River Soar and canal skirting Aylestone – and along the Mile Straight, bordering the city itself – was of an inky, opaque blackness far removed from the image of a burbling, infant stream. This off-putting and unnatural phenomenon served only to reinforce the perception that Leicester was not a city to linger in. In reality the cause was trade effluent from several dye works, established in Wigston since the year dot, passing straight through the local sewerage treatment works. New legislation had, however, imposed colour conditions on discharges amounting to full colour removal: a real challenge for the fledgling Environment Agency's hard-pressed chemists.

Yet what remained was the puzzle of the problem's relatively recent origins. One plausible explanation lay in the changing nature of the fashion industry. Once, ostensibly, buyer-led (we responded to the length of a skirt or the cut of a suit) our sartorial whims became firmly orchestrated by the industry itself: colour consistently being its key device. In unison went a definite movement towards man-made fibres and their reactive dye processes: bright colours predominated in wardrobes, their turgid residues lingered in rivers.

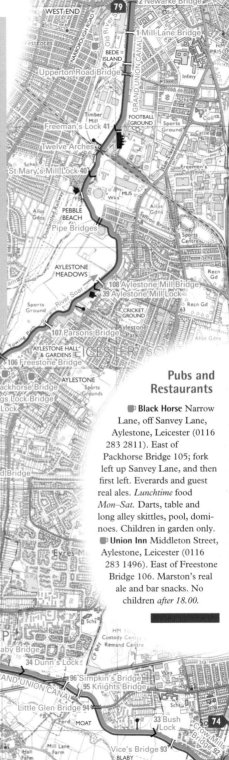

Pubs and Restaurants

🍺 **Black Horse** Narrow Lane, off Sanvey Lane, Aylestone, Leicester (0116 283 2811). East of Packhorse Bridge 105; fork left up Sanvey Lane, and then first left. Everards and guest real ales. *Lunchtime* food *Mon–Sat.* Darts, table and long alley skittles, pool, dominoes. Children in garden only.

🍺 **Union Inn** Middleton Street, Aylestone, Leicester (0116 283 1496). East of Freestone Bridge 106. Marston's real ale and bar snacks. No children *after 18.00.*

Leicester

For almost all of its journey through the city of Leicester, the navigation pursues a course quite separate from the river, the navigation having been rebuilt towards the end of the 19thC as part of Leicester's flood prevention scheme. For more than $^1/_2$ mile south of West Bridge, the navigation, a section known locally as the Mile Straight, is like a formal avenue, tree-lined and crossed by several ornamental iron bridges, but where it curves under the old Great Central Railway it begins to follow a less public course through the nether regions of Leicester. A combination of locks, once-derelict canal basins (some now restored for moorings), tall factory buildings and a substantial stretch of parkland adds up to a stretch of urban canal that offers a greater variety of interest than exists in most other cities. At Belgrave Lock the canal joins the Soar, which proceeds to meander carelessly through the city's outskirts. The city centre is remarkably compact, and there are some gems amongst the façades jostled together along its main thoroughfares, with everything surprisingly close to the moorings at Castle Gardens. As is the case with all large towns, if you moor at an unprotected site make sure your boat is securely locked if you leave it unattended. Birstall provides a useful mooring and place to shop to the north of the city: tie up near the lock and walk up beside the White Horse.

NAVIGATIONAL NOTES

It is worth remembering that the River Soar may flood at any time, so boaters travelling after heavy rainfall should enquire about the navigational conditions in advance in order to avert the risk of running aground in the middle of a water meadow.

● **Leicester**
MD Wed, Fri, Sat. All services. A prosperous city with two universities. Fortunes were founded on the hosiery and the boot and shoe trades, but now a variety of light industries flourish in Leicester. There are a great many things to see, for this was the Roman town of Ratae and there is plenty of evidence of the Roman buildings, plus a castle that dates from 1088, with the delightful church of St Mary de Castro next to it. The travel agent Thomas Cook started business in Leicester; in 1841 he organised the first publicly advertised excursion by train. It was a great success, and Cook made the organising of such trips a regular occupation. Leicester has a particularly good selection of museums, and it is fortunate that most of these are near the Grand Union Canal which forms the western boundary of Castle Park. The city should be commended, both for the comprehensive manner in which it markets its copious wealth of attractions and for promoting its cultural diversity in such a positive fashion. The opportunities to sample Asian cuisine, produce, jewellery, cloth, faith and festivals must be second to none outside the Indian sub-continent and could, alone, fill this page. With the provision of secure visitor moorings at Castle Gardens and, in the near future, at Memory Lane Wharf, the boater has no reason to ignore a city that has so much to offer.
Abbey Park Abbey Park Road, Leicester. All that remains of the abbey is a mansion built from the ruins and the old stone wall surrounding the grounds. Cardinal Wolsey was buried here in 1530. The park itself, very much in the Victorian mould, has a boating lake, Chinese garden, bandstand and riverside café and is the setting for music festivals and fairs. There is a landing stage in Abbey Park Basin. *Open daily.*
Abbey Pumping Station Corporation Road, Abbey Lane, Leicester (0116 266 1330). Dating from 1891 this refurbished site features the Victorian steam-powered beam engines that used to pump the city's sewerage to the nearby treatment plant. Also a unique public health exhibition and the manager's house circa World War II. *Open Mon–Sat 10.00–17.30 & Sun 14.00–17.30. Closed G. Fri, Xmas Day & Box. Day.* Free. Partial disabled access. Moorings. It is expected that during 2000 the National Space Centre will open alongside the Pumping Station site. For further details contact the Tourist Information Centre.
Belgrave Hall and Gardens Church Road, Belgrave, Leicester (0116 266 6590). Three-storey Queen Anne house dating from 1709 with attractive period and botanical gardens, and 18th- and 19th-C room settings including kitchen, drawing room and nursery. *Open Mon–Sat 10.00–17.30, Sun 14.00–17.30. Closed G. Fri, Xmas Day & Box. Day.* Free. Disabled access to gardens and ground floor only. Moorings.

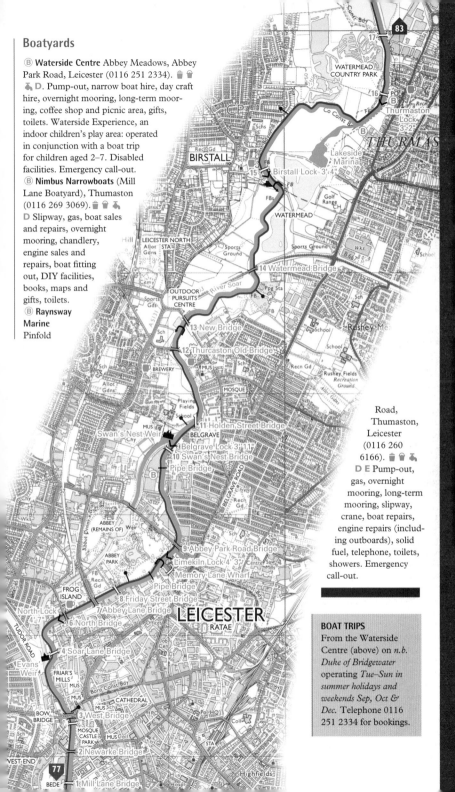

Boatyards

Ⓑ **Waterside Centre** Abbey Meadows, Abbey Park Road, Leicester (0116 251 2334). 🛁 🚻 🛒 **D**. Pump-out, narrow boat hire, day craft hire, overnight mooring, long-term mooring, coffee shop and picnic area, gifts, toilets. Waterside Experience, an indoor children's play area: operated in conjunction with a boat trip for children aged 2–7. Disabled facilities. Emergency call-out.

Ⓑ **Nimbus Narrowboats** (Mill Lane Boatyard), Thumaston (0116 269 3069). 🛒 🚻 🛁 **D** Slipway, gas, boat sales and repairs, overnight mooring, chandlery, engine sales and repairs, boat fitting out, DIY facilities, books, maps and gifts, toilets.

Ⓑ **Raynsway Marine** Pinfold Road, Thumaston, Leicester (0116 260 6166). 🛒 🚻 🛁 **D E** Pump-out, gas, overnight mooring, long-term mooring, slipway, crane, boat repairs, engine repairs (including outboards), solid fuel, telephone, toilets, showers. Emergency call-out.

BOAT TRIPS

From the Waterside Centre (above) on *n.b. Duke of Bridgewater* operating *Tue–Sun in summer holidays and weekends Sep, Oct & Dec.* Telephone 0116 251 2334 for bookings.

Castle Gardens & Castle Motte Riverside between St Nicholas Circle and The Newarke. Once a low-lying marshy area of reeds and willows it was drained in the late 19thC as part of the city's flood alleviation scheme and initially used as allotments. The public gardens were established in 1926. The raised mound, or Motte, dates from the 11thC and would originally have been surmounted by a timber fortification. Garden *open daily during daylight hours and as an access for boaters to secure moorings.*

Cathedral Guildhall Lane, Leicester (0116 262 5294). Originally the parish church of St Martin's, it was extended in the 14th and 15thC, restored in the 19thC and became the cathedral in 1927. *Open daily.* Donations. Disabled toilets.

De Montfort Hall Granville Road, Leicester (0116 233 3111). Prime venue for touring opera and ballet companies and for orchestras and soloist alike.

Eco House Western Park, Hinckley Road, Leicester (0116 285 6675/4047). Environment-friendly show home featuring energy efficient, sustainable living with emphasis on renewable energy, organic garden, water conservation and health. Playground, shop and refreshments. *Open all year, Wed–Fri 14.00–17.00, weekends 10.00–17.00.* Donations appreciated. Bus service.

Golden Mile An area centred on Belgrave Road, to the north of the city centre, where the focus lies on the superb range of Asian cultural delights and cuisine, reflecting Leicester's status as a truly cosmopolitan city. Excellent guide entitled *A Taste of Asia* available from Tourist Information Centre (see page 81). Free.

Guildhall Guildhall Lane, Leicester (0116 253 2569). Built by the Guild of Corpus Christi and dating from the 14thC it contains fine oak panelling and an elaborately carved chimney-piece from 1637. It includes the Old Town Library, 19th-C police cells and a Great Hall with civic murals. *Open Mon–Sat 10.00–17.30 & Sun 14.00–17.30. Closed G. Fri, Xmas Day & Box. Day.* Free. Disabled toilets.

Guru Nanak Gurdwara & Sikh Museum 9 Holy Bones, Leicester (0116 262 8606). An impressive Sikh Temple in a transformed hosiery factory. Also spectacular models of shrines, manuscripts, paintings, coins, photographic portrayal of the part played by Sikh soldiers in both World Wars in a museum depicting the history of the Sikh nation. *Open to devotees daily.* Museum *open Thu 13.00–16.00. Other times by appointment.* Free.

Haymarket Theatre Belgrave Gate, Leicester (0116 253 9797). Venue for hit shows bound for the West End, with the emphasis on musicals. Also hard-hitting modern drama and the classics. **Studio Theatre** is home to more

avant garde productions. Café and bar.

Jain Centre 32 Oxford Street, Leicester (0116 254 3091). A fine example of traditional Indian architecture in the western world and a place of pilgrimage for Jains. Shrines of white marble, hand-carved pillars, stained glass, mirror walls, a dome and ceilings in sandstone. *Open Mon–Fri 14.00–17.30.* Donations appreciated.

Jewry Wall Museum St Nicholas Circle, Leicester (0116 247 3021). Collection of the county's archaeology from early times through to the Middle Ages overlooking the Jewry Wall, a small portion of which remains. This is thought to have been part of a basilica or Roman baths dating from the 2ndC. Two Roman mosaic pavements can be seen in situ. *Open Mon–Sat 10.00–17.30 & Sun 14.00–17.30. Closed G. Fri, Xmas Day & Box. Day.* Free. Disabled access (and toilet) via entrance in Holy Bones.

Little Theatre Dover Street, Leicester (0116 255 1302). Amateur dramatics, social activities and theatre workshops.

Markets Market Place, Leicester (0116 252 6776). The Food Hall selling fresh meat, poultry, dairy produce and fish from all over the world is *open Tue–Sat 06.30–18.00.* The retail market, composed of over 300 covered stalls, is *open Mon–Sat 07.00–18.00.*

Museum & Art Gallery New Walk, Leicester (0116 255 4100). Italian, Spanish and Flemish old masters. 18th–20thC English paintings. Also French Impressionists and German Expressionists, ceramics, silver, archives, natural history and geology. *Open Mon–Sat 10.00–17.30, Sun 14.00–17.30. Closed G. Fri, Xmas Day & Box. Day.* Free. Disabled access.

Newarke Houses Museum The social history of the area from 1500 to the present day. Locally made clocks and a clockmaker's workshop. Also shows the history of the hosiery, costume and lace industries. There is a reconstructed Victorian street scene. *Open Mon–Sat 10.00–17.30 & Sun 14.00–17.30. Closed G. Fri, Xmas Day & Box. Day.* Free. Disabled access difficult.

Phoenix Arts Centre Newarke Street, Leicester (0116 255 4854). Cinema and live performances of contemporary dance, mime, jazz and folk. Café serving a varied menu *lunchtimes and evenings.*

Royal Infirmary Museum Knighton Street Nurses Home, Royal Infirmary, Leicester (01858 565532). History of the Infirmary from 1771 including medical and surgical equipment. *Open Tue & Wed 12.00–14.00.* Donations appreciated.

Shires Shopping Centre High Street, Leicester (0116 251 2461). All the usual big name (and not so big) stores under one high, glass-arched roof plus cafés, pizzeria and gelateria. *Open Mon,*

Tue, Thu & Fri 09.00–17.30, Wed 09.00–20.00, Sat 09.00–18.00 & B. Hols 10.00–17.00. Disabled access.

St Martins Square & Loseby Lane Between Cank Street and Silver Street, Leicester (0116 253 8247). Speciality shopping centre in the heart of the city. Food, fashion, wine and flowers amongst which to placidly browse, take in some street entertainment or simply unwind. Most shops *open Mon–Sat 09.00–17.00.*

St Mary de Castro Castle Yard, Leicester. Founded in 1107 with excellent examples of Norman glass, stone and wood carving. Henry VI was knighted here in 1426 and Geoffrey Chaucer was probably married here.

St Nicholas Church St Nicholas Circle, Leicester. The oldest church in the city dating back to Anglo-Saxon times, and retaining examples of Saxon construction and Roman brickwork in the tower. *Open for services.*

Wygston's House Museum of Costume 12 Applegate, St Nicholas Circle, Leicester (0116 247 3056).

'Y' Theatre YMCA East Street, Leicester (0116 255 6507). A mixed programme of largely local productions.

Tourist Information Centre Every Street, Town Hall Square, Leicester (0116 265 0555). *Open Mon 10.00–17.30, Tue–Fri 09.00–17.30, Sat 09.00–17.00, B. Hols & Sun during summer 10.00–16.00.* Leicestershire also offers a comprehensive range of guided walks throughout the year, some of which are based in the Leicester area. Contact the Tourist Information Centre for further details.

● **Thumaston**
Leics. PO, tel, stores, garage. This unexciting suburb stretches along the Roman road, the old Fosse Way, now bypassed by a dual carriageway. However, the opportunity thus afforded to Thumaston has not been exploited. Evidence of Roman habitation was discovered in 1955, when excavation of an Anglo-Saxon cemetery brought to light 95 urns dating from 50 years after Julius Caesar's invasion.

Pubs and Restaurants

In a large city such as Leicester there is a wide range of pubs and restaurants to choose from; those listed are close to the waterway.

🍺 **Red Lion** 19 Highcross Street (off High Street), Leicester (0116 262 0368). Small, town local serving Burtonwood and Foreshaw's real ale. Comfortable lounge. Pool and pub games. *Closed Sun evenings.*

🍺 **Hat & Beaver** 60 Highcross Street (off High Street), Leicester (0116 262 2157). Close to the Shires shopping centre, a basic and friendly pub serving Hardys and Hansons real ale and good bar snacks. Beer garden and pub games.

🍺 **Wilkie's** 29 Market Street, Leicester (0116 255 6877). Continental-style bar with up to 120 imported bottled beers and Adnams, Fuller's, Shepherd Neame, Boddingtons and guest real ales. German food *lunchtimes.* Draught cider.

🍺 **Salmon** 19 Butt Close Lane, Leicester (0116 253 2301). Near to St Margaret's bus station. Typical Banks's pub serving their Mild and Bitter in friendly surroundings. Bar food *lunchtimes.* Beer garden.

🍺 **Northbridge Tavern** 1 Frog Island, Leicester (0116 251 2508). Canalside at North Lock. Busy, wood-panelled bars

dispensing Hoskins and Oldfield, Marston's, Tetley and Boddingtons real ale. Food *all day.* Beer garden and pub games.

✕♀ **Joe Rigatoni** St Martins Square, Leicester (0116 253 3977). Stylish pizza and pasta house offering good value meals. *L & D, closed Sun.*

✕♀ **Golden Mile** Consult *A Taste of Asia* (see page 80 under Golden Mile) for a wide-ranging selection of excitingly different and authentic eating experiences. This is a detailed and comprehensive selection numbering nearly 30 establishments.

🍺 **White Horse** White Horse Lane, off Front Street, Birstall, Leicester (0116 267 4490). Tetley, Marston's and Ansells real ale served in a large, friendly, riverside pub. A wide variety of grills, snacks and meals available *lunchtimes and evenings (Mon–Sat) & 12.00– 17.00 Sun.* Moorings and garden. Darts, dominoes and cards. Close to Watermead Country Park.

🍺 **Taverna Inn** Melton Road, Thumaston, Leicester. Just up the lane from Nimbus Narrowboats. Unassuming pub serving John Smith's real ale and inexpensive bar snacks and meals.

Mountsorrel

North of Thumaston the canal leaves the river and heads north through an area scarred by busy gravel workings. Just beyond the boatyard, the River Wreake flows in from the north east; the name of the nearby boatyard and the next lock hints at the significance of this little river. The River Soar rejoins the canal by Cossington Lock. The villages of Cossington and Rothley are one mile away from Cossington Lock, on opposite sides of the Soar. The Rothley Brook joins the canal north of the lock. At Sileby Lock is another water mill. There has been a mill here since 1608 and the present building has been restored as a private residence. From here it is a short distance to Mountsorrel. The lock here is very much a waterways showplace, and the extensive moorings and lockside pub make it a busy one.

● **Rothley**
Leics. PO, tel, stores, garage. Lies in the valley of the Rothley Brook which runs to the south of the village and through the grounds of Rothley Temple, once a preceptory for the Knights Templar. In the churchyard is a tall Anglo-Saxon cross, thought to be over 1000 years old.

● **Cossington**
Leics. Tel. A mile east of Cossington Lock, this is a pretty village with wide, well-kept grass verges and plenty of trees.

● **Sileby**
Leics. PO, tel, stores, takeaways, garage, chemist, bank, station. Once a thriving community based around hosiery manufacture this large village is much swollen by dormitory housing for neighbouring Leicester and Loughborough.

● **Mountsorrel**
Leics. PO, tel, stores, take-away, off-licence, garage. It is but a few yards from the lock here to the centre of the village with its long main street. **Busline** (0116 251 1411). For full details on bus travel to local (and not so local) attractions.
The Melton Mowbray Navigation & the Oakham

Canal This waterway was opened in 1797 as a broadlocked river navigation from the canal north of Syston to Melton Mowbray, 15 miles away to the east. Beyond Melton the Oakham Canal, constructed in 1802, extended the navigation as far as Oakham, in Rutland. When the railways were built the two waterways could not compete and the Oakham Canal was closed as early as 1841. More than a century later, some lengths still hold water; in other places the former canal bed is only a faint depression. The Melton Mowbray Navigation was closed to traffic in 1877.

Stonehurst Family Farm and Museum
Loughborough Road, Mountsorrel (01509 413216). A chance to see a working farm, a museum of memorabilia and old cars, and for children to cuddle and stroke small animals. Teashop serving light lunches and cream teas. Farm shop selling fresh produce, home-made bread and preserves. *Open daily 09.30–17.00.* Charge. Shop and tearoom *open all year.* Disabled visitors telephone for assistance.

Boatyards

Ⓑ **L.R. Harris & Son** Old Junction Boatyard, Meadow Lane, Syston (0116 269 2135). 🛢 🚻 ⚓ Gas, overnight and long-term mooring, chandlery and extensive spares, slipway, winter storage, boat sales and repairs, boat building and fit-outs, inboard and outboard engines sales and repairs. Welding specialists. Toilets and showers. Emergency call-out.

Ⓑ **Sileby Mill Boatyard** Mill Lane, Sileby (01509 813583). 🛢 🚻 ⚓ D E Pump-out, gas, narrow boat hire, day craft hire, overnight mooring, long-term mooring, winter storage, slipway, crane, boat sales and repairs (including outboards), engineering, welding and structural repairs, wooden boat repair specialists, chandlery, engine sales and repairs, DIY facilities, books, maps and gifts, ice creams, toilets, showers.

Ⓑ **Meadow Farm Marina** Huston Close, Barrow upon Soar (01509 816035/812215) 🛢 🚻 ⚓ Gas, long-term mooring (20–60ft boats), slipway, crane, boat sales, toilets, showers. Private club for moorers. Disabled facilities.

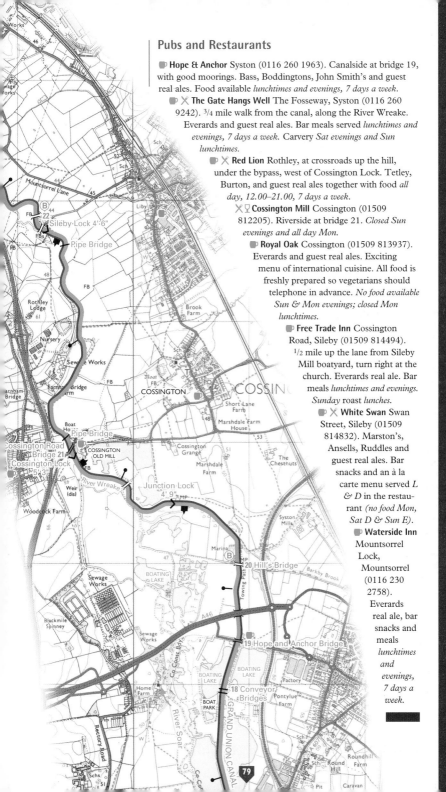

Pubs and Restaurants

🍺 **Hope & Anchor** Syston (0116 260 1963). Canalside at bridge 19, with good moorings. Bass, Boddingtons, John Smith's and guest real ales. Food available *lunchtimes and evenings, 7 days a week.*

🍺 ✕ **The Gate Hangs Well** The Fosseway, Syston (0116 260 9242). 3/4 mile walk from the canal, along the River Wreake. Everards and guest real ales. Bar meals served *lunchtimes and evenings, 7 days a week.* Carvery *Sat evenings and Sun lunchtimes.*

🍺 ✕ **Red Lion** Rothley, at crossroads up the hill, under the bypass, west of Cossington Lock. Tetley, Burton, and guest real ales together with food *all day, 12.00–21.00, 7 days a week.*

✕ 🍷 **Cossington Mill** Cossington (01509 812205). Riverside at bridge 21. *Closed Sun evenings and all day Mon.*

🍺 **Royal Oak** Cossington (01509 813937). Everards and guest real ales. Exciting menu of international cuisine. All food is freshly prepared so vegetarians should telephone in advance. *No food available Sun & Mon evenings; closed Mon lunchtimes.*

🍺 **Free Trade Inn** Cossington Road, Sileby (01509 814494). 1/2 mile up the lane from Sileby Mill boatyard, turn right at the church. Everards real ale. Bar meals *lunchtimes and evenings. Sunday roast lunches.*

🍺 ✕ **White Swan** Swan Street, Sileby (01509 814832). Marston's, Ansells, Ruddles and guest real ales. Bar snacks and an à la carte menu served *L & D in the restaurant (no food Mon, Sat D & Sun E).*

🍺 **Waterside Inn** Mountsorrel Lock, Mountsorrel (0116 230 2758). Everards real ale, bar snacks and meals *lunchtimes and evenings, 7 days a week.*

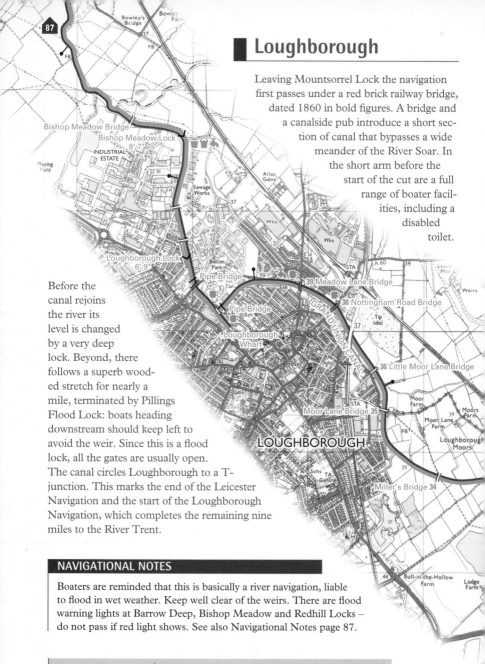

Loughborough

Leaving Mountsorrel Lock the navigation first passes under a red brick railway bridge, dated 1860 in bold figures. A bridge and a canalside pub introduce a short section of canal that bypasses a wide meander of the River Soar. In the short arm before the start of the cut are a full range of boater facilities, including a disabled toilet.

Before the canal rejoins the river its level is changed by a very deep lock. Beyond, there follows a superb wooded stretch for nearly a mile, terminated by Pillings Flood Lock: boats heading downstream should keep left to avoid the weir. Since this is a flood lock, all the gates are usually open. The canal circles Loughborough to a T-junction. This marks the end of the Leicester Navigation and the start of the Loughborough Navigation, which completes the remaining nine miles to the River Trent.

NAVIGATIONAL NOTES

Boaters are reminded that this is basically a river navigation, liable to flood in wet weather. Keep well clear of the weirs. There are flood warning lights at Barrow Deep, Bishop Meadow and Redhill Locks – do not pass if red light shows. See also Navigational Notes page 87.

BOAT TRIPS

Barrow Boating 14 Bridge Street, Barrow on Soar (at the former mill) offer a variety of craft for hire by the hour. *Open daily during the summer 11.00–18.00.* Also day boats *summer and winter, and daily* boat trips *during the summer,* leaving Barrow on Soar *at 18.30 and returning 21.00.* Charter trips.

n.b. Will Scarlet offers canal trips from outside the Albion Pub, Loughborough. Telephone 01509 213952 for further details.

- **Barrow upon Soar**
  Leics. PO, tel, stores, garage, station.
- **Loughborough**
  Leics. MD Thu, Sat. All services (including laundrette). A busy industrial town. There is a bric-a-brac market held in the Queens Hall, Granby Street *every Friday.*
  Bell Foundry Museum Freehold Street, Nottingham Road, Loughborough (01509 233414). South of bridge 38. Gift shop. Partial disabled access. *Open Tue–Sat & B. Hol Mon 10.00–12.30 & 13.30–16.30. Sun (Apr–Oct) 11.00–12.30 & 13.30–16.30; Nov–Apr 13.30–16.30.* Charge.

Carillon & War Memorial Queens Park, Loughborough (01509 634704). *Open daily Good Fri–Sep 14.00–18.00.* Carillon recitals *Sun & B. Hols. 15.30 & Thu 13.00.* Charge.
Great Central Railway Great Central Road, Loughborough (01509 230726). South of bridge 36. Eight miles of preserved main line taking you back to the days of express steam haulage. *Open every weekend throughout the year and weekdays May–Aug.* Charge. Telephone for details of special events.
Tourist Information Centre John Storer House, Wards End, Loughborough (01509 218113).

Pubs and Restaurants

- **Navigation** Mill Lane, Barrow on Soar (01509 412842). Shipstone's, Marston's, Banks's and guest real ales. Home-made *lunchtime* food *(weekdays)* and *weekend* barbecues *(lunchtimes and evenings) weather permitting.*
- **Soar Bridge Inn** Barrow on Soar (01509 412686). Near Barrow Deep Lock. Everards and guest real ales. Bar meals are available *lunchtimes and evenings, 7 days a week except Sun evening.* Vegetarians and children catered for.
- ✕ **Riverside** Barrow on Soar (01509 412260). Riverside, below Barrow Deep Lock. John Smith's, Courage and Ruddles real ales. Wide range of food

available *lunchtimes and evenings, 7 days a week except Sun evenings.*
- **Boat** Meadow Lane, Loughborough (01509 214578). Canalside, at bridge 39. Marston's and Banks's real ales. Traditional bar food available *lunchtimes, 7 days a week. Sunday* roasts. *Shops, take-away, station and PO nearby.*
- ✕ ⚲ **Lynroys** Loughborough (01509 215698). Canalside 100yds north of Loughborough Wharf, offering a 7 course *evening* menu. *Open Mon–Fri 19.00–23.00, weekends 19.00–24.00.*
- **Swan in the Rushes** 21 The Rushes, Loughborough (01509 217014). Archers, Marston's, Castle Rock, Tetley and guest real ales. Food *lunchtimes and evenings (no food Sat & Sun evenings).* Draught cider. Disabled access. B & B.
- **Three Nuns** 30 Churchgate, Loughborough (01509 213660). Everards and guest real ales. *Daily lunchtime* food and excellent breakfasts available *from 09.00, Thu–Sat.* Disabled access.
- **Albion Inn** Canal Bank, Loughborough (01509 213952). ¼ mile north of Loughborough Wharf. Mansfield, Samuel Smith and guest real ales. Food available *lunchtimes and evenings, 7 days a week.* Canalside seating and pub games. Beer cruises.

Kegworth

The Loughborough Navigation has the same physical characteristics as the Leicester Navigation. It continues the fall towards the Trent with the same pattern of meandering river reaches and the occasional canal cut, with locks bypassing the weirs. Normanton on Soar is visible some way away because of its prominent church steeple; on approaching, one finds the church is only a matter of yards from the river bank. However the inhabitants of Normanton guard their waterfront jealously, making it extremely difficult to get ashore. Below Normanton is the settlement of Zouch which has a certain weary and less conventional charm, easier access and more facilities. At Devil's Elbow boats heading downstream should keep right to stay in the main navigation channel. At the point where the A6 and the Soar almost touch there is a riverside pub and a boatyard. North of the pub a willow-lined reach leads to a stone mansion with spreading lawns where the channel divides. To the left (nearer Kegworth) is a maze of shallow and weedy backwaters, weirs and a water mill; boats should keep to the right for Kegworth Deep Lock where a new lock has been constructed beside the old as part of a flood prevention scheme. After another sharp swing to the north the channel divides again, and northbound boats should once more bear right for Kegworth Shallow Lock.

● **Whatton House**
Visible from the river near the Devil's Elbow, this mansion was built about 1802, damaged by fire and restored in 1876. Its fine 25-acre gardens are *open summer, Sun 14.00–18.00.* Charge.

● **Normanton on Soar**
Notts. PO, tel. A quiet and carefully preserved village with wide grass verges and some discreetly pretty buildings. The cruciform church has a central tower and spire, rare in so small a church. On the east wall of the nave there are some excellent stone carvings; the centre one is an elaborate coat of arms with a quizzical lion in the middle. The plain glass windows make the church enjoyably light. A ferry here once again links Nottinghamshire to Leicestershire.

● **Kegworth**
Leics. PO, tel, stores, chemist, take-aways. Kegworth has an attractive situation up on a wooded hill that is crowned by the church spire, but although it is close to the river, access is easy only from Kegworth Shallow Lock.

Kegworth Museum 52 High Street, Kegworth (01509 673620). Award-winning displays include Victorian parlour, local school, saddlers, knitting industry, Royal British Legion war memorabilia and local transport history. *Open Easter–Sep, Sun, Wed & B. Hol. Mon 14.00–17.00.* Small charge.

● **Kingston on Soar**
Notts. Tel. Situated east of the railway embankment, this is a small quiet estate village which looks much as it must have done 50 years ago. The church, still very much the focus of the village, is a pretty building of 1900.

Boatyards

Ⓑ **East Midlands Boat Services** London Road, Kegworth (01509 672385). 🚽 ⛽ D Pump-out, gas, overnight mooring, long-term mooring, slipway, winter storage, boat sales and repairs, engine sales and repairs, boat building and fitting out, chandlery, DIY facilities, emergency call-out.

Ⓑ **Forster Marine** The Boatyard, Bridgefields, Kegworth (01509 672084). D Long-term mooring, boat repairs, engine repairs and sales, boat fitting out.

Ⓑ **Kegworth Marine** Kingston Lane, Kegworth (01509 672300). ⛽ D Day hire craft, gas, long-term mooring, covered slipway, boat and engine repairs, DIY facilities, wet dock (60').

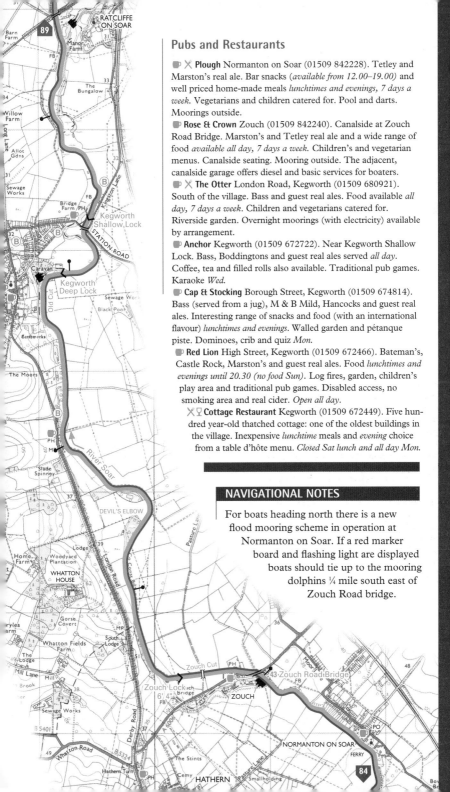

Pubs and Restaurants

▶ ✕ **Plough** Normanton on Soar (01509 842228). Tetley and Marston's real ale. Bar snacks (*available from 12.00–19.00*) and well priced home-made meals *lunchtimes and evenings, 7 days a week*. Vegetarians and children catered for. Pool and darts. Moorings outside.

▶ **Rose & Crown** Zouch (01509 842240). Canalside at Zouch Road Bridge. Marston's and Tetley real ale and a wide range of food *available all day, 7 days a week*. Children's and vegetarian menus. Canalside seating. Mooring outside. The adjacent, canalside garage offers diesel and basic services for boaters.

▶ ✕ **The Otter** London Road, Kegworth (01509 680921). South of the village. Bass and guest real ales. Food available *all day, 7 days a week*. Children and vegetarians catered for. Riverside garden. Overnight moorings (with electricity) available by arrangement.

▶ **Anchor** Kegworth (01509 672722). Near Kegworth Shallow Lock. Bass, Boddingtons and guest real ales served *all day*. Coffee, tea and filled rolls also available. Traditional pub games. Karaoke *Wed*.

▶ **Cap & Stocking** Borough Street, Kegworth (01509 674814). Bass (served from a jug), M & B Mild, Hancocks and guest real ales. Interesting range of snacks and food (with an international flavour) *lunchtimes and evenings*. Walled garden and pétanque piste. Dominoes, crib and quiz *Mon*.

▶ **Red Lion** High Street, Kegworth (01509 672466). Bateman's, Castle Rock, Marston's and guest real ales. Food *lunchtimes and evenings until 20.30 (no food Sun)*. Log fires, garden, children's play area and traditional pub games. Disabled access, no smoking area and real cider. *Open all day*.

✕ ♀ **Cottage Restaurant** Kegworth (01509 672449). Five hundred year-old thatched cottage: one of the oldest buildings in the village. Inexpensive *lunchtime* meals and *evening* choice from a table d'hôte menu. *Closed Sat lunch and all day Mon*.

NAVIGATIONAL NOTES

For boats heading north there is a new flood mooring scheme in operation at Normanton on Soar. If a red marker board and flashing light are displayed boats should tie up to the mooring dolphins ¼ mile south east of Zouch Road bridge.

Grand Union Canal – River Soar Kegworth

Ratcliffe on Soar

From Kegworth Shallow Lock to the Trent the navigation is somewhat more isolated, but two notable landmarks are the spire of Ratcliffe on Soar church and the eight cooling towers and vast chimney of the Ratcliffe Power Station that totally dominate the landscape for miles around. The navigation skirts round the west side of Red Hill. The last lock here has a well-painted bridge on which are shown the flood levels for 1955 and 1960, explaining the necessity for the flood prevention works. A few hundred yards below Red Hill Lock the Soar flows into the River Trent and loses its identity in this much bigger waterway.

NAVIGATIONAL NOTES

Boats negotiating the junction of the rivers Soar and Trent should keep well away from Thrumpton Weir, which is just east (downstream) of the big iron railway bridge. Navigators are reminded that the main line of the Trent Navigation is the Cranfleet Cut. This begins 200yds upstream of the mouth of the Soar, right by the large, wooden building which houses one of the many sailing clubs on the Trent. The entrance to the Erewash Canal is also here, marked by a lock and a cluster of buildings. If the warning light at Redhill Lock shows red – do not pass.

● **Ratcliffe on Soar**
Notts. Tel. A tiny village with a spired church dating from the 13thC. The interior of the nave is pleasantly uncluttered and rather spartan. There is no stained glass to darken it, and the white-washed walls accentuate the bold and ancient arches. In the chancel, on the other hand, there is a profusion of stone effigies and wall memorials, many of them to the Sacheverell family.

● **Trent Lock**
A busy and unusual boating centre at the southern terminus of the Erewash Canal (see page 55). There are two boatyards and two pubs here as well as the Waterway Manager's office.

● **Sawley**
Notts. PO, tel, stores, garage. The tall church spire attracts one across the river to Sawley, and in this respect the promise is fulfilled, for the medieval church is very beautiful and is approached by a formal avenue of lime trees leading to the 600-year-old doorway. But otherwise Sawley is an uninteresting main road village on the outskirts of Long Eaton.

● **Sawley Cut**
In addition to a large marina and a well-patronised BW mooring site, the Derby Motor Boat Club have a base on the Sawley Cut. All kinds of boats are represented here:

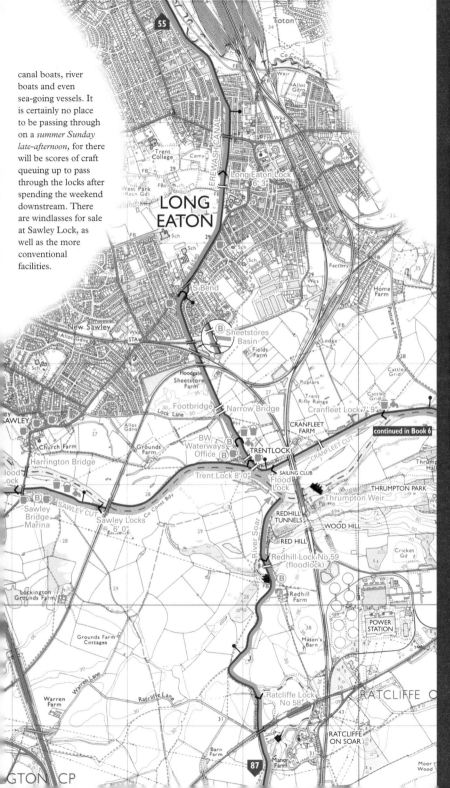

canal boats, river boats and even sea-going vessels. It is certainly no place to be passing through on a *summer Sunday late-afternoon*, for there will be scores of craft queuing up to pass through the locks after spending the weekend downstream. There are windlasses for sale at Sawley Lock, as well as the more conventional facilities.

continued in Book 6

Boatyards

Ⓑ **Redhill Marine Ltd** Redhill Marina, Radcliffe on Soar, Nottingham (01509 672770). ⛽ 🔧 Gas, long-term mooring winter storage, crane, slipway, slipway, hoist, chandlery, DIY facilities, toilets.

Ⓑ **Midland Boat Sales** Redhill Marina, Radcliffe on Soar, Nottingham (01509 673888). Overnight mooring, crane, boat sales and repairs, engine sales and repairs, boat refurbishment, DIY facilities, emergency call-out, café, toilets, groceries.

Ⓑ **Sawley Bridge Marina** Above Sawley Locks (0115 973 4278). 🚿 🚽 🔧 ⚡E Pump-out, gas, narrow boat hire, day hire boats, extensive moorings, two slipways, winter storage, 8 ton crane, chandlery, boat sales and repairs, engine sales and repairs, boat building and maintenance, books, maps and gifts, groceries, toilet, showers, telephone, café and pub. Maintains a watch on marine VHF.

Ⓑ **n.b. Jackal** and **butty Hereford** Trent Lock (0860 828723). Moored outside BW Waterway Office, above the lock. Windlasses, solid fuel, canalware, books, gifts, fenders, BW sanitary station and handcuff lock keys *available out of hours*. Decorative boat painting. Sometimes cruising during *summer months* so telephone to check before visiting.

Ⓑ **Trent Lock Marine Services** Trent Lock, Lock Lane, Sawley, Long Eaton (01159 727936). Boat and engine repairs, boat building, fitting out, dry and wet docks, DIY facilities.

Ⓑ **Mills Dockyard**, Trent Lock, Lock Lane, Long Eaton (0115 973 2595). Overnight and long-term mooring, winter storage, engine repairs, dry dock, wooden boat restoration and repairs, general boat maintenance, fitting out and repairs, houseboat construction.

The towpath
Once the River Trent is reached the towpath comes to an abrupt halt and there is no right of way along the south bank of the river. Originally there would probably have been a bridge here; more recently there was certainly a ferry. Walkers and cyclists will have to retrace their steps and make a lengthy detour (¼ mile north west of Ratcliffe Lock take the footpath south west to eventually cross under the motorway – then north, under the motorway again, meeting the Trent at Sawley Marina) if they wish to follow the waterways system further. This is a pity as it is the only break in an otherwise continuous path linking London to Nottingham and the Humber estuary to the north east and Burton on Trent, and ultimately Manchester, in the north west.

Pubs and Restaurants

🍺 ✕ **Chandlery Restaurant** Sawley Marina (0115 973 4278). Part of the marina complex this new pub serves food *all day, every day,* specialising in large portions at low prices serving a predictable Italian fare.

🍺 **Plank & Leggit** Tamworth Road, Sawley (0115 972 1515). A new pub 200 yds south of Sawley Cut, behind the marina, serving Courage, Mansfield, Marston's, Theakston and guest real ales. A wide ranging, inexpensive menu, majoring on healthy eating, is available *all day* as are inexpensive children's and special menus (wide vegetarian choice). Indoor and outdoor children's play areas, outside seating and summer barbecues. Dogs welcome on outdoor patio area.

🍺 ✕ **Harrington Arms** Sawley (0115 973 2614). North of the flood lock. Hardys & Hansons real ales and inexpensive bar and restaurant meals served *lunchtimes and evenings* in this cosy, 400-year-old coaching inn. Traditional *Sunday lunch;* children and vegetarians catered for. Outside seating. B & B.

🍺 **Nag's Head** Sawley (0115 973 2983). North of the Flood Lock. Marston's real ale and *lunchtime* sandwiches. Children welcome, outside seating.

🍺 ✕ **White Lion** Sawley (0115 973 3961). North of the flood lock. Marston's real ale and food available *lunchtimes and evenings*. Children and vegetarians catered for. Outside seating. Traditional pub games.

🍺 **Navigation Inn** Trent Lock (0115 973 2984). Large, popular, family pub with a garden and play area. Home, Marston's and guest real ales. Wide range of reasonably priced food available *lunchtimes and evenings, 7 days a week*. Vegetarians catered for. Moorings.

🍺 **Steamboat Inn** Trent Lock, on the Erewash Canal (0115 946 3955). Built by the canal company in 1791, when it was called the Erewash Navigation Inn, it is now a busy and popular venue. The bars have been handsomely restored and decorated with suitably nautical objects. Theakston, Marston's, Morland and guest real ales. Bar meals available *lunchtimes and evenings (not Sun evenings)*. Garden, animal farm and children's playground. Quiz *Mon*. Attached to the pub is Trattoria il Nautica.

GRAND UNION CANAL – MAIN LINE

MAXIMUM DIMENSIONS

Norton Junction to Camp Hill
Top Lock (Birmingham)
Length: 72'
Beam: 7'
Headroom: 7' 6"
Craft up to 12' 6" beam are permitted between Norton Junction and Camp Hill but all craft of this size must seek advice before proceeding. Permission must be obtained from BW for passage through the tunnels.

Camp Hill to Aston Junction and Salford Junction
Length: 70'
Beam: 7'
Headroom: 6' 6"

MANAGERS

Norton Junction to Napton: (01788) 890666
Napton to Camp Hill: (01564) 784634
Camp Hill to Salford Junction: 0121 506 1300

MILEAGE

Norton Junction to:
Braunston Turn: 4$^{1}/_{4}$ miles
Napton Junction: 9$^{1}/_{4}$ miles
Kingswood Junction: 31 miles
Bordesley Junction: 45$^{1}/_{2}$ miles
Salford Junction: 48 miles
Locks: 68

The whole length of the Grand Union Canal is unique among English canals in being composed of at least eight separate canals, linking London with Birmingham, Leicester and Nottingham. Up to the 1920s all these canals were owned and operated by quite separate companies: five between London and Birmingham alone.

The original – and still the most important – part of the system was the Grand Junction Canal, constructed at the turn of the 18thC to provide a short cut between Braunston on the Oxford Canal and Brentford, west of London on the Thames. Previously, all London-bound traffic from the Midlands had to follow the Fazeley, Coventry and Oxford canals down to Oxford, there to tranship into lighters to make the 100-mile trip down river to Brentford and London. The new Grand Junction Canal cut this distance by fully 60 miles, and with its 14ft wide locks and numerous branches to important towns rapidly became busy and profitable. The building of wide locks to take 70-ton barges was a brave attempt to persuade neighbouring canal companies – the Oxford, Coventry and the distant Trent & Mersey – to widen their navigations and establish a 70-ton barge standard throughout the waterways of the Midlands. Unfortunately, the other companies were deterred by the cost of widening, and to this day those same canals – and many others – can only pass boats 7ft wide. The mere proposal of the building of the Grand Junction Canal was enough to generate and justify plans for other canals linked to it. Before the Grand Junction itself was completed, independent canals were built linking it in a direct line to Warwick and Birmingham, and a little later a connection was established from the Grand Junction to Market Harborough and Leicester, and thence via the canalised River Soar to the Trent. Unfortunately, part of this line was built with narrow locks, thereby sealing the fate of the Grand Junction's wide canals scheme.

These canals made up the spine of southern England's transport system until the advent of the railways. When, in this century, the Regent's Canal Company acquired the Grand Junction and others, the whole system was integrated as the Grand Union Canal Company in 1929. In 1932 the new company, aided by the Government, launched a massive programme of modernisation: widening the 52 locks from Braunston to Birmingham. But when the grant was all spent, the task was unfinished and broad beam boats never became common on the Grand Union Canal.

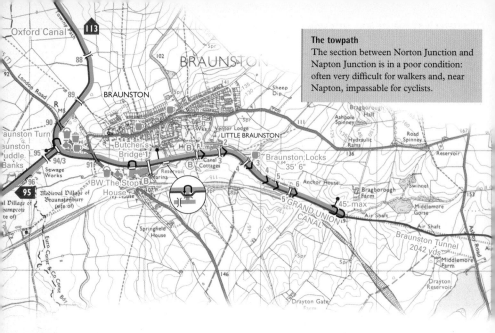

The towpath
The section between Norton Junction and
Napton Junction is in a poor condition:
often very difficult for walkers and, near
Napton, impassable for cyclists.

Braunston

From Norton Junction to Braunston the canal runs westward through hills and wooded
country, then into a wooded cutting which leads to Braunston Tunnel. There is a
good track over the top of the hill, which passes the brick tops of the ventilation shafts.
A cutting follows the tunnel, and then the landscape opens out although the hills stay
present on either side. Long rows of moored craft flank the canal, but there is usually
plenty of space to moor, and a fine selection of old buildings at Braunston. Note especially the iron side-bridge and the 18th-C dry dock. The arm in fact was part of the old
route of the Oxford Canal before it was shortened by building a large embankment
(Braunston Puddle Banks) across the Leam Valley to Braunston Turn. The entrance to
this arm was thus the original Braunston Junction. The Waterway Office in the Stop
House was originally the Toll Office between the Oxford Canal and the Grand Junction
Canal.

Pubs and Restaurants

X **White Horse** High Street, Welton (01327
702820). 3/4 mile from the canal at bridge 6.
Webster's, Marston's, Courage and guest real
ales. Bar meals and snacks served *lunchtimes,*
with restaurant meals available *D every day and
Sun L only.* Vegetarian options. Large garden.

X **Admiral Nelson** Dark Lane, Little
Braunston (01788 890075). By lock 3. Food
*lunchtimes and evenings, every day (except Mon in
winter)* John Smith's real ale. Canalside seating.
Cottage crafts are sold nearby.

Wheatsheaf The Green, Braunston. A locals'
pub with a warm atmosphere. Everards, Flowers,
Wadworth's and guest real ales. Meals are

served *18.30–22.00 daily.* Children welcome, and
a garden with a barbecue.

X **Old Plough** 82 High Street, Braunston
(01788 890000). A fine pub dating from 1672,
serving Ansells, Burton and guest real ales. Good
food *lunchtimes and evenings every day,* with a
vegetarian menu. Children are welcome, and
there is a garden. Quiz every other *Sun.*

X **The Mill House** Braunston (01788 890450).
Once the Rose & Castle. Bass and Worthington
real ale. Food *Mon–Sun 12.00–21.30 (21.00
Sun).* Children's room and fine canalside
garden with swings. Overnight mooring for
patrons.

NAVIGATIONAL NOTES

Braunston Tunnel – two boats of 7ft beam can pass in this tunnel, but wide beam boats *must get permission from BW* on (01788) 890666 to arrange a passage.

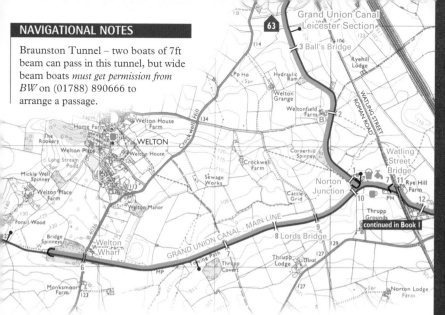

continued in Book I

- **Welton**
  Northants. Tel. The village climbs up the side of a steep hill, which makes it compact and attractive, especially around the church.
- **Braunston Tunnel**
  Opened in 1796, to bore through the Northamptonshire heights, the tunnel is 2042yds long. Its construction was hindered by quicksands, and a mistake in direction whilst building has given it a slight S bend.
- **Braunston**
  Northants. PO, tel, stores, butcher, fish & chips. Set up on a hill to the north of the canal. The village is really a long main street a little separate from the canal, with houses of all periods. A well known canal centre, it is no less significant today than when the Oxford and Grand Junction canals were first connected here. British Waterways reopened the Stop House as the local Waterway Office in 1990, and there is a small information room and gift shop within.

BOAT TRIPS

Rachael Operating from Braunston Marina, this licensed restaurant boat can accommodate 20 people. It makes regular *3-hour evening trips during the summer* on the Oxford Canal, and can also be chartered for *lunchtime* cruises. Telephone 07071 880784 for details.
The Rambler Operating from The Mill House (see below). Seating 12 people, this boat provides *lunchtime* cruises, *afternoon* cream tea cruises, and *evening* trips to the Napton Bridge Inn *Fri-Sat*, plus *hourly trips each Sun, throughout the summer.* It is also available for private charter. Details from Braunston Cruises, 14 Countryside, braunston (01788 890373). Booking is essential.

Boatyards

The Boat Shop (01788 891310). Started on board a boat moored at Braunston Turn, this is now a shop by Braunston Top Lock selling basic chandlery, coal, groceries, fruit and vegetables and canal ware, brass ware and much more. *Open mid-Mar–mid-Oct 08.00–20.00; rest of the year 08.00–18.00.*
Ⓑ **Braunston Boats** Bottom Lock, Braunston (01788 891079). **D** Pump-out, gas, long-term mooring, winter storage, slipway.
Ⓑ **Union Canal Carriers** Canalside at Braunston

Pump House, Dark Lane (01788 890784).
🚿 ⚓ **D** Pump-out, gas, narrow boat hire, dry dock, engine sales, boat and engine repairs.
Ⓑ **Braunston Marina** The Wharf, Braunston (01788 891373). Through the fine bridge dated 1834 and into an historic canal wharf. 🚽 🚿 ⚓ **D E** Gas, pump-out, overnight and long-term mooring, dry and wet dock, chandlery, boat building sales and repairs, engineering – all services. Toilets and showers, public telephone, chandlery, gift shop selling books and maps. Laundrette.

Napton Junction

The canal now passes through open countryside with a background of hills, and is very quiet and empty following all of the waterway activity around Braunston. The land is agricultural, with just a few houses in sight. There are initially no locks, no villages and the bridges are well spaced, making this a very pleasant rural stretch of canal running south west towards Napton Junction, on a length once used by both the Grand Junction Company and the Oxford Canal Company. As the Oxford Canal actually *owned* this stretch, they charged excessive toll rates in an attempt to get even with their rival, whose more direct route between London and the Midlands had attracted most of the traffic. At Napton Junction the Oxford Canal heads to the south while the Grand Union Canal strikes off north towards Birmingham. The empty landscape rolls on towards Stockton, broken only by Calcutt Locks. The windmill on top of Napton Hill can be seen from Napton Junction.

Boatyards

Ⓑ **Napton Narrowboats** Napton Marina, Stockton (01926 813644). 🚿 🚽 🔧 D Pump-out, gas, narrow boat hire, overnight and long-term mooring, boat & engine repairs, toilets, chandlery, gifts.

Ⓑ **Calcutt Boats** Calcutt Top Lock (01926 813757). 🚿 🚽 🔧 D Pump-out, gas, narrow boat hire, day boat hire, overnight mooring, long-term mooring, slipway, crane, dry dock, boat and engine sales and repairs, toilets, chandlery, solid fuel, breakdown service.

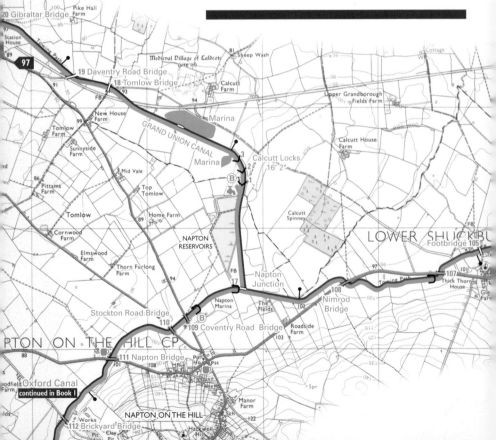

Pubs and Restaurants

Napton Bridge Inn (01926 812466). Canalside at bridge 111 on the Oxford Canal. Excellent food is served *lunchtimes and evenings every day,* with restaurant meals *L & D*. You can choose from steaks to fish to spicy pasta. Vegetarians are well looked after, and children are welcomed. Flowers, Tetley's and a guest real ale are available. There is a pleasant garden with a children's play area, and often entertainment during *the summer months.*

Ye Olde Kings Head Napton-on-the-Hill (01926 812202). Just 200yds south of bridge 109. Marston's, Morland's plus seven constantly changing real ales and a wide range of bar and restaurant meals *lunchtimes and evenings every day (all day at weekends, when there is a Sunday carvery).*

Children are welcome, there is a children's menu, and a large garden.

Old Olive Bush Flecknoe (01788 891134). A village pub serving meals *Tue–Sun evenings,* and bar snacks *Sat & Sun lunchtimes.* Vegetarian options, children welcome, and there is a garden. *Closed Mon–Fri lunchtimes.*

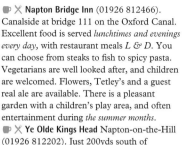

Lower Shuckburgh
Warwicks. PO box. A tiny village along the main road. The church, built in 1864, is attractive in a Victorian way, with great use of contrasting brickwork inside.

The towpath
The section between Napton Junction and Norton Junction is in a poor condition: often very difficult for walkers and, near Napton, impassable for cyclists.

Stockton

Continuing west, the canal passes to the north of Stockton and descends Stockton Locks, where you will notice the remains of the old narrow locks beside the newer wide ones. Around here there is a change in landscape, with the hills coming much closer to the canal, broken by old quarries and thick woods along the south bank. The quarries produced blue lias, a local stone, and cement which was used in the construction of the Thames Embankment. Huge fossils have been found in the blue lias clay, which is the lowest layer from the Jurassic period. This section contrasts greatly with the open landscape that precedes and follows it. The canal passes Long Itchington, a village with a large number of pubs, including two on the canal, all the while flanked by open arable land backed on both sides by hills. This pleasant emptiness is broken only by further locks continuing the fall to Warwick. Of particular interest are the top two locks at Bascote, just beyond the pretty toll house, which form a staircase. Then once again the canal is in quiet, wooded, countryside.

● **Stockton**
Warwicks PO, tel, stores, fish & chips, Indian take-away. Stockton is a largely Victorian village in an area which has been dominated by the cement works to the west. St Michael's church is built of blue lias, quarried near Stockton Locks, although the tower is of red sandstone.

● **Long Itchington**
Warwicks. PO, tel, stores, garage. A large housing estate flanks the busy A423; the village proper lies

a short walk to the north west, and is very attractive. Apart from several pubs there are houses of the 17th and 18thC, and impressive poplars around the village pond. St Wulfstan, who later became Bishop of Worcester, was born here in 1012.
Holy Trinity A largely 13th-C church whose tall spire was blown down in a gale in 1762, and replaced with a stump. Parts of the south aisle date from the 12thC, although the 13th-C windows are perhaps the building's best feature. There is a 14th-C screen.

Boatyards

Ⓑ **Blue Lias Marina** Stockton (01926 854976). By bridge 20. 🚽 🚰 ⛽ D Pump-out, gas, overnight and long-term mooring, winter storage, slipwqay, crane, boatbuilding, telephone, chandlery, solid fuel, DIY facilities.

Ⓑ **Warwickshire Fly Boat Company** Stop Lock Cottage, Stockton (01926 812093). By the Kayes Arm. 🚰 ⛽ D Pump-out, gas, overnight mooring, long-term mooring, winter storage, dry dock, boat and engine sales and repairs, boatbuilding, telephone, toilets, showers, chandlery, solid fuel, laundrette.

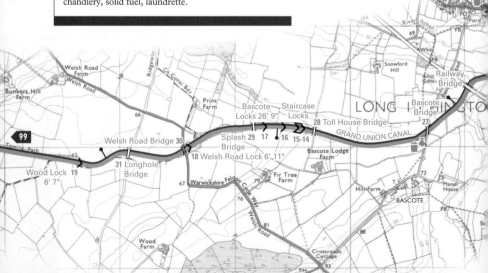

Pubs and Restaurants

Boat Birdingbury Wharf, Rugby Road (01926 812349). Canalside at bridge 21. A pleasant old pub with a fine canalside map, painted by Dusty Miller, around the top of the bar. Bass and guest real ales. Grills and bar meals *lunchtimes and evenings* with a vegetarian menu. Canalside garden with play area.

Blue Lias Stockton. (01926 812249). Canalside at bridge 23. A well kept and attractive pub, with a pleasant canalside garden with ponies, donkeys and rabbits. Be prepared for the uneven interior brickwork, which may look straighter when you have enjoyed one of the four real ales they regularly keep. Bar meals *lunchtimes and evenings every day*, with vegetarian choices. Live music *Sat evenings in summer*. Children are welcome.

Barley Mow School Street, Stockton (01926 812713). Banks's, Bass and a guest real ale modernised pub. Bar meals *lunchtimes and evenings (not Mon)*, with a vegetarian menu. Outside seating on the green, opposite the church. Children welcome.

Two Boats Inn Southam Road, Long Itchington (01926 812640). Canalside at bridge 25. A good selection of real ale including Bass, Greene King and Hook

Norton are available in this fine pub, built in 1743. At one time there was a forge and stables here for the boat horses. Bar meals and grills *lunchtimes and evenings* with vegetarian choices. Children welcome. Garden with fine views of the canal. Live music *Sat* with folk evening *first Sun in every month*.

Green Man Church Road, Long Itchington (01926 812208). Just past the church, this is a fine traditional country pub with a very low ceiling in the corridor. Bass and Tetley's real ale and bar meals *lunchtimes and evenings (but not Tue: bookings only for Sun)*, with a vegetarian menu. Family room and garden.

Harvester Church Road, Long Itchington (01926 812698). Opposite the village store. Small, popular local serving Hook Norton and guest real ales. Bar and restaurant meals *lunchtimes and evenings,* with a selection of vegetarian dishes. Outside seating. Children welcome. Young Farmers meet here on *Wed evening*.

Jolly Fisherman The Green, Long Itchington (01926 812296). A large pub overlooking the village green and pond. Garden. Queen Elizabeth I once stayed in the black and white timbered building opposite.

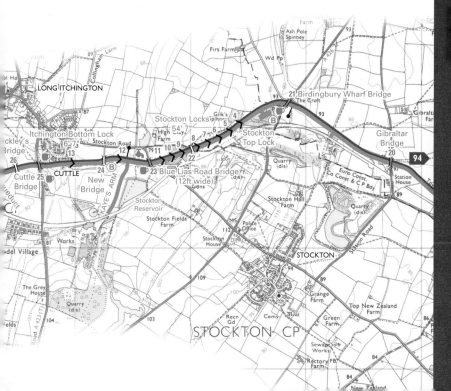

Royal Leamington Spa

The waterway makes its descent through the quiet Fosse Locks and continues west through attractive and isolated country to pass to the north of Radford Semele, where there is a fine wooded cutting. Emerging from the cutting, the canal joins a busy road for a short while, then carves a fairly discreet course through Leamington. Midway through the town the canal enters a deep cutting that hides it from the adjacent main road and railway. Leaving Leamington the canal swings north west under a main road and crosses the railway and the River Avon on aqueducts, to immediately enter the outskirts of Warwick. There are good moorings, shops and two Indian take-aways by bridge 40.

Pubs and Restaurants

🍺 **Stags Head** Welsh Road, Offchurch (01926 425801). A thatched 15th-C pub, serving Bass, Flowers and Tetley's real ale and food *lunchtimes and evenings daily*, with vegetarian options. Children welcome, and garden with swings. *Sun evening* quiz.

🍺 **Old White Lion** Southam Road, Kingshurst, Radford Semele (01926 425770). Greenalls, Marston's and Tetley's real ales, and meals served *all day every day*, with vegetarian options. Garden with play area. Occasional quiz nights. Children welcome in the restaurant.

🍺 **The Fusilier** Sydenham Drive, Leamington Spa (01926 336048). No real ale, no children, but dogs are welcome. Karaoke *Sat*, quiz and disco *Sun*. Lawn at the back. Fish & chips next door, and shops nearby.

🍺 **Bridge** Brunswick Street, Leamington Spa (01926 425674). Canalside at bridge 40. Bass and Whitbread real ale and bar meals *lunchtimes and evenings every day,* with vegetarian choices. Children welcome when dining. Big garden, barbecue and canalside terrace. Mooring for patrons.

✕♀ **Grand Union & JJs Restaurant** 66 Clemens Street (01926 421323). At bridge 40, overlooking the canal. English dinner and à la carte menu. *D only, and a champagne Sun lunch.* Booking essential for the Grand Union, not essential for JJs.

🍺 **The Tiller Pin** Queensway, Leamington Spa (01926 435139). By bridge 43. M & B and Bass real ale. Food is available *Mon–Fri lunchtimes and evenings, and all day until 21.00 at weekends.* Children are welcome if you are having a meal. Large garden.

🍺 ✕ **The Moorings** (01926 425043). By bridge 43. Banks's, Marston's and Camerons real ale. Food available in bar or restaurant *all day every day.* Children are welcome. BBQs in *summer.* Mooring.

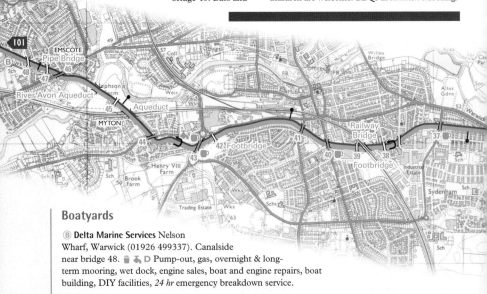

Boatyards

Ⓑ **Delta Marine Services** Nelson Wharf, Warwick (01926 499337). Canalside near bridge 48. 🚿 ⛽ D Pump-out, gas, overnight & long-term mooring, wet dock, engine sales, boat and engine repairs, boat building, DIY facilities, *24 hr* emergency breakdown service.

● **Offchurch**
Warwicks. Tel. A scattered residential village reflecting the proximity of Leamington. It takes its name from Offa, the Saxon King of Mercia, reputedly buried near here. The church, with its tall grey stone tower, contains some Norman work. To the west lies Offchurch Bury, whose park runs almost to the canal. Originally this was a 17th-C house, but is has since been entirely rebuilt. The façade is now early 19th-C Gothic.

● **Radford Semele**
Warwicks. PO, tel, stores, garage. A main road suburb of Leamington, Radford Semele takes no notice of the canal that runs below the village, alongside the River Leam and what was once the railway line to Rugby. Among the bungalows are some fine large houses, including Radford Hall, a reconstructed Jacobean building. The Victorian church of St Nicholas is set curiously by itself, seeming to be in the middle of a field.

● **Royal Leamington Spa**
Warwicks. PO, tel, stores (by bridge 40), garage, station, cinema. During the 19thC the population of Leamington increased rapidly, due to the late 18th and 19thC fashion for spas generally. As a result the town is largely mid-Victorian, and a number of Victorian churches and hotels dominate it, several designed by J. Cundall, a local architect of some note who also built the brick and stone Town Hall. The long rows of villas, elegant houses in their own grounds spreading out from the centre, all express the Victorian love of exotic styles – Gothic, Classical, Jacobean, Renaissance, French and Greek are all mixed here with bold abandon. Since the Victorian era, however, much industrialisation has taken place.
Assembly Rooms, Art Gallery & Museum Royal Pump Rooms, The Parade, Royal Leamington Spa (01926 742700). British, Dutch and Flemish paintings of the 16th and 17thC. Also a collection of modern art, pottery and porcelain through the ages and a specialist series of 18th-C English drinking glasses. Victorian costumes and objects. *Open Wed, Fri & Sat 10.30–17.00, Tue & Thu 13.30–20.00, Sun 11.00–16.00. Closed Mon.* Free.
All Saints' Church Bath Street. Begun in 1843 to the design of J. C. Jackson, who was greatly influenced by the then vicar, Dr John Craig. It is of Gothic style, apparently not always correct in detail. The north transept has a rose window patterned on Rouen Cathedral; the west window is by Kempe. The scale of the building is impressive, being fully 172 feet long and 80 feet high.
Jephson Gardens Alongside Newbold Terrace, north of bridge 40. Beautiful ornamental gardens named after Dr Jephson (1798–1878), the local practitioner who was largely responsible for the spa's high medical reputation.
Tourist Information Centre Royal Pump Rooms, The Parade, Royal Leamington Spa (01926 742762).

BOAT TRIPS

Prince Regent II is a 50-seater wide-beam Edwardian luxury dining boat, available for private charter and public trips *evenings and Sun lunchtimes.* Good food and wine, and entertainment can be arranged. It operates from Offchurch Wharf. Telephone 01926 450317 for details or contact Ham Farm, Welsh Road, Offchurch, Leamington Spa CV33 9AB.

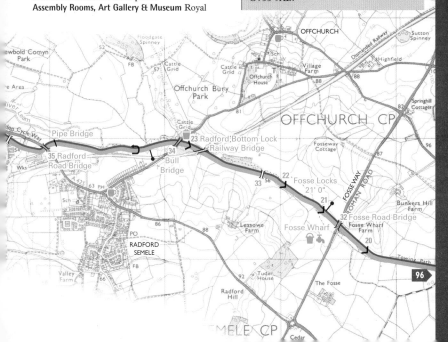

Warwick

The canal passes around the north side of central Warwick, so if you wish to visit the town centre, it is best to approach from bridge 49 (walking to the south for a little over half a mile), or from the Saltisford Canal Centre (see below). After climbing the two Cape Locks, the canal swings south to Budbrooke Junction, where the old Warwick and Napton Canal joined the Warwick and Birmingham Canal. A short section of the arm to the east of the junction has been restored, and has a winding hole, moorings and other facilities. To the west of the junction, beyond a large road bridge, is the first of the 21 locks of the Hatton flight, with its distinctive paddle gear and gates stretching up the hill ahead, a daunting sight for even the most resilient boatman. Consolation is offered by the fine view of the spires of Warwick as you climb the flight. There is a small shop selling maps and canalia between locks 45 and 46. On reaching the top, the canal turns to the west, passing the wooded hills that conceal Hatton village and Hatton Park. The canal then enters the wooded cutting that leads to Shrewley Tunnel.

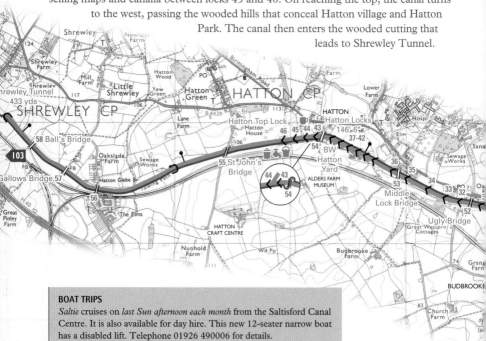

BOAT TRIPS
Saltie cruises on *last Sun afternoon each month* from the Saltisford Canal Centre. It is also available for day hire. This new 12-seater narrow boat has a disabled lift. Telephone 01926 490006 for details.

Boatyards

Ⓑ **Saltisford Canal Centre** Budbrooke Road, Warwick (01926 490006). 🚿 🚽 ⚓ Pump-out, day hire craft, overnight mooring, long-term mooring, telephone nearby, toilets, gifts, small laundrette. Gardens, picnic places, BBQ and snacks available. Small museum and information centre. An excellent place in its own right, with good access to Warwick.

Ⓑ **Kate Boats Warwick** The Boatyard, Nelson Lane, Warwick (01926 492968). 🚽 ⚓ D Pump-out, gas, narrow boat hire, overnight mooring, long-term mooring, boat and engine repairs, boatbuilding, telephone, toilets, chandlery.

Get Knotted Lower Cape (01926 410588). Next door to the Cape of Good Hope pub. Rope fender making specialist, plus general ropework and an expanding chandlery.

Ⓑ **Stephen Goldsbrough Boats** Hatton (01564 778210). Dry dock on the Hatton flight, boat painting and repairs, DIY facilities.

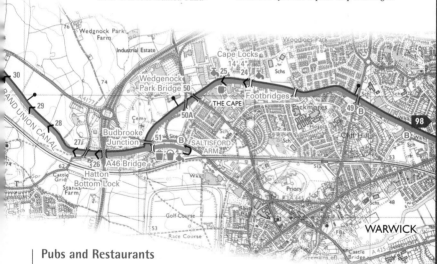

● **Warwick**
Warwicks. MD Sat. All services. Virtually destroyed by fire in 1694 the town rose again, with Queen Anne styles now mixed with the medieval buildings which survived the blaze.
Warwick Castle Castle Hill (telephone 01926 406600 for information line). Built on the site of a motte and bailey constructed by William the Conqueror in 1068, the present exterior is a famous example of a 14th-C fortification, with the tall Caesar's Tower rising to a height of 147ft. The castle grounds were laid out by Capability Brown. *Open daily 10.00–17.30. Closed Xmas.* Charge. Programme of events *throughout the year.*
Collegiate Church of St Mary's Of Norman origin. The most striking feature of the rebuilt church is its pseudo-Gothic tower, built 1698–1704. Climb to the top to enjoy the view *(May–Sep, 10.00–16.00 weather permitting).* Church *open summer 10.00–18.00; winter 10.00–16.00.* Free (charge for tower).
Warwick County Museum Market Place (01926 412500). Housed in the Market Hall. Includes the Sheldon tapestry map of Warwickshire, which dates from 1588. *Open May–Sep, Mon–Sat 10.00–17.30, Sun 11.00–17.00.* Free.
Lord Leycester Hospital High Street (01926 491422). A superbly preserved group of 14th-C timber-framed build-ings. Chapel of St James, Great Hall and galleried courtyard. The Museum of the Queen's Own Hussars is also here. *Open Tue–Sun & B. Hol Mons 10.00–17.00 (16.00 winter).* The newly restored gardens are *open during the summer.* Charge.
Oken's House & Doll Museum Castle Street (01926 412500). A superb collection of early dolls housed in one of the few timber buildings that survived the great fire. *Open Easter–Oct, Mon–Sat 10.00–17.00, Sun 13.00–17.00; Nov–Easter, Sat only 10.00–dusk.* Charge.
Tourist Information Centre The Court House, Jury Street, Warwick (01926 492212). Guided walks are arranged from here *during the summer.*

● **Hatton**
Warwicks. A heavily wooded village.
Hatton Country World George's Farm, Hatton (01926 843411). South of bridge 55. Rare breeds, craft workshops and a children's play area. *Open daily 10.00–17.00 (closed Xmas).* Entrance to the Craft village is free, but a charge is made for the Farm Park.

● **Shrewley**
Warwicks. PO, tel, stores. Best approached from the north-western end of the Shrewley Tunnel, through an exciting, but slippery, towpath tunnel.
Shrewley Tunnel 433yds long, the tunnel was opened in 1799 with the completion of the Warwick and Birmingham Canal. *This tunnel allows two 7ft boats to pass: keep to the right.*

Pubs and Restaurants

There are many pubs and restaurants in Warwick which will repay exploration.
● **Cape of Good Hope** Cape Locks, 66 Lower Cape (01926 498138). Good food is served *lunchtimes and evenings every day*, and there are three regular real ales plus a guest. Lockside seating.
● ✕ **The Waterman** Birmingham Road (A4177), Hatton (01926 492427). An excellent and extensive bar menu, with vegetarian choices, is available *lunchtimes and evenings every day* in this pub, which has a comfortable beamed bar and fine views over the Hatton flight. Bass, Tetley's and a guest real ale. Large garden. Children welcome. Regular live music.

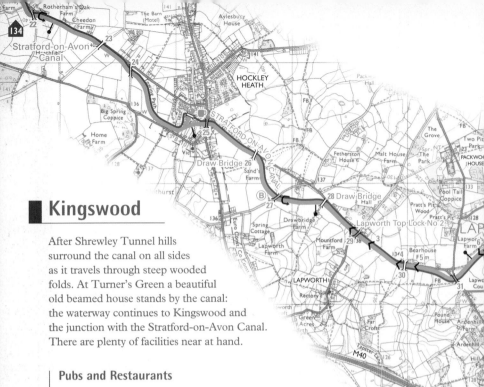

Kingswood

After Shrewley Tunnel hills
surround the canal on all sides
as it travels through steep wooded
folds. At Turner's Green a beautiful
old beamed house stands by the canal:
the waterway continues to Kingswood and
the junction with the Stratford-on-Avon Canal.
There are plenty of facilities near at hand.

Pubs and Restaurants

Durham Ox Shrewley Common, Shrewley
(01926 842283). Greene King and Marston's real
ale, and bar and restaurant meals served
lunchtimes and evenings, with vegetarian options.
Children are welcome, and there is a large garden.

Cock Horse Old Warwick Road, Rowington
(01926 842183). Boddingtons, Flowers and
Wadworth's real ale and meals *lunchtimes every
day, and evenings Tue-Sat.* Children welcome, and
there is a garden.

The Case is Altered Case Lane, Just off Five
Ways, Haseley Knob (01926 484206). A 45-
minute walk from bridge 62, but worth it to
find this old-fashioned ale house. Pass
Rowington Hall, then north-east past South
Lawn. Ansells, Flowers and Greene King real
ale. Outside seating.

**Tom o' the
Wood** Finwood
Road, Rowington
(01564 782252).
Flowers, Morland's and
Tetley's real ale, and bar
and restaurant meals
*lunchtimes and evenings every
day,* with vegetarians well catered
for. Garden, and children welcome.

Navigation Old Warwick Road,
canalside at Kingswood (01564
783337). M & B, Bass and guest real
ales and real draught cider. Bar meals
lunchtimes and evenings daily, with a
vegetarian menu. Children welcome.
Moorings.

● **Rowington**
Warwicks. Tel. Near the canal the 13th-C church
retains some furnishings and a fine peal of bells.

● **Kingswood**
Warwicks. Tel, garage, station. The village is
scattered over a wide area from the Grand Union
Canal to the Stratford-on-Avon Canal. The centre
is a mile to the west, around the ambitious 15th-C
church.
Packwood House *NT property* (01564 782024).
Hockley Heath, 2 miles west of bridge 66. Timber-

framed Tudor house, dating from the late 16thC
and enlarged in the 17thC, where Cromwell's
general, Henry Ireton, slept before the Battle of
Edgehill in 1642. *Open Apr–Sep, Wed–Sun 14.00–
17.30; Oct, Wed–Sun 14.00–16.00.* Charge.
Events are staged *during the summer.*

● **Baddesley Clinton**
Warwicks. Tel, stores. The village is a mile from
the canal at bridge 66, but nearer are the church
and the hall, set amid parkland. The church is
mostly 16th- and 17th-C.

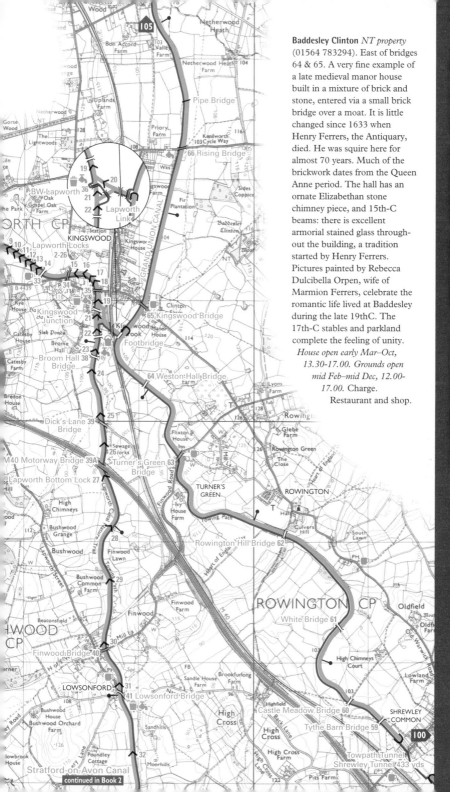

Baddesley Clinton *NT property* (01564 783294). East of bridges 64 & 65. A very fine example of a late medieval manor house built in a mixture of brick and stone, entered via a small brick bridge over a moat. It is little changed since 1633 when Henry Ferrers, the Antiquary, died. He was squire here for almost 70 years. Much of the brickwork dates from the Queen Anne period. The hall has an ornate Elizabethan stone chimney piece, and 15th-C beams: there is excellent armorial stained glass throughout the building, a tradition started by Henry Ferrers. Pictures painted by Rebecca Dulcibella Orpen, wife of Marmion Ferrers, celebrate the romantic life lived at Baddesley during the late 19thC. The 17th-C stables and parkland complete the feeling of unity. *House open early Mar–Oct, 13.30-17.00. Grounds open mid Feb–mid Dec, 12.00-17.00.* Charge. Restaurant and shop.

Knowle

The canal now continues its northerly route, passing through countryside which is surprisingly peaceful. Knowle Locks introduce more hilly countryside again, and this green and pleasant land continues right through to Solihull, concealing the nearness of Birmingham. The flight of five wide locks at Knowle used to be six narrow ones, until the 1930 improvements: the remains of the old ones can still be seen alongside the new, together with the side ponds (originally built to save water). The locks are comparatively deep, and are well maintained and pleasantly situated. They are also the northernmost wide locks for many miles now, since all the Birmingham canals have narrow locks. Knowle is set back from the canal, but warrants a visit, especially to see the church. Continuing north west through wooded country, the canal passes under the M42 motorway and crosses the River Blyth on a small aqueduct.

● **Knowle**
W. Midlands. All services. Despite its proximity to Birmingham, Knowle still survives as a village, albeit rather self-consciously. A number of old buildings thankfully remain, some dating from the Middle Ages and including such gems as Chester House (now the library), which illustrate the advances in timber frame construction from the 13th to the 15thC. Have a look at the splendid knot garden around the back. Half-a-mile north of the village is Grimshaw Hall, a gabled 16th-C house noted for its decorative brickwork. There are good views of it from the canal.
Church of St John the Baptist, St Lawrence and St Anne Knowle. This remarkable church was built as a result of the efforts of Walter Cook, a wealthy man who founded a chapel here in 1396, and completed the present church in 1402. Prior to its building the parishioners of Knowle had to make a 6-mile round trip each Sunday to the church at Hampton-in-Arden. This involved crossing the River Blythe, an innocuous brook today, but in medieval times 'a greate and daungerous water' which 'noyther man nor beaste can passe wt. owte daunger of peryshing'. The building is built in the Perpendicular style, with a great deal of intricate stonework. There is much of interest to be seen inside, including the roof timbers, the original font and a medieval dug-out chest. Behind the church is the three-acre 'Children's Field', given to the National Trust by the Reverend T. Downing 'to be used for games'.

WE ARE THE OVALTINE-EES . . .

Dr George Wander founded the company which was to manufacture Ovaltine in Switzerland in 1864. Finding a ready market in England, the company established a factory at Kings Langley, beside what is now the Grand Union Canal. In 1925 they decided to build their own fleet of narrow boats to bring coal to this factory from Warwickshire. Their boats were always immaculately maintained, with the words 'Drink delicious Ovaltine for Health' emblazoned in orange and yellow on a very dark blue background. The last boat arrived at Kings Langley on 17 April 1959.

Pubs and Restaurants

● **Black Boy** Warwick Road, at bridge 69 (01564 772655). A traditional pub, built in 1793, sporting a canalside garden with children's play area. Bass real ale and excellent bar meals with a choice of 72 main courses served *lunchtimes and evenings every day.* Vegetarian choices. Children welcome.

● ✕ **Wilsons Arms** Warwick Road, Knowle (01564 772559). A Toby Carvery pub which dates from the 16thC. The older part still retains much of its character. Bass and M & B real ale, and carvery served *lunchtimes and evenings every day,* with a vegetarian menu. Outside seating. Children welcome.

● **Heron's Nest** (01564 771177). Canalside at bridge 75. A friendly pub serving Bass and M & B real ale. Bar meals *lunchtimes and evenings every day.* Children welcome. Garden.

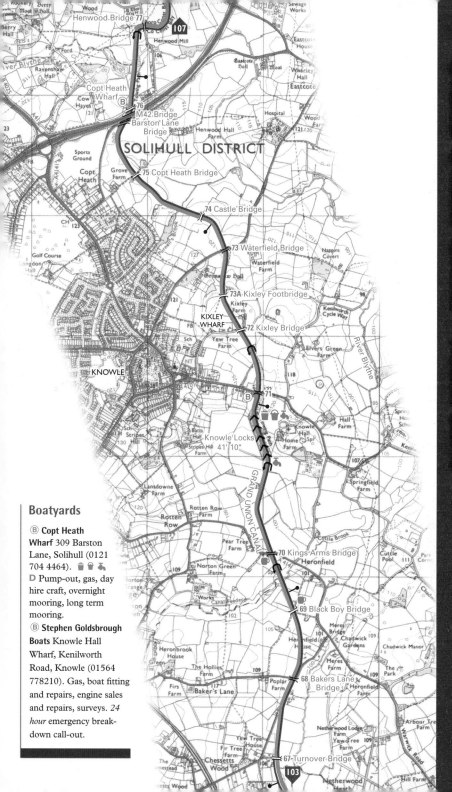

Henwood Bridge 77

107

Copt Heath Wharf

B 76
M42 Bridge
Barston Lane
Bridge

SOLIHULL DISTRICT

75 Copt Heath Bridge

74 Castle Bridge

73 Waterfield Bridge

73A Kixley Footbridge

KIXLEY WHARF

72 Kixley Bridge

KNOWLE

B 71

Knowle Locks
41' 10"

GRAND UNION CANAL

70 Kings Arms Bridge
Heronfield

69 Black Boy Bridge

68 Bakers Lane Bridge

67 Turnover Bridge

103

Boatyards

Ⓑ **Copt Heath
Wharf** 309 Barston
Lane, Solihull (0121
704 4464).
D Pump-out, gas, day
hire craft, overnight
mooring, long term
mooring.

Ⓑ **Stephen Goldsbrough
Boats** Knowle Hall
Wharf, Kenilworth
Road, Knowle (01564
778210). Gas, boat fitting
and repairs, engine sales
and repairs, surveys. *24
hour* emergency break-
down call-out.

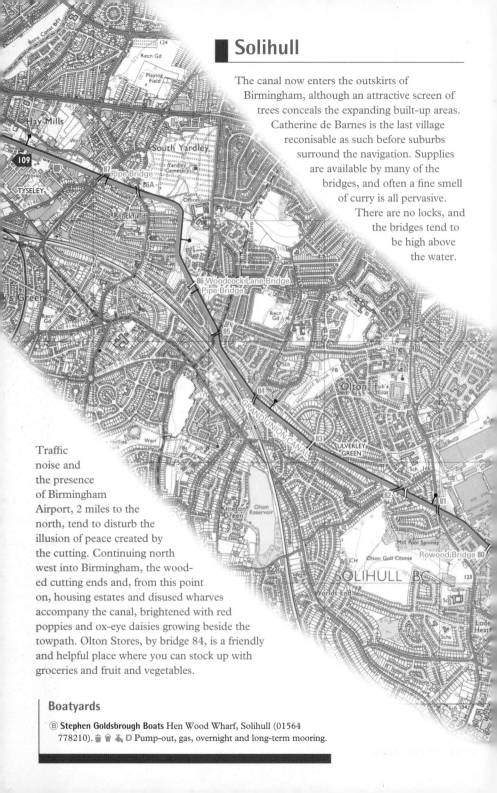

Solihull

The canal now enters the outskirts of Birmingham, although an attractive screen of trees conceals the expanding built-up areas. Catherine de Barnes is the last village reconisable as such before suburbs surround the navigation. Supplies are available by many of the bridges, and often a fine smell of curry is all pervasive. There are no locks, and the bridges tend to be high above the water.

Traffic noise and the presence of Birmingham Airport, 2 miles to the north, tend to disturb the illusion of peace created by the cutting. Continuing north west into Birmingham, the wooded cutting ends and, from this point on, housing estates and disused wharves accompany the canal, brightened with red poppies and ox-eye daisies growing beside the towpath. Olton Stores, by bridge 84, is a friendly and helpful place where you can stock up with groceries and fruit and vegetables.

Boatyards

Ⓑ **Stephen Goldsbrough Boats** Hen Wood Wharf, Solihull (01564 778210). 🖀 🖀 🕭 D Pump-out, gas, overnight and long-term mooring.

Catherine de Barnes
W. Midlands. PO, tel, stores, garage. A higgledy-piggledy village far from the romanticism implied by the name. However, a convenient supply centre with easy access from the canal before the bulk of Birmingham begins to make its presence felt.

Elmdon Heath
W. Midlands. PO, tel, stores, garage. A suburb of Solihull useful for supplies.

Solihull
W. Midlands. PO, tel, stores, garage, cinema, station. A modern commuter development, with fine public buildings. What used to be the town centre, dominated by the tall spire of the parish church, is now a shopping area.
St Alphege Church Solihull. Built of red sandstone, it is almost all late 13th-C and early 14th-C. The lofty interior contains work of all periods, including a Jacobean pulpit, a 17th-C communion rail, 19th-C stained glass and a few notable monuments.
Tourist Information Centre Central Library, Homer Road, Solihull (0121 704 6130).

Pubs and Restaurants

Boat Inn Catherine de Barnes (0121 705 0474). A well kept and friendly pub, offering real ale, together with bar meals *all day, every day*, including vegetarian dishes. Children are welcome, and there is a garden.

Longfellows English Restaurant Catherine de Barnes (0121 705 0547). *L Tue-Fri, D Tue-Sat.*

The Barge Stop Tyseley. Between bridges 87 and 88. Food served all day.

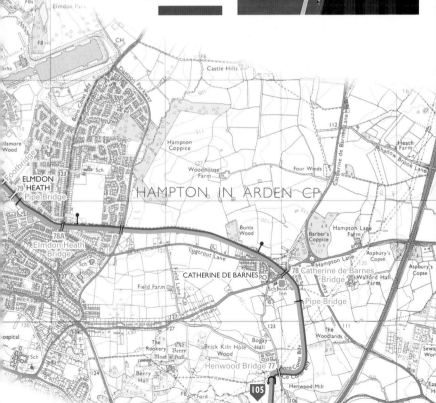

Birmingham

The canal curves past the large Energy from Waste plant and the Ackers Trust Basin before reaching Camp Hill Locks. These, and all the succeeding locks, are narrow. After passing through subterranean vaults formed by the criss-crossing of railway viaducts Bordesley Junction is reached. Ahead, beyond the Junction, the canal continues towards the Birmingham Canal Main Line, joining the Birmingham & Fazeley Canal at Aston Junction, passing a very fine collection of old wharf buildings on the way. Heading north from Bordesley Junction, the Grand Union is accompanied by pleasantly transformed surroundings to join the Birmingham & Fazeley Canal at Salford Junction

Pubs and Restaurants

🍺 **The Marlborough** Anderton Road, Sparkbrook (0121 772 2459). West of bridge 90. A large red-brick pile, marked with a prominent clock-tower. Snacks, children welcome.

✕ **Café Bond** 180-182 Fazeley Street (0121 771 0222). Canalside, between Bordesley Junction and Typhoo Basin, and handy for meals and snacks. *Open 08.00-14.15 daily.*

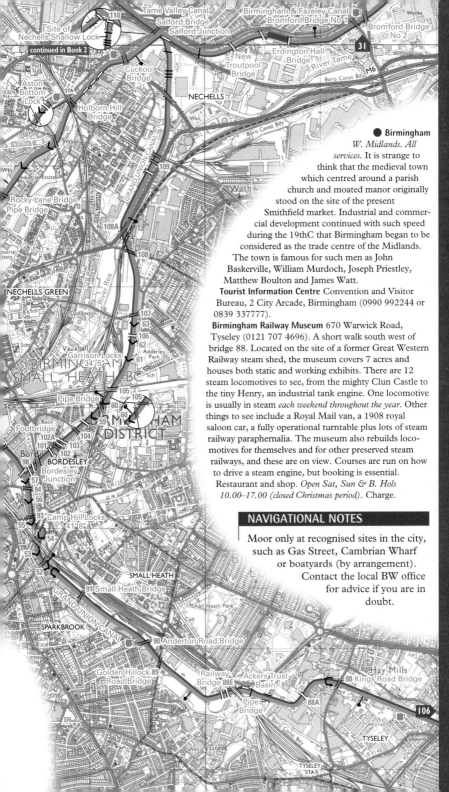

● **Birmingham**
*W. Midlands. All
services.* It is strange to
think that the medieval town
which centred around a parish
church and moated manor originally
stood on the site of the present
Smithfield market. Industrial and commercial development continued with such speed
during the 19thC that Birmingham began to be
considered as the trade centre of the Midlands.
The town is famous for such men as John
Baskerville, William Murdoch, Joseph Priestley,
Matthew Boulton and James Watt.

Tourist Information Centre Convention and Visitor
Bureau, 2 City Arcade, Birmingham (0990 992244 or
0839 337777).

Birmingham Railway Museum 670 Warwick Road,
Tyseley (0121 707 4696). A short walk south west of
bridge 88. Located on the site of a former Great Western
Railway steam shed, the museum covers 7 acres and
houses both static and working exhibits. There are 12
steam locomotives to see, from the mighty Clun Castle to
the tiny Henry, an industrial tank engine. One locomotive
is usually in steam *each weekend throughout the year.* Other
things to see include a Royal Mail van, a 1908 royal
saloon car, a fully operational turntable plus lots of steam
railway paraphernalia. The museum also rebuilds locomotives for themselves and for other preserved steam
railways, and these are on view. Courses are run on how
to drive a steam engine, but booking is essential.
Restaurant and shop. *Open Sat, Sun & B. Hols
10.00–17.00 (closed Christmas period).* Charge.

NAVIGATIONAL NOTES

Moor only at recognised sites in the city,
such as Gas Street, Cambrian Wharf
or boatyards (by arrangement).
Contact the local BW office
for advice if you are in
doubt.

Braunston, at the junction of the Grand Union and Oxford Canals

OXFORD CANAL

MAXIMUM DIMENSIONS
Length: 70'
Beam: 7'
Headroom: 7'

MILEAGE
BRAUNSTON TURN to:
Hillmorton Bottom Lock: $7^{1}/_{2}$
Rugby Wharf Arm: $10^{1}/_{4}$
Stretton Stop: $15^{3}/_{4}$

HAWKESBURY JUNCTION Coventry
Canal): $22^{3}/_{4}$ miles
Locks: 4

MANAGER
(01788) 890666

The Oxford Canal was one of the earliest and, for many years, one of the most important canals in southern England. It was authorised in 1769, when the Coventry Canal was in the offing, and was intended to fetch coal southwards from the Warwickshire coalfield to Banbury and Oxford, at the same time giving access to the River Thames. James Brindley was appointed engineer: he built a winding contour canal 91 miles long that soon began to look thoroughly outdated and inefficient for the carriage of goods. Brindley died in 1772, and was replaced by Samuel Simcock: he completed the line from Longford, where a junction was made with the Coventry Canal, to Banbury, in 1778. After a long pause, the canal was finally brought into Oxford in 1790, and thereafter through traffic flowed constantly along this important new trade route.

In 1780, however, the Grand Junction Canal opened (excepting the tunnel at Blisworth) from London to Braunston, and the Warwick & Napton and Warwick & Birmingham Canals completed the new short route from London to Birmingham. This had the natural – and intended – effect of drawing traffic off the Oxford Canal, especially south of Napton Junction, but the Oxford Company protected itself very effectively against this powerful opposition by charging outrageously high rates for their $5^{1}/_{2}$-mile stretch between Braunston and Napton, which had become part of the new London-Birmingham through route. Thus the Oxford Canal maintained its revenue and very high dividends for many years to come.

By the late 1820s, however, the Oxford Canal had become conspicuously out of date with its extravagant winding course; and under the threat of various schemes for big new canals which, if built, would render the Oxford Canal almost redundant, the company decided to modernise the northern part of their navigation. Tremendous engineering works were therefore carried out which completely changed the face of the canal north of Braunston. Aqueducts, massive embankments and deep cuttings were built, carrying the canal in great sweeps through the countryside and cutting almost 14 miles off the original 36 miles between Braunston Junction and the Coventry Canal. Much of the old main line suddenly became a series of loops and branches leading nowhere and crossed by elegant new towpath bridges inscribed Horseley Ironworks 1828.

This very expensive programme was well worthwhile. Although toll rates, and thus revenue, began to fall because of keen competition from the railways, dividends were kept at a high level for years – indeed a respectable profit was still shown right through to the 20thC.

Braunston and Willoughby

North of Braunston the Oxford Canal soon leaves behind the excitement and interest of the village to run through wide open country, backed by bare hills to the east. It is an ancient landscape, and by bridge 87 medieval ridge and furrow field patterns are in evidence. These were created as villagers cleared forested land, and each ploughed strips throwing soil towards the centre. Gradually a collection of strips, all running parallel to each other, made up a furlong or cultura. This was then enclosed by a low bank and an access track (usually difficult to identify today) was created. Fields, consisting of dozens of furlongs, were then sometimes fenced. Skirting round Barby Hill, the canal swings north east towards Hillmorton and Rugby. The M45 makes a noisy crossing after Barby Hill.

Boatyards

All the following are on the *Grand Union Canal* at Braunston.
The Boat Shop (01788 891310). Started on board a boat moored at Braunston Turn, this is now a shop by Braunston Top Lock selling basic chandlery, coal, groceries, fruit and vegetables canal ware, brass ware and much more. *Open Jun–Sep, 08.00–20.00, Oct–May 08.00–18.00.*
Ⓑ **Braunston Boats** Bottom Lock, Braunston (01788 891079). 🛠 D Pump-out, gas, narrow boat hire, long-term mooring by arrangement only.
Ⓑ **Union Canal Carriers** Canalside at Braunston pump house, Dark Lane (01788 890784). D Pump-out, gas, narrow boat hire, overnight

mooring by arrangement, books and maps, boat building, boat and engine sales and repairs. *24hr breakdown service (telephone 01788 812156 outside working hours).*
Ⓑ **Braunston Marina** The Wharf, Braunston (01788 891373). Through the fine bridge dated 1834 and into an historic canal wharf. 🛆 🛆 🛠 D E Gas, pump-out, overnight and long-term mooring, dry and wet dock, chandlery, boat building sales and repairs, engineering – all services. Toilets and showers, public telephone, chandlery, gift shop selling books and maps. Laundrette.
Ⓑ **Midland Chandlers** Canalside, Braunston Turn (01788 891401). A wide range of chandlery.

BOAT TRIPS
Rachael Operating from Braunston Marina, this licensed restaurant boat can accommodate 20 people. It makes regular *3-hour evening trips during the summer* on the Oxford Canal, and can also be chartered for *lunchtime* cruises. Telephone 07071 880784 for details.
The Rambler Operating from The Mill House (see below). Seating 12 people, this boat provides *lunchtime* cruises, *afternoon* cream tea cruises, and *evening* trips to the Napton Bridge Inn *Fri-Sat*, plus *hourly trips each Sun, throughout the summer.* It is also available for private charter. Details from Braunston Cruises, 14 Countryside, Braunston (01788 890373). Booking is essential.

Pubs and Restaurants

📶 ✕ **Rose Inn** Main Street, Willoughby (01788 890567). An attractively maintained thatched village pub, offering Courage real ale. Bar, restaurant and carvery meals *lunchtimes and evenings (not Mon & Wed lunchtime or Sun evenings)*, with vegetarian choices. Outside seating with children's play area. Regular entertainment with theme nights.
📶 ✕ **The Mill House** London Road, Braunston (01788 890450). Once the Rose & Castle, now a comfortable and friendly modern pub/restaurant. Bass and Worthington real ale, and food *7 days 12.00–21.30 (Sun 21.00)*. Children's room and fine canalside garden. Overnight mooring for patrons.

📶 **Wheatsheaf** The Green, Braunston (01788 890748). A locals' pub with a warm atmosphere, and traditional bar games. Everards, Flowers and guest real ales. Food *lunchtimes and evenings*, along with some interesting wines. Children welcome until early evening.
📶 ✕ **Old Plough Inn** High Street, Braunston (01788 890000). Popular village pub of great character, with an open fire. Built around 1672, it has had only thirteen landlords since then. Wadworth's real ale, with good food *lunchtimes and evenings every day*, including vegetarian dishes. Children are welcome, and there is a garden.

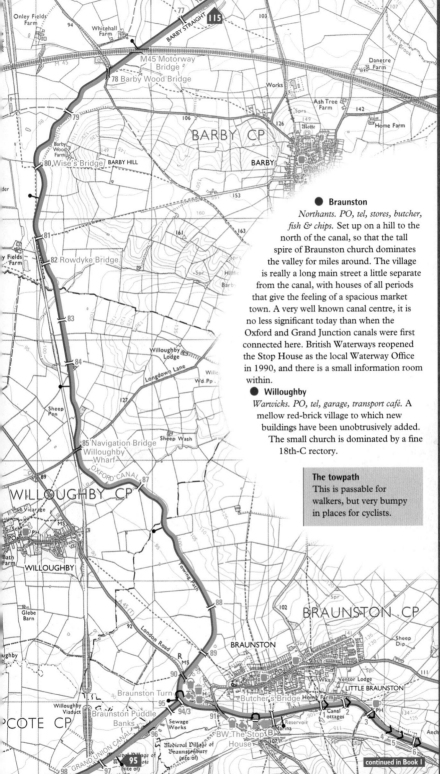

● **Braunston**

Northants. PO, tel, stores, butcher, fish & chips. Set up on a hill to the north of the canal, so that the tall spire of Braunston church dominates the valley for miles around. The village is really a long main street a little separate from the canal, with houses of all periods that give the feeling of a spacious market town. A very well known canal centre, it is no less significant today than when the Oxford and Grand Junction canals were first connected here. British Waterways reopened the Stop House as the local Waterway Office in 1990, and there is a small information room within.

● **Willoughby**

Warwicks. PO, tel, garage, transport café. A mellow red-brick village to which new buildings have been unobtrusively added. The small church is dominated by a fine 18th-C rectory.

The towpath
This is passable for walkers, but very bumpy in places for cyclists.

continued in Book 1

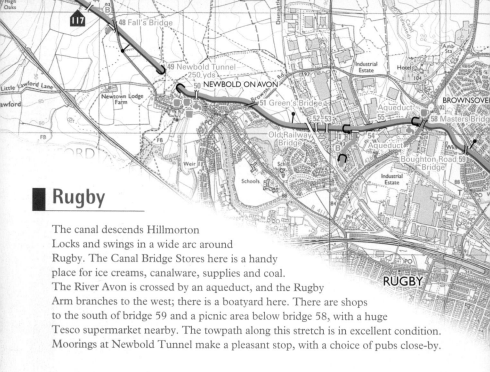

Rugby

The canal descends Hillmorton
Locks and swings in a wide arc around
Rugby. The Canal Bridge Stores here is a handy
place for ice creams, canalware, supplies and coal.
The River Avon is crossed by an aqueduct, and the Rugby
Arm branches to the west; there is a boatyard here. There are shops
to the south of bridge 59 and a picnic area below bridge 58, with a huge
Tesco supermarket nearby. The towpath along this stretch is in excellent condition.
Moorings at Newbold Tunnel make a pleasant stop, with a choice of pubs close-by.

Boatyards

Ⓑ **Club Line Cruisers** Hillmorton Wharf, Crick Road, Rugby (01788 577300). Long-term mooring, dry dock with hydraulic lift.

Ⓑ **Hillmorton Boat Services** The Locks, Hillmorton (01788 578661). 🚽 🚿 ⚓ Wet dock and dry dock, boat sales, boat and engine repairs, boat repainting, engineering services, sign-writing, boat covers. *24 hour* boat emergency breakdown call-out.

Ⓑ **Clifton Cruisers** Clifton Wharf, Vicarage Hill, Clifton on Dunsmore (01788 543570). 🚽 ⚓ D Pump-out, gas, narrow boat hire, overnight

mooring, boat and engine repairs, boatbuilding, toilets, showers, gifts.

Ⓑ **Willow Wren Hire Cruisers** Rugby Wharf, off Consul Road, Leicester Road, Rugby (01788 562183). 🚽 ⚓ D Pump-out, gas, narrow boat hire, overnight and long-term mooring, toilets and showers, gifts.

Ⓑ **T. F. Yates** Falls Bridge Works, Cathiron Lane, Newbold-on-Avon (01788 569140). East of bridge 44. 🚿 D Pump-out, gas, crane, engine sales, boat and engine repairs, full engineering services, real chandlery.

● **Hillmorton**
Warwicks. PO, tel, stores, garage, take-aways, but all a fair distance from the canal.

● **Rugby**
Warwicks. MD Mon, Fri, Sat. PO, tel, stores, garage, station, theatre, cinema, leisure centre. There is a pedestrianised shopping centre, a leisure centre and an open market with a town crier. Look out for the tiny shop in Chapel Street, which has stood for over 500 years and is reputedly the oldest building in the town.
James Gilbert Rugby Football Museum 5 St Matthews Street, Rugby (01788 542426).

Founded by the nephew of William Gilbert, who made boots and shoes for Rugby School in his original shop in the High Street. *Open Mon–Fri 10.00–17.00, Sat 10.00–14.00. Closed Sun. Free.*
Rugby School Museum 10 Little Church Street, Rugby (01788 574117). Opposite the Temple Speech Room, opened in 1909 by King Edward VII and named after a headmaster of the school who later became Archbishop of Canterbury. Guided tours. *Open daily 10.30–16.30. Charge.*
Tourist Information Centre Rugby Library, St Matthew's Street, Rugby (01788 535348).

Pubs and Restaurants

Old Royal Oak Crick Road, Hillmorton Wharf (01788 561401). Canalside at bridge 73. Marston's and Ansells real ale and bar meals *all day,* with a vegetarian menu. Children's room and play area. Mooring for patrons.

Clifton Inn Clifton Road, Rugby (01788 542338). South of bridge 66. Ansells, Marston's, Morland's and Tetleys real ales, bar and restaurant meals *lunchtimes and evenings every day,* with a vegetarian menu. Live music *Fri & Sat*, with a quiz on *Sun.*

Bell & Barge Brownsover Road, Rugby (01788 569466). Bridge 58. A Harvester serving Bass and M&B real ale and food *lunchtimes and evenings every day,* with vegetarian options. Garden. Children welcome.

Boat Main Street, Newbold Wharf (01788 576995). By Bridge 50. Bass and Greenalls real ale. Menu, including vegetarian food, *lunchtimes and evenings every day.* Pleasant garden and moorings. A fine variety of entertainment with traditional bar games, and Morris Dancers *in the summer.*

Barley Mow Main Street, Newbold-on-Avon (01788 544174). Canalside pub serving Bass real ale. Bar and restaurant meals and snacks available *lunchtimes and evenings every day.* Vegetarian menu. Children welcome, and there is a canalside garden with a bouncy castle. Regular entertainment, and *weekend* piano sing-alongs.

● **Newbold on Avon**
Warwicks. PO, tel, stores, garage, fish & chips. At the wharf near the tunnel mouth are two fine pubs right next door to each other.

Newbold Quarry Park
Newbold Road, Rugby (02476 302912). A local nature reserve beside the canal, on the site of an old limestone quarry. There are wildflowers, butterflies and birds to look out for, together with muntjac deer. Take care near the water, it is deep!

● **Newbold Tunnel**
This 250yd long tunnel was built during the shortening of the Oxford Canal in the 1820s.

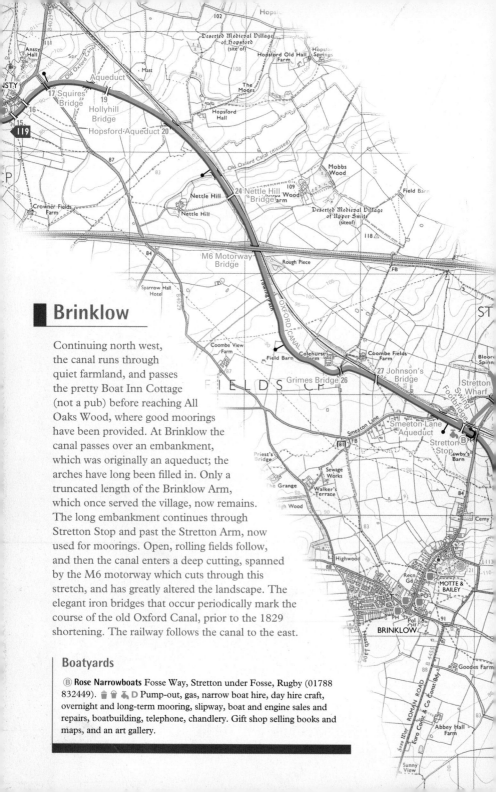

Brinklow

Continuing north west, the canal runs through quiet farmland, and passes the pretty Boat Inn Cottage (not a pub) before reaching All Oaks Wood, where good moorings have been provided. At Brinklow the canal passes over an embankment, which was originally an aqueduct; the arches have long been filled in. Only a truncated length of the Brinklow Arm, which once served the village, now remains. The long embankment continues through Stretton Stop and past the Stretton Arm, now used for moorings. Open, rolling fields follow, and then the canal enters a deep cutting, spanned by the M6 motorway which cuts through this stretch, and has greatly altered the landscape. The elegant iron bridges that occur periodically mark the course of the old Oxford Canal, prior to the 1829 shortening. The railway follows the canal to the east.

Boatyards

Ⓑ **Rose Narrowboats** Fosse Way, Stretton under Fosse, Rugby (01788 832449). Pump-out, gas, narrow boat hire, day hire craft, overnight and long-term mooring, slipway, boat and engine sales and repairs, boatbuilding, telephone, chandlery. Gift shop selling books and maps, and an art gallery.

Harborough Magna

Warwicks. PO box, tel, stores. Quiet red-brick village one mile to the north of the canal from bridges 43 or 48. The 13th–14thC church has a Victorian west tower and many Victorian additions, including an interesting stained-glass window depicting Christ rising, with two angels, against a dark blue background.

Brinklow

Warwicks. PO, tel, stores, garage, fish & chips. A spacious pre-industrial village built along a wide main street. The church of St John Baptist is of late Perpendicular style, and has some interesting 15th-C stained glass depicting birds, including a peacock. Its sloping floor climbs 12 feet from west to east. Alongside is the substantial mound of a motte and bailey castle, built to defend the Fosse Way.

Pubs and Restaurants

White Lion Broad Street, Brinklow (01788 832579). A welcoming local pub with a plush lounge and an old-fashioned bar, serving Banks's real ale and bar snacks *lunchtimes Mon–Fri*. Garden and children's room. Traditional bar games, theme and quiz nights. B & B.

Bulls Head Broad Street, Brinklow (01788 832355). A smartly furnished family pub. Food. Garden.

Raven Broad Street, Brinklow (01788 832655). A friendly family pub at the top of the village, with Banks's and Marston's real ale available. Extensive range of bar meals *lunchtimes and evenings every day*, with a vegetarian menu and traditional *Sunday lunch*. Garden.

Dun Cow Coventry Road, Brinklow (01788 832358). A locals' pub serving Boddingtons and M & B real ale with food available in the restaurant or bar, including vegetarian choices, *lunchtimes and evenings every day*. Children welcome in the lounge. Garden.

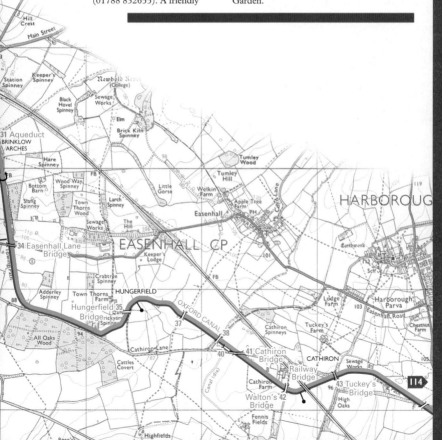

Hawkesbury Junction

The open landscape continues beyond Ansty, although the motorway is never far away. Soon the first signs of Coventry appear, with views of pylons and housing estates. The new Wyken Colliery Arm leaves to the west: it was built to replace the old one eaten up by the motorway which comes alongside the canal at this point: it is now used by the Coventry Cruising Club. Sharp bends then lead to the stop lock before Hawkesbury Junction, the end of the Oxford Canal where it joins the Coventry Canal. This last stretch of the Oxford Canal is characterised by the 1820s shortenings; straight cuttings and embankments date from this period, while the cast iron bridges mark the old route.

Pubs and Restaurants

Rose and Castle Main Road, Ansty (02476 612822). A friendly and welcoming canalside pub serving Bass, Courage, Tetley's and guest real ales. An extensive range of good food is available *lunchtimes and evenings every day*. Children welcome, play area and canalside garden. Moorings and 🐕.

Elephant & Castle 445 Aldermans Green Road (02476 364606). Canalside, by Tusses Bridge 4. There is a good choice of real ale in this recently refurbished friendly local community pub. Bar meals are served *lunchtimes*, with snacks available *the rest of the time*. Vegetarians can usually be catered for. Huge garden with a children's play area.

Old Crown Aldermans Green Road (02476 365894). South of Tusses Bridge (no. 4). A cosy pub with carved woodwork, beams, brasses, and snug settees, serving Marston's, a guest and a choice of bottled real ales. Food *lunchtimes and evenings*, with a vegetarian choices. Children welcome, garden.

✕ Greyhound Hawkesbury Junction (02476 363046). A fascinating pub beside the junction, decorated with canal and rugby memorabilia, together with an immense collection of Toby jugs, warmed by log fires in winter. An imaginative selection of food, especially pies and salads, is served in the bar or restaurant *lunchtimes and evenings every day*, with a vegetarian menu, and a choice of real ales is available. Canalside garden and safe children's play area. Folk music on *third Thu each month*.

Boat Inn Black Horse Road, Longford (02476 361438). A fine friendly pub with unspoilt rooms and a cosy lounge, all decorated with antiques, just a 3 minute walk from the junction. Ansells, Greene King and Tetley's real ales, and also real draught cider. *Lunchtime* bar snacks. Children welcome. Garden for the summer and a real fire for the winter.

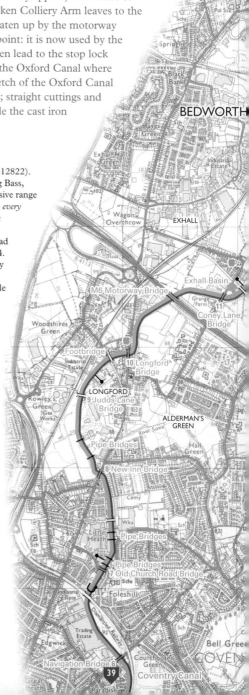

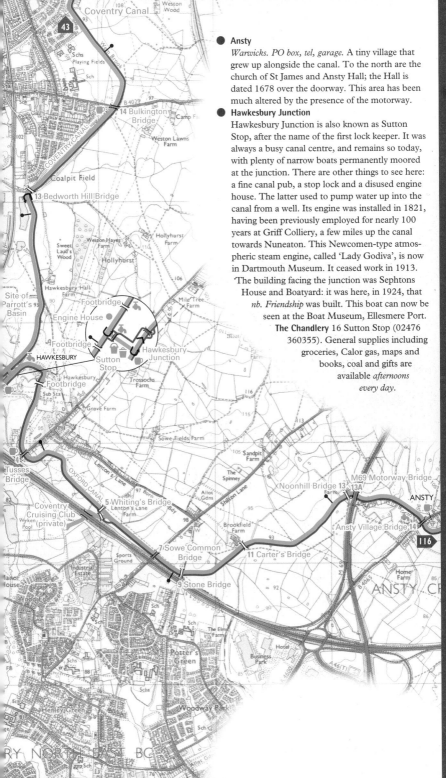

● **Ansty**

Warwicks. PO box, tel, garage. A tiny village that grew up alongside the canal. To the north are the church of St James and Ansty Hall; the Hall is dated 1678 over the doorway. This area has been much altered by the presence of the motorway.

● **Hawkesbury Junction**

Hawkesbury Junction is also known as Sutton Stop, after the name of the first lock keeper. It was always a busy canal centre, and remains so today, with plenty of narrow boats permanently moored at the junction. There are other things to see here: a fine canal pub, a stop lock and a disused engine house. The latter used to pump water up into the canal from a well. Its engine was installed in 1821, having been previously employed for nearly 100 years at Griff Colliery, a few miles up the canal towards Nuneaton. This Newcomen-type atmospheric steam engine, called 'Lady Godiva', is now in Dartmouth Museum. It ceased work in 1913. The building facing the junction was Sephtons House and Boatyard: it was here, in 1924, that *nb. Friendship* was built. This boat can now be seen at the Boat Museum, Ellesmere Port.

The Chandlery 16 Sutton Stop (02476 360355). General supplies including groceries, Calor gas, maps and books, coal and gifts are available *afternoons every day.*

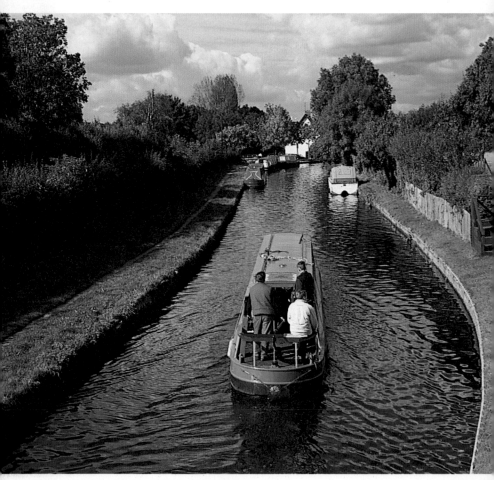

View from Cross Green Bridge, near Coven (see page 122)

STAFFORDSHIRE & WORCESTERSHIRE CANAL: NORTH

MAXIMUM DIMENSIONS	MILEAGE
Length: 70'	AUTHERLEY JUNCTION to
Beam: 7'	*GREAT HAYWOOD JUNCTION:* 20¹/₂ miles
Headroom: 6' 6"	
	Locks: 12
MANAGER	
(01785) 284253	

Construction of this navigation was begun immediately after that of the Trent & Mersey, to effect the joining of the rivers Trent, Mersey and Severn. Engineered by James Brindley, the Staffordshire & Worcestershire was opened throughout in 1772, at a cost of rather over £100,000. It stretched 46 miles from Great Haywood on the Trent & Mersey to the River Severn, which it joined at Stourport. The canal was an immediate success. It was well placed to bring goods from the Potteries down to Gloucester, Bristol and the West Country; while the Birmingham Canal, which joined it halfway along at Aldersley Junction, fed manufactured goods northwards from the Black Country to the Potteries via Great Haywood. In 1815 the Worcester & Birmingham Canal opened, offering a more direct but heavily locked canal link between Birmingham and the Severn. The Staffs & Worcs answered this threat by gradually extending the opening times of the locks, until by 1830 they were open 24 hours a day. When the Birmingham & Liverpool Junction Canal was opened from Autherley to Nantwich in 1835, traffic bound for Merseyside from Birmingham naturally began to use this more direct, modern canal. The Staffs & Worcs lost a great deal of traffic over its length as most of the boats now passed along only the ¹/₂-mile stretch of the Staffs & Worcs Canal between Autherley and Aldersley Junctions. The company levied absurdly high tolls for this tiny length. The B & LJ Company therefore cooperated with the Birmingham Canal Company in 1836 to promote in Parliament a Bill for the Tettenhall & Autherley Canal and Aqueduct. This project was to be a canal flyover, going from the Birmingham Canal right over the profiteering Staffs & Worcs and locking down into the Birmingham & Liverpool Junction Canal. The Staffs & Worcs company had to give way, and reduced its tolls to an acceptable level.

In spite of this set back, the Staffs & Worcs maintained a good profit, and high dividends were paid throughout the rest of the 19thC. From the 1860s onwards, railway competition began to bite, and the company's profits began to slip. Several modernisation schemes came to nothing, and the canal's trade declined. Now the canal is used almost exclusively by pleasure craft. It is covered in full in Book 2.

Autherley Junction

Autherley Junction is marked by a big white bridge on the towpath side. The stop lock just beyond marks the entrance to the Shropshire Union: there is a useful boatyard just to the north of it. Leaving Autherley the Staffordshire & Worcestershire runs through a very narrow cutting in rock: there is only room for boats to pass in the designated places, so a good look out should be kept for oncoming craft. After passing the motorway and a rather conspicuous sewage works at Coven Heath, the navigation leaves behind the suburbs of Wolverhampton and enters pleasant farmland. The bridges need care: although the bridgeholes are reasonably wide, the actual arches are rather low.

● **Autherley Junction**
A busy canal junction with a full range of boating facilities close by.

● **Coven**
Staffs. PO, tel, stores, garage, fish & chips. The only true village on this section, Coven lies beyond a dual carriageway north west of Cross Green Bridge. There are a large number of shops, including a launderette.

Gailey Lock (see page 125)

Boatyards

Ⓑ **Water Travel** Autherley Junction, Oxley Moor Road, Wolverhampton (01902 782371). 🚿 🔧 D Pump-out, gas, narrow boat hire, slipway, boat and engine repairs, chandlery, toilets.

The towpath
This is generally in good condition.

BOAT TRIPS
Nb. Stafford Public trips on the *first Sun each month*, plus private charter. For details telephone (01902) 789522.

Pubs and Restaurants

🍺 ✕ **Anchor Inn** (01902 790466). Canalside by Cross Green Bridge. A large family-friendly pub with a roof-top terrace, tastefully decorated with wood and stained glass. Morland's and Tetleys real ale, and meals are *available all day*, with vegetarian options. The food is good, and includes a balti choice. Children's menu, garden and good moorings.

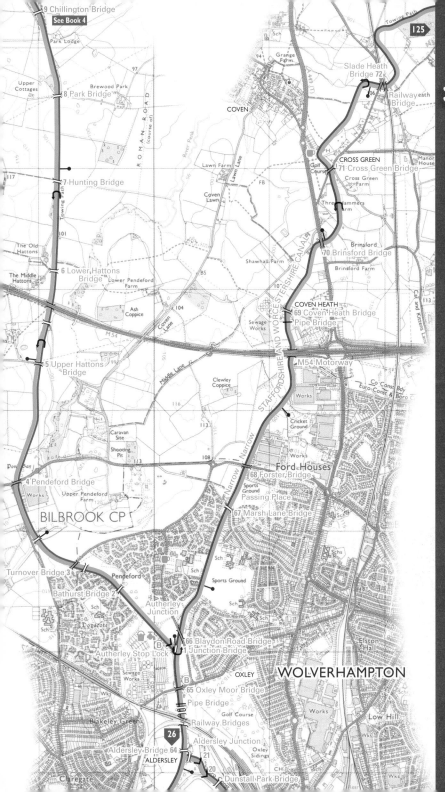

Staffordshire & Worcestershire Canal

Autherley Junction

9 Chillington Bridge
See Book 4
Park Lodge

Upper Cottages

8 Park Bridge

Slade Heath Bridge 72

Railway Bridge

COVEN

CROSS GREEN
71 Cross Green Bridge

Three Hammers Farm

7 Hunting Bridge

Lawn Farm

Lawn Lane

FB

Coven Peak

Golf Course

Cross Green Farm

Manor House

The Old Hattons

Coven Lawn

Brinsford

70 Brinsford Bridge

Brinsford Farm

The Middle Hattons

6 Lower Hattons Bridge

Lower Pendeford Farm

Shawhall Farm

BS

COVEN HEATH
69 Coven Heath Bridge
Pipe Bridge

Ash Coppice

Coven Lane

Sewage Works

M54 Motorway

5 Upper Hattons Bridge

Middle Lane

Clewley Coppice

Works

Cricket Ground

Co Const Bdy
Euro Const & Boro

Cat and Kittens Lane

Caravan Site
Shooting Pit

Works

Ford Houses

Narrow Narrow

68 Forster Bridge

Don Bay

4 Pendeford Bridge

Upper Pendeford Farm

Sports Ground
Passing Place

67 Marsh Lane Bridge

Works

BILBROOK CP

Sch

Sports Ground

Turnover Bridge 3

Pendeford

Bathurst Bridge 2

Autherley Junction

66 Blaydon Road Bridge
1 Junction Bridge

Elston Hall

Autherley Stop Lock

OXLEY

WOLVERHAMPTON

Sewage Works

65 Oxley Moor Bridge
Pipe Bridge

Golf Course

Low Hill

Works

Blakeley Green

Railway Bridges

26

Aldersley Junction

Aldersley Bridge 64

21

Oxley Sidings

ALDERSLEY

20

Chargate

Dunstall Park Bridge

Towing Path

125

Sch

Grange Farm

Slade Heath

Gailey Wharf

The considerable age of this canal is shown by its extremely twisting course, revealed after passing the railway bridge. There are few real centres of population along this stretch, which comprises largely former heathland. Hatherton Junction marks the entrance of the former Hatherton Branch of the Staffs & Worcs Canal into the main line. This branch used to connect with the Birmingham Canal Navigations. It is closed above the derelict second lock, although the channel remains as a feeder for the Staffs & Worcs Canal. There is a marina at the junction. A little further along, a chemical works is encountered, astride the canal in what used to be woodlands. Gailey Wharf is about a mile further north: it is a small canal settlement that includes a boatyard and a large, round, toll keeper's watch-tower, containing a useful canal shop. The picturesque Wharf Cottage opposite has been restored as a bijou residence. The canal itself disappears under Watling Street and then falls rapidly through five locks towards Penkridge. These locks are very attractive, and some are accompanied by little brick bridges. The M6 motorway comes alongside for $1/2$ mile, screening the reservoirs which feed the canal.

Pillaton Old Hall South east of bridge 85. Only the gate-house and stone built chapel remain of this late 15th-C brick mansion built by the Littleton family, although there are still traces of the hall and courtyard. The chapel contains a 13th-C wooden carving of a saint. Visiting is by appointment only: telephone (01785) 712200. The modest charge is donated to charity.
Gailey and Calf Heath reservoirs $1/2$ mile east of Gailey Wharf, either side of the M6. These are feeder reservoirs for the canal, though rarely drawn on. The public has access to them as nature reserves to study the wide variety of natural life, especially the long-established heronry which is thriving on an island in Gailey Lower reservoir. In Gailey Upper, fishing is available to the public from the riparian owner. In Gailey Lower a limited number of angling tickets are available on a season ticket basis each year from BW. There is club sailing on two of the reservoirs.

Boatyards

Ⓑ **Otherton Boat Haven** Otherton Hall Farm, Offerton (01785 712515). 🛆 🛆 🔧 D Pump-out, gas, overnight and long-term mooring, crane, boat and engine sales and repairs, toilets.
Ⓑ **Gailey Marine** The Wharf, Watling Street, Standeford (01902 790612). 🛆 🛆 🔧 Pump-out, gas, narrow boat hire, long-term mooring, boat & engine repairs, boatbuilding, public telephone. Boatbuilding on site at J.D. Boat Services, contact as above. Gifts and provisions opposite in the Roundhouse.
Ⓑ **Calf Heath Marina** (01902 790570). 🔧 D Pump-out, gas, overnight and long-term moorings, telephone, toilet.

Pubs and Restaurants

✕ ⏱ **Misty's Bar & Restaurant** Calf Heath Marina (01902 790570). Licensed restaurant, serving excellent and reasonably priced food *L & D*. Children welcome, garden.
🍺 **Spread Eagle** Watling Street, Gailey (01902 790212). About $1/2$ mile west of Gailey Wharf. A large road house serving Banks's real ale and food *lunchtimes and evenings*. Enormous garden.
🍺 **Cross Keys** Filance Lane (01785 712826). Canalside, at Filance Bridge (84). Once a lonely canal pub, now it is modernised and surrounded by housing estates. Family orientated, it serves Banks's, Bass, M & B and Worthington real ale and food *lunchtimes and evenings*. Garden, with *summer* barbeques. 🔧 There is a useful Spar shop 100yds north, on the estate.

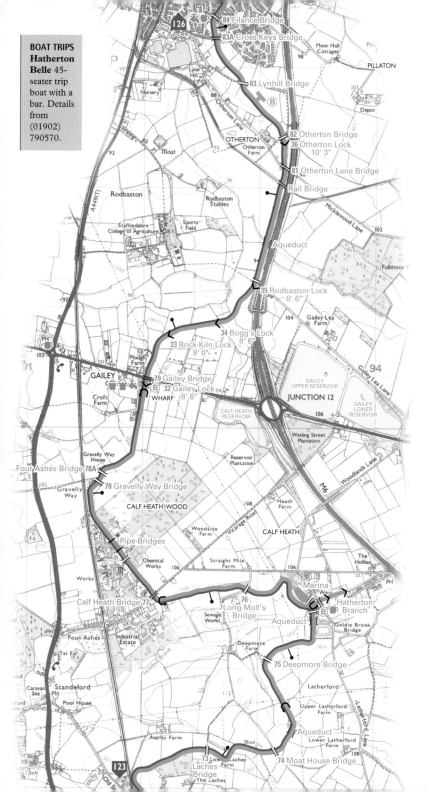

BOAT TRIPS
Hatherton Belle 45-seater trip boat with a bar. Details from (01902) 790570.

126

84 Filance Bridge
83A Cross Keys Bridge

Moor Hall Cottages

PILLATON

83 Lynhill Bridge

OTHERTON
Otherton Farm

82 Otherton Bridge
36 Otherton Lock 10' 3"

81 Otherton Lane Bridge

Rail Bridge

Micklewood Lane

Fullmoor

Aqueduct

Rodbaston

Rodbaston Stables

Staffordshire College of Agriculture

Sports Field

35 Rodbaston Lock 8' 6"

Gailey Lea Farm

34 Bogg's Lock 8' 6"

33 Brick-Kiln Lock 8' 0"

Plough Farm

Gailey Lea Lane

94

GAILEY

Croft Farm

79 Gailey Bridge

WHARF

32 Gailey Lock 8' 6"

GAILEY UPPER RESERVOIR

JUNCTION 12

GAILEY LOWER RESERVOIR

CALF HEATH RESERVOIR

Watling Street Plantation

Gravelly Way House

Four Ashes Bridge 78A

78 Gravelly Way Bridge

Gravelly Way

CALF HEATH WOOD

Reservoir Plantation

M6

Woodlands Lane

Heath Farm

CALF HEATH

Pipe Bridges

Woodside Farm

Chemical Works

Straight Mile Farm

The Hollies

PH

Works

Calf Heath Bridge 77

76 Long Moll's Bridge

Sewage Works

Aqueduct

Marina Weir

Hatherton Branch

Goldie Brook Bridge

Four Ashes

Industrial Estate

Deepmore Farm

75 Deepmore Bridge

Latherford

Standeford

Pool House

Upper Latherford Farm

Lower Latherford Farm

Aqueduct

Latherford Lane

Aspley Farm

Moat

73 Lower Laches Bridge

The Laches

74 Moat House Bridge

123

Penkridge

The navigation now passes through Penkridge and is soon approached by the little River Penk: the two water courses share the valley for the next few miles. Apart from the noise of the motorway this is a pleasant valley: there are plenty of trees, a handful of locks and the large Teddesley Park alongside the canal. At Acton Trussell the M6 roars off to the north west and once again peace returns to the waterway.

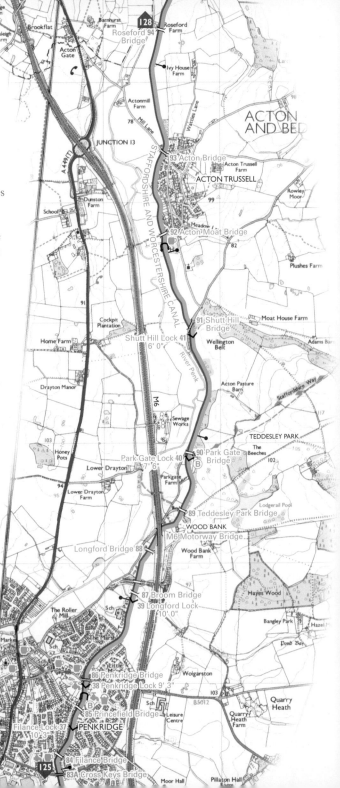

● **Penkridge**
*Staffs. MD Mon. PO, tel, stores, garage, bank,
station.* Above Penkridge Lock is a good place
to tie up in this relatively old village. It is
bisected by a trunk road, but luckily most of
the village lies to the east of it. The church of
St Michael is tall and sombre, and is well kept.
An harmonious mixture of styles, the earliest
dates from the 11thC, but the whole was
restored in 1881. There is a fine Dutch
18th-C wrought iron screen brought from
Cape Town, and the tower is believed to date
from about 1500. There are fine monuments
of the Littletons of Pillaton Hall (see the

previous section), dating from 1558 and
later.
Teddesley Park On the east bank of the canal.
The Hall, once the family seat of the Littletons,
was used during the last war as a prisoner-of-
war camp, but has since been demolished. Its
extensive wooded estate still remains.
● **Acton Trussell**
Staffs. PO, tel, stores. A village overwhelmed
by modern housing: much the best way to see
it is from the canal. The church stands to the
south, overlooking the navigation. The west
tower dates from the 13thC, topped by a spire
built in 1562.

Boatyards

Ⓑ **Teddesley Boat Company** Park Gate Lock,
Teddesley Road, Penkridge (01785 714692).
D Pump-out, gas, narrow boat hire, day boat
hire, overnight & long-term mooring, winter
storage, crane, boat & engine sales & repairs,

boat building. *Closed Sun.* For chandlery
telephone 01785 712437.
Ⓑ **Tom's Moorings** Cannock Road, Penkridge
(01543 414808). Above Penkridge Lock. ♨
Pump-out, gas, overnight and long-term mooring.

The Moat House, Acton Trussell

Pubs and Restaurants

🍺 **The Boat** Cannock Road (01785 714178).
Canalside, by Penkridge Lock. A mellow and
friendly red-brick pub dating from 1779, with
plenty of brass and other bits and pieces in the
homely bars. Ansells, Marston's and
Morland's and food *lunchtimes and evenings
(not Sunday evenings)*. Children welcome.
🍺 **Star** Market Place, Penkridge (01785
712513). A very fine old pub, tastefully
renovated and serving Banks's real ale and bar
meals *lunchtimes and evenings*, with a vegetarian
menu. Outside seating. Children welcome.
🍺 **White Hart** Stone Cross, Penkridge (01785
712242). This historic former coaching inn,
visited by Mary, Queen of Scots and Elizabeth
I, has an impressive frontage, timber framed
with three gables. It serves Banks's and Bass

real ale and meals *lunchtimes and evenings,
along with traditional Sunday lunch.* Garden.
🍺 **Railway** Wolverhampton Road, Penkridge
(01785 712685). Tetley's, Banks's, Porter and
guest real ales are available in this listed
historic main road pub, along with meals
*lunchtimes and evenings, including special Sunday
lunches,* with a vegetarian choice. Children
welcome. Garden. Karaoke nights.
🍺 ✕ **The Moat House** Bridge 92, Acton
Trussell (01785 712217). Very attractive
14thC pub with a conservatory and 6 acres of
landscaped garden. Banks's and Marston's
real ale. Restaurant meals *L & D* and bar
meals *Mon–Sat lunchtimes and Sun–Fri
evenings,* including a vegetarian menu.
Children welcome. Pleasant moorings. B & B.

Tixall

Continuing north along the shallow Penk valley, the canal soon reaches Radford Bridge, the nearest point to Stafford. It is about $1^1/2$ miles to the centre of town: there is a frequent bus service. A mile further north the canal bends around to the south east and follows the pretty valley of the River Sow. At Milford the navigation crosses the Sow via an aqueduct – an early structure by James Brindley, carried heavily on low brick arches. Dedging around here revealed the presence of great numbers of fresh water mussels. Tixall Lock offers some interesting views in all directions: the castellated entrance to Shugborough Railway Tunnel at the foot of the thick woods of Cannock Chase and the distant outline of Tixall Gatehouse. The canal now completes its journey to the Trent & Mersey Canal at Great Haywood. It is a length of waterway quite unlike any other. Proceeding along this very charming valley, the navigation enters Tixall Wide – an amazing and delightful stretch of water more resembling a lake than a canal, and navigable to the edges. The Wide is noted for its kingfisher population. On the low hill to the north is the equally remarkable Tixall Gatehouse, while woods across the valley conceal Shugborough Hall. The River Trent is met, on its way south from Stoke-on-Trent, and crossed on an aqueduct.

There is a wharf, and fresh produce can be purchased at the farm near here: gifts are sold in the old canal toll booth. The Trent & Mersey Canal is entered through an elegantly arched bridge, the subject of a famous photograph taken by the canal historian Eric de Maré.

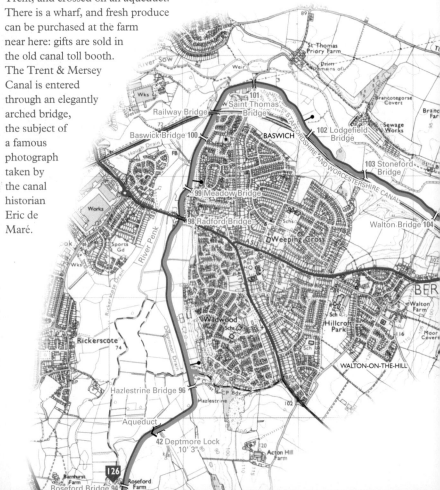

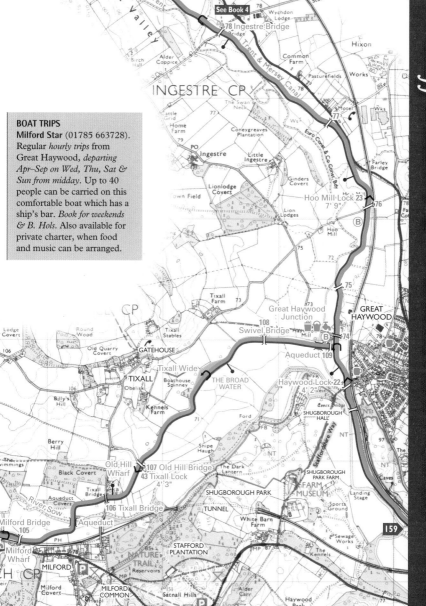

BOAT TRIPS
Milford Star (01785 663728).
Regular *hourly trips* from
Great Haywood, *departing
Apr–Sep on Wed, Thu, Sat &
Sun from midday.* Up to 40
people can be carried on this
comfortable boat which has a
ship's bar. *Book for weekends
& B. Hols.* Also available for
private charter, when food
and music can be arranged.

Boatyards

Ⓑ **Anglo Welsh** The Canal Wharf, Mill Lane, Great Haywood (01889
881711). 🚽 🎁 ♿ D Pump-out, gas, narrow boat hire, day hire craft, overnight
mooring, long term mooring, boat and engine repairs, toilets, gifts.

Stafford

Staffs. MD Tue, Fri, Sat. All services. This town is well worth visiting, since there is here a remarkable wealth of fine old buildings. These include a handsome City Hall complex of ornamental Italianate buildings, c1880. The robust-looking gaol is nearby; and the church of St Mary stands in very pleasing and spacious grounds. There are some pretty back alleys: Church Lane contains a splendid-looking eating house, and at the bottom of the lane a fruiterer's shop is in a thatched cottage built in 1610.

The Shire Hall Gallery Market Square, Stafford (01785 278345). A stimulating variety of work by local artists, craftsmen, printmakers, jewellers, photographers and others. *Open Mon-Sat 10.00-17.00.*

Tourist Information Centre The Ancient High House, Greengate Street, Stafford (01785 240204).

● **The Stafford Branch**

Just west of bridge 101 there was once a lock taking a branch off the Staffs & Worcs to Stafford. One mile long, it was unusual in that it was not a canal but the canalised course of the River Sow.

● **Milford**

Staffs. PO, tel, stores, garage. Best reached from Tixall Bridge (106). Milford Hall is hidden by trees.

● **Tixall**

Staffs. Tel, stores. Just to the east are the stables and the Gatehouse of the long-vanished Tixall Hall. This massive square Elizabethan building dates from 1598 and is fully four storeys high. It stands alone in a field and is considered to be one of the most ambitious gatehouses in the country. The Gatehouse is now available for holiday lets: telephone the Landmark Trust (01628 825925) for details.

● **Great Haywood**

Staffs. PO, tel, stores. Centre of the Great Haywood and Shugborough Conservation Area, the village is not particularly beautiful, but it is closely connected in many ways to Shugborough Park, to which it is physically linked by the very old Essex Bridge, where the crystal clear waters of the River Sow join the Trent on its way down from Stoke.

Shugborough Hall *National Trust property.* Walk south along the road from bridge 106 to the A513 at Milford Common. The main entrance is on your left. The present house dates from 1693, but was substantially altered by James Stuart around 1760 and by Samuel Wyatt around the turn of the 18thC. The Trust has leased the whole to Staffordshire County Council who now manage it. The house has been restored at great expense. There are some magnificent rooms and treasures inside.

Museum of Staffordshire Life This excellent establishment, which is Staffordshire's County Museum, is housed in the old stables adjacent to Shugborough Hall. Open since 1966, it is superbly laid out and contains all sorts of exhibits concerned with old country life in Staffordshire.

Shugborough Park There are some remarkable sights in the large park that encircles the hall. Thomas Anson, who inherited the estate in 1720, enlisted in 1744 the help of his famous brother, Admiral George Anson, to beautify and improve the house and the park. In 1762 he commissioned James Stuart, a neo-Grecian architect, to embellish the grounds. 'Athenian' Stuart set to with a will, and the spectacular results of his work can be seen scattered round the park.

The Park Farm Designed by Samuel Wyatt, it contains an agricultural museum, a working mill and a rare breeds centre. Traditional country skills such as bread-making, butter-churning and cheese-making are demonstrated.

Shugborough Hall, Grounds, Museum and Farm (01889 881388). *Open late Mar–late Sep, daily 11.00–17.00.* Charge. Parties must book.

Pubs and Restaurants

🍺 **Clifford Arms** Main Road, Great Haywood (01889 881321). Friendly village local with a real fire, once a coaching house, now serving Bass real ale and bar and restaurant meals *lunchtimes and evenings every day.* Garden.

🍺 **Fox & Hounds** Main Road, Great Haywood (01889 881252). Plush village pub serving Ansells, Marston's, Tetley's and guest real ales.

Food *lunchtimes and evenings.* Vegetarians are catered for. Garden. Children welcome.

✕ 🍷 **Lockhouse Restaurant** Trent Lane, Great Haywood (01889 881294). *L every day* and home-cooked English food *D, Wed–Sat only (booking advisable).* Vegetarians catered for. Marston's real ale. Just a couple of minutes walk from the centre of the village.

STRATFORD-ON-AVON CANAL

MAXIMUM DIMENSIONS	MILEAGE
King's Norton to Kingswood	*KING'S NORTON JUNCTION to*
Length: 70'	Hockley Heath: 9³/4 miles
Beam: 7'	*KINGSWOOD* Junction with Grand Union
Headroom: 7' 3"	Canal: 12¹/2
MANAGER	Locks: 14
(01564) 784634	

he opening of the Oxford Canal in 1790 and of the Coventry Canal throughout shortly
terwards opened up a continuous waterway from London to the rapidly developing
dustrial area based on Birmingham. It also gave access, via the Trent & Mersey Canal, to
e expanding pottery industry based around Stoke-on-Trent, to the Mersey, and to the
ast Midlands coalfield. When the Warwick & Birmingham and Warwick & Napton
anals were projected to pass within 8 miles of Stratford-on-Avon, the business interests of
at town realised that the prosperity being generated by these new trade arteries would
ss them by unless Stratford acquired direct access to the network. And so on 28 March
'93 an Act of Parliament was passed for the construction of the Stratford-on-Avon Canal,
start at King's Norton on the Worcester & Birmingham Canal.

ogress was rapid at first, but almost the total estimated cost of the complete canal was
ent in the first three years, on cutting the 9³/4 lock-free miles to Hockley Heath. It took
other four years, more negotiations, a revision of the route and another Act of
rliament to get things going again. By 1803 the canal was open from King's Norton
nction to its junction with the Warwick & Birmingham Canal (now part of the Grand
nion main line) near Lapworth. Cutting recommenced in 1812, the route being revised
t again in 1815 to include the present junction with the River Avon at Stratford.

its most prosperous period, the canal's annual traffic exceeded 180,000 tons, including
,000 tons of coal through the complete canal, down to Stratford. By 1835 the canal was
ffering from railway competition. This grew so rapidly that in 1845 the Canal Company
cided to sell out to the Great Western Railway. In 1890 the tonnage carried was still a
arter of what it had been 50 years before, but the fall in ton-miles was much greater.
his pattern of decline continued in the 20thC, and by the 1950s only an occasional work-
g boat used the northern section; the southern section (Lapworth to Stratford) was badly
ted, some locks were unusable and some of the short pounds below Wilmcote were dry.
ter World War II interest began to grow in boating as a recreation. In 1955 a Board of
rvey had recommended sweeping canal closures, including the southern section of the
ratford Canal, but public protest was such that a Committee of Enquiry was set up in
58, and this prompted the start of a massive campaign to save the canal. The campaign
s successful: the decision not to abandon it was announced by the Ministry on 22 May
59. On 16 October of the same year the National Trust announced that it had agreed a
se from the British Transport Commission under which the Trust would assume
ponsibility for restoring and maintaining the southern section.

e reopening ceremony was performed by Queen Elizabeth the Queen Mother on 11 July
64, after more than four years of hard work by prison labourers, canal enthusiasts, Army
its and a handful of National Trust staff. On the 1st April 1988 control of the southern
tion of the Stratford-on-Avon Canal was passed to the British Waterways Board (now
itish Waterways).

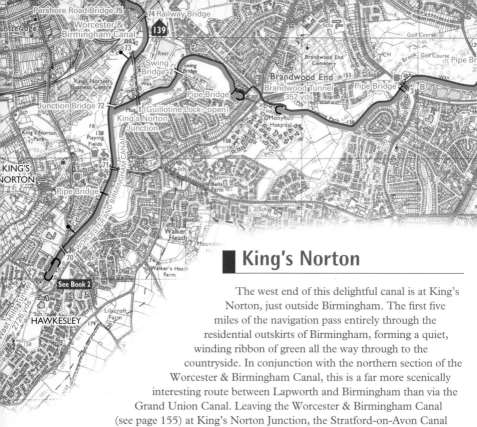

King's Norton

The west end of this delightful canal is at King's Norton, just outside Birmingham. The first five miles of the navigation pass entirely through the residential outskirts of Birmingham, forming a quiet, winding ribbon of green all the way through to the countryside. In conjunction with the northern section of the Worcester & Birmingham Canal, this is a far more scenically interesting route between Lapworth and Birmingham than via the Grand Union Canal. Leaving the Worcester & Birmingham Canal (see page 155) at King's Norton Junction, the Stratford-on-Avon Canal proceeds straight to the well-known King's Norton Stop Lock. In the days of the private canal companies, stop locks were common at junctions, as one canal sought to protect its water supply from any newcomer; but King's Norton Stop Lock is unusual in having two wooden guillotine gates mounted in iron frames, balanced by chains and counterweights. The machinery is not now used, and boats pass under the two gates without stopping. The next bridge is a small (but very heavy) swing bridge, followed by Brandwood Tunnel. Further east is a beautiful tree-lined cutting, then a bridge with a pub beside it (*petrol and telephone nearby*) and the remains of an old arm just beyond it. Passing over a small aqueduct, the canal reaches a steel lift bridge, which is raised and lowered electrically (see note below). Then beyond a railway bridge the canal begins to shed all traces of the suburbs, maintaining its twisting course in wooded cuttings through quiet countryside. The bridges over the navigation are mostly the generous brick-arched bridges typical of the canal between King's Norton and Lapworth Locks (in contrast to the much smaller bridges further south), but few roads of any significance come near the canal. At bridge 16 the canal emerges from a long cutting and is joined by a feeder from the nearby Earlswood Reservoir. Boats are moored along this, since this is the base of the Earlswood Motor Yacht Club. There are no villages along this rural stretch of canal, but at Salter Street there is a modern school and a strange Victorian church.

NAVIGATIONAL NOTES

You will need a BW key and a windlass to operate bridge 8.

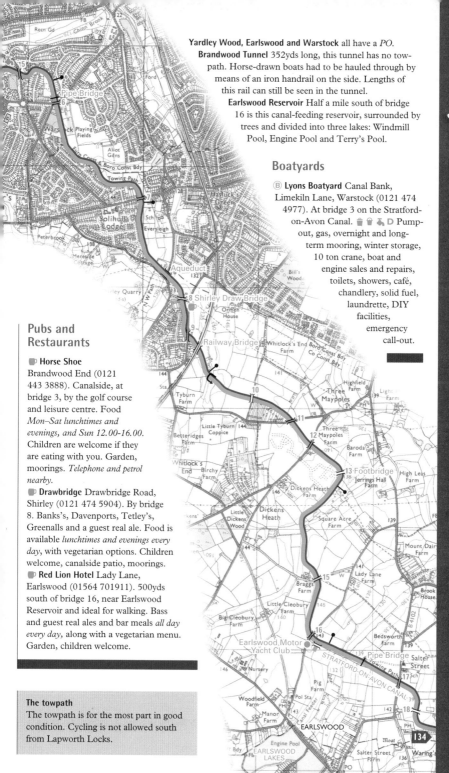

Yardley Wood, Earlswood and Warstock all have a *PO*.
Brandwood Tunnel 352yds long, this tunnel has no towpath. Horse-drawn boats had to be hauled through by means of an iron handrail on the side. Lengths of this rail can still be seen in the tunnel.

Earlswood Reservoir Half a mile south of bridge 16 is this canal-feeding reservoir, surrounded by trees and divided into three lakes: Windmill Pool, Engine Pool and Terry's Pool.

Boatyards

Ⓑ **Lyons Boatyard** Canal Bank, Limekiln Lane, Warstock (0121 474 4977). At bridge 3 on the Stratford-on-Avon Canal. 🚿 🚽 🛠 D Pumpout, gas, overnight and longterm mooring, winter storage, 10 ton crane, boat and engine sales and repairs, toilets, showers, café, chandlery, solid fuel, laundrette, DIY facilities, emergency call-out.

Pubs and Restaurants

🍺 **Horse Shoe** Brandwood End (0121 443 3888). Canalside, at bridge 3, by the golf course and leisure centre. Food *Mon–Sat lunchtimes and evenings, and Sun 12.00-16.00.* Children are welcome if they are eating with you. Garden, moorings. *Telephone and petrol nearby.*

🍺 **Drawbridge** Drawbridge Road, Shirley (0121 474 5904). By bridge 8. Banks's, Davenports, Tetley's, Greenalls and a guest real ale. Food is available *lunchtimes and evenings every day,* with vegetarian options. Children welcome, canalside patio, moorings.

🍺 **Red Lion Hotel** Lady Lane, Earlswood (01564 701911). 500yds south of bridge 16, near Earlswood Reservoir and ideal for walking. Bass and guest real ales and bar meals *all day every day,* along with a vegetarian menu. Garden, children welcome.

The towpath
The towpath is for the most part in good condition. Cycling is not allowed south from Lapworth Locks.

134 ▶

Lapworth Locks

The canal continues on its south-easterly course, passing through quiet countryside interrupted only by the incessant roar of the M42 motorway, crossing overhead. There are no locks, and the bridges – especially those in the cuttings – are still the big brick arches worthy of a broader canal. At Hockley Heath (bridge 25) there is a tiny arm that once served a coal wharf. Nearby the Wharf Inn overlooks the canal. East of here things change dramatically, for the first of the locks down to Kingswood Junction is reached.

The top lock is numbered 2, as the old stop lock at King's Norton is number 1. The surroundings of the top lock are indeed pleasant: a white house enclosed by walls and hemmed in by trees stands beside the lock, while a cottage with a delightful garden faces the towpath just below. To the south west can be seen the spire of Lapworth church. After the first four locks, there is a 1/2-mile breathing space: then the Lapworth flight begins in earnest, with each of the next nine locks spaced only a few yards from its neighbour. There is a useful canal shop by lock 14 selling groceries, home-made bread and cakes, brassware and gifts. The short intervening pounds

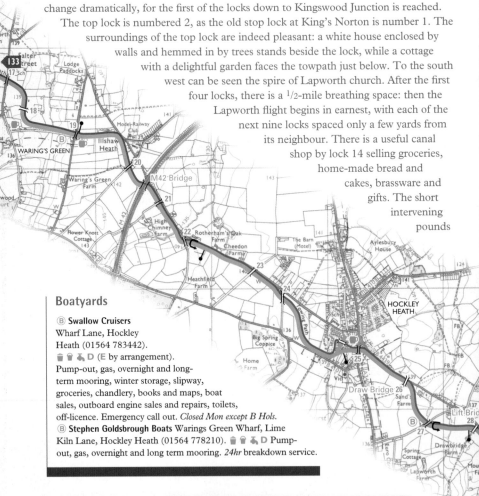

Boatyards

Ⓑ **Swallow Cruisers**
Wharf Lane, Hockley
Heath (01564 783442).
🚿 🚽 ♿ D (E by arrangement).
Pump-out, gas, overnight and long-term mooring, winter storage, slipway, groceries, chandlery, books and maps, boat sales, outboard engine sales and repairs, toilets, off-licence. Emergency call out. *Closed Mon except B Hols.*
Ⓑ **Stephen Goldsbrough Boats** Warings Green Wharf, Lime Kiln Lane, Hockley Heath (01564 778210). 🚿 🚽 ♿ D Pump-out, gas, overnight and long term mooring. *24hr breakdown service.*

NAVIGATIONAL NOTES

1. Bank erosion is a serious problem on all canals, and especially so on this one. *Please go slowly* to minimise your wash.
2. Bridges 26 and 28 operate hydraulically, using a lock windlass.
3. Due to rebuilding, the chamber of lock 15 on the Lapworth flight is now over 2ft shorter than the other locks. Those in full length boats should take extra care when descending.

have been enlarged to provide a
bigger working reservoir of water,
so that one side of each lock is
virtually an isthmus. The locks have
double bottom gates and are not
heavy going. They are interspersed
with the old cast iron split bridges that
are such a charming feature of the
Stratford-on-Avon Canal. These bridges
are built in two halves, separated by a one
inch gap so that the towing line between a
horse and a boat could be dropped through
the gap without having to disconnect the
horse. Below lock 19 is Kingswood Junction:
boats heading for Stratford should keep
right here. A short branch to the left leads
under the railway line to the Grand
Union Canal, or you can use the
Lapworth Link after lock 22 if you are
heading north to the GU, avoiding
unnecessary lockage.

Hockley Heath

Warwicks. PO, tel, stores, garage. A featureless place, but the several shops are conveniently close to the canal bridge, and the pub is pleasant.

Lapworth

Warwicks. PO, tel, stores, garage, station. Indivisible from Kingswood, this is more a residential area than a village. Two canals pass through Lapworth: the heavily locked Stratford-on-Avon Canal and, to the east, the main line of the Grand Union Canal. These two waterways, and the short spur that connects them, are easily the most interesting aspect of Lapworth. The canalside buildings are attractive and there are two small reservoirs at the junction. The mostly 15th-C church is quite separate from the village and is 1½ miles west of the junction; it contains an interesting monument by Eric Gill, 1928.

Packwood House *NT property* (01564 782024). Hockley Heath, 2 miles west of bridge 66. Timber-framed Tudor house, dating from the late 16thC and enlarged in the 17thC, where Cromwell's general, Henry Ireton, slept before the Battle of Edgehill in 1642. Owned by the Featherstones until 1869, it was eventually purchased by Alfred Ash, who repaired the house and reinstated the gardens. Collection of tapestry, needlework and furniture. Park with formal grounds and 17th-C yew garden possibly laid out to represent the Sermon on the Mount, the trees taking the place of Jesus and his followers. *House open Wed–Sun, Mar, Apr & Oct 12.30–16.30; May–Sep 13.30–17.30. Garden open Wed-Sun, Mar, Apr & Oct 10.00–16.30; May–Sep 10.00–17.30.* Charge. Events are staged *during the summer.*

Pubs and Restaurants

Bull's Head Lime Kiln Lane, Salter Street (01564 702335). ¼ mile south of bridge 17. Pleasant, low-ceilinged country pub in converted cottages, serving traditional and continental food *Mon–Sat lunchtimes and evenings, and Sun 12.00–18.00.* Vegetarian choices and children's helpings. Ansells, Tetley's and a guest real ale. Games in the cupboard, and dominoes are played *Thu & Sun.* Garden with a water pump, and there is a resident ghost – a 17th-C limekiln worker who appears during Jul & Aug (to attract visitors?).

Blue Bell Cider House Warings Green Road, Hockley Heath (01564 702328). Canalside, at bridge 19. A pretty traditional cider house serving real draught cider and a couple of guest real ales. It is a drinkers pub, but bar meals and snacks are available *Mon–Sat lunchtimes and*

evenings and Sun lunchtime with children's and vegetarian menus. Garden with playground. Good mooring jetty for patrons. *Wed* is quiz night.

Wharf Tavern Stratford Road, Hockley Heath (01564 782075). Canalside, at bridge 25. A smart pub with a pleasant canalside garden and adventure playground, offering Marston's and John Smith's real ales and bar meals (carvery) *lunchtimes and evenings every day,* with vegetarian options. Children welcome, moorings.

Boot Inn Old Warwick Road, Lapworth (01564 782464). Near lock 14. Quaint cosmopolitan country pub serving Morland, Tetley's, Boddingtons, Whitbread and guest real ales. Fashionable bar meals from chargrill to oysters *lunchtimes and evenings every day,* with vegetarian dishes. Garden with gas heaters for cooler nights!

Canada Geese, Edgbaston (see page 140)

WORCESTER & BIRMINGHAM CANAL

MAXIMUM DIMENSIONS

Maximum dimensions
Length: 71' 6"
Beam: 7'
Headroom: 8'

MANAGER

(01564) 784634

MILEAGE

KING'S NORTON JUNCTION to:
BIRMINGHAM Gas Street Basin: 5½ miles
No locks

The Bill for the Worcester & Birmingham Canal was passed in 1791 in spite of fierce opposition from the Staffordshire & Worcestershire Canal proprietors, who saw trade on their route to the Severn threatened. The supporters of the Bill claimed that the route from Birmingham and the Black Country towns would be much shorter, enabling traffic to avoid the then notorious shallows in the Severn below Stourport. The Birmingham Canal Company also opposed the Bill and succeeded in obtaining a clause preventing the new navigation from approaching within 7ft of their water. This resulted in the famous Worcester Bar separating the two canals in the centre of Birmingham.

Construction of the canal began at the Birmingham end following the line originally surveyed by John Snape and Josiah Clowes. Even at this early stage difficulties with water supply were encountered. The company was obliged by the Act authorising the canal to safeguard water supplies to the mills on the streams south of Birmingham. To do this, and to supply water for the summit level, ten reservoirs were planned or constructed. The high cost of these engineering works led to a change of policy: instead of building a broad canal, the company decided to build it with narrow locks, in order to save money in construction and water in operation.

The canal was completed in 1815. In the same year an agreement with the Birmingham Canal proprietors permitted the cutting of a stop lock through Worcester Bar. The canal had cost £610,000, exceeding its original estimate by many thousands of pounds. Industrial goods and coal were carried down to Worcester, often for onward shipping to Bristol, while grain, timber and agricultural produce were returned to the growing towns of the Midlands. However the opening of railways in the 1840s and 1850s reduced traffic considerably and had a profound effect on the fortunes of the canal.

By the early 1900s the commercial future of the canal was uncertain, although the works were in much better condition than on many other canals. Schemes to enlarge the navigation as part of a Bristol-Birmingham route came to nothing. Commercial carrying continued until about 1964, the traffic being mostly between the two Cadbury factories of Bournville and Blackpole, and to Frampton on the Gloucester & Sharpness Canal. After nationalisation, several proposals were made to abandon the canal, but the 1960s brought a dramatic increase in the number of pleasure boats using the waterway thus securing its future use. The whole of the canal is covered in Book 2.

King's Norton

To the north of King's Norton Junction, where the Stratford-on-Avon Canal (see page 132) joins the Worcester & Birmingham Canal, the canal passes through an industrial area, but thankfully seems to hold the factories at bay on one side, while a railway line, the main line from Worcester and the south west to Birmingham, draws alongside on its west flank. Canal and railway together drive through the middle of Cadbury's Bournville works, which is interesting rather than oppressive. Beyond it is Bournville station, followed by a cutting.

Bournville Garden Factory The creation of the Cadbury family, who moved their cocoa and chocolate manufacturing business south from the centre of Birmingham. The Bournville estate was begun in the late 1800s and is an interesting example of controlled suburban development. There were once old canal wharves here, which became disused when most of the ingredients travelled by rail – but the sidings closed in the late 1960s and now regrettably everything comes by road.

Cadbury World Linden Road (Information line 0121 451 4180). It is by the factory and signposted from the canal, where there are moorings. An exhibition dedicated to the history and the love of chocolate. Audio visual displays, a jungle to explore, and Victorian Birmingham. *Open Mon–Fri 10.00–15.00, Sat & Sun 09.30–16.30*

(restricted hours in winter – please telephone). Reservation for admission is advised, telephone 0121 451 4159. Charge.

Selly Manor and Minworth Greaves Sycamore Road, Bournville (0121 472 0199). Two half-timbered Birmingham houses of the 13th and early 14thC re-erected in the 1920s and 1930s in Bournville. They contain a collection of old furniture and domestic equipment. *Open all year Tue–Fri 10.00–17.00; also Apr–Oct, Sat & Sun 14.00–17.00; Nov–Mar, closed Sat-Mon.* Charge. The nearest point of access from the canal is at Bournville station: walk west to the Cadbury's entrance. There is a public right of way (Birdcage Walk) through the works: bear right at the fork, then turn right at the village green. The two houses are close by, on the left. Selly Oak and Bournville both have a PO.

King's Norton Tunnel

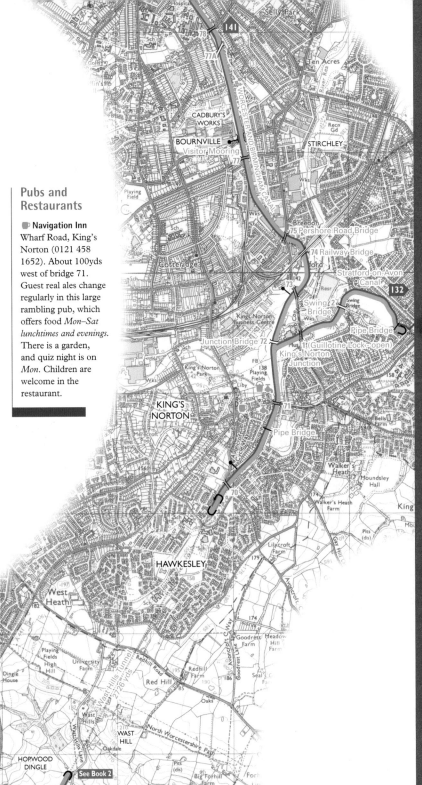

Pubs and Restaurants

🍺 **Navigation Inn**
Wharf Road, King's
Norton (0121 458
1652). About 100yds
west of bridge 71.
Guest real ales change
regularly in this large
rambling pub, which
offers food *Mon–Sat
lunchtimes and evenings*.
There is a garden,
and quiz night is on
Mon. Children are
welcome in the
restaurant.

Birmingham

Soon the railway vanishes briefly behind the buildings of Selly Oak. Between bridge 80 and the next, skewed, railway bridge is the site of the junction with the Dudley Canal, but no trace remains here now of either the junction or the canal itself. North of here the canal and railway together shrug off industry and town, and head north on an embankment towards Birmingham in splendid isolation and attractive surroundings. Below on either side is the green spaciousness of residential Edgbaston, its botanical gardens and woods. A hospital is on the west side. The University of Birmingham is on the east side; among its many large buildings the most conspicuous is the Chamberlain Campanile Tower, which was erected in 1900. At one of the bridges near the University, two Roman forts used to stand; but most evidence of them was obliterated by the building of the canal and railway. Only a reconstructed part of the larger fort now exists. There is a useful Sainsbury's just south of bridge 80. Past the University's moorings, canal and railway enter a cutting, in which their enjoyable seclusion from the neighbourhood is complete; the charming old bridges are high, while the cutting is steep, and always lined by overhanging foliage. It is a remarkable approach to Birmingham. The railway is the canal's almost constant companion, dipping away here and there to reappear a short distance further on; but trains are not too frequent, and in a way their occasional appearance heightens the remoteness that attaches to this length of canal. At one stage the two routes pass through short tunnels side by side: the canal's tunnel, Edgbaston, is the northernmost of the five on this canal and the only one with a towpath through it. It is a mere 105yds long. The Worcester & Birmingham Canal now completes its delightful approach to Birmingham. The railway disappears underneath in a tunnel to New Street station, while the canal passes Holiday Wharf and makes a sharp left turn to the basin. The terminus of the Worcester & Birmingham Canal is the former stop lock at Gas Street Basin; this is known as Worcester Bar, for originally there was a physical barrier here between the Worcester & Birmingham Canal and the much older Birmingham Canal. The latter refused to allow a junction, and for several years goods had to be transhipped at this point from one canal to the other. This absurd situation was remedied by an Act of Parliament in 1815, by which time a stop lock was allowed to be inserted to connect the two canals. Nowadays the stop gates are kept open and one can pass straight through, on to the Birmingham Canal (see page 21). Don't leave your boat unattended in this area.

The Dudley Canal This canal used to join the Worcester & Birmingham Canal at Selly Oak, thus providing a southern bypass round Birmingham. The eastern end of the canal has been closed for many years, and will certainly remain so. The tremendously long (3795yd) Lappal Tunnel, now collapsed, emerged 2 miles from Selly Oak. This bore was more like a drainpipe than a navigable tunnel – it was only 7ft 9in wide, a few inches wider than the boats that used it, and headroom was limited to a scant 6ft. Boats were assisted through by a pumping engine flushing water along the tunnel, but it must still have been a nightmarishly claustrophobic trip for the boatmen.

● **Edgbaston**
West Midlands. PO. A desirable residential suburb of Birmingham, Edgbaston is bisected by the canal.
Botanical Gardens Edgbaston. Founded over 100 years ago. Alpine Garden, lily pond and a collection of tropical birds. *Open daily.*
Perrott's Folly Waterworks Road, off Monument Road, Edgbaston. About ¾ mile west of bridge 86, not far from the Plough & Harrow Hotel. This seven-storey tower was built in 1758 by John Perrott and claims to be Birmingham's most eccentric building. One theory as to its origin is that Mr Perrott could, from its height, gaze upon his late wife's grave 10 miles away. One of the Two Towers of Gondor, featured in J.R.R. Tolkien's *Lord of the Rings,* is thought to have been based upon this building. Tolkien's last address in Birmingham was at 4 Highfield Road, opposite the Plough & Harrow. From 1884-1984 the folly was used as a weather station and was subsequently renovated. *Open Easter–Sep, Sun and B. Hols 14.00–17.00.* Modest charge. Tea room.

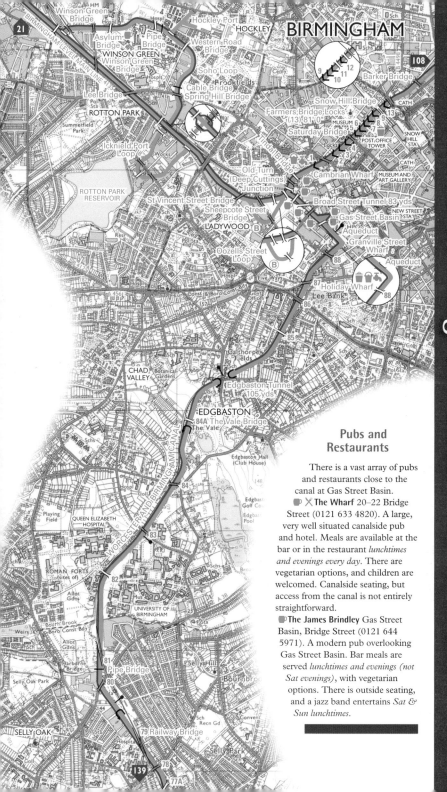

BIRMINGHAM

Pubs and Restaurants

There is a vast array of pubs and restaurants close to the canal at Gas Street Basin.

The Wharf 20–22 Bridge Street (0121 633 4820). A large, very well situated canalside pub and hotel. Meals are available at the bar or in the restaurant *lunchtimes and evenings every day*. There are vegetarian options, and children are welcomed. Canalside seating, but access from the canal is not entirely straightforward.

The James Brindley Gas Street Basin, Bridge Street (0121 644 5971). A modern pub overlooking Gas Street Basin. Bar meals are served *lunchtimes and evenings (not Sat evenings)*, with vegetarian options. There is outside seating, and a jazz band entertains *Sat & Sun lunchtimes*.

New Inn at Shardlow (see page 144)

TRENT & MERSEY CANAL

MAXIMUM DIMENSIONS

Derwent Mouth to Burton upon Trent
Length: 72'
Beam: 10'
Headroom: 7'

Burton upon Trent to south end of Harecastle Tunnel
Length: 72'
Beam: 7'
Headroom: 6' 3"

MANAGER
Derwent Mouth to Colwich: (01283) 790236
Colwich to Great Haywood: (01785) 284253

MILEAGE
DERWENT MOUTH to
Swarkestone Lock: 7 miles
Willington: $12^{1/4}$ miles
Horninglow Wharf: $16^{1/2}$ miles
Barton Turn: $21^{1/4}$ miles
Fradley, junction with Coventry Canal: $26^{1/4}$ miles
Great Haywood, junction with Staffs & Worcs Canal: 39 miles

Locks: 76

This early canal was originally conceived partly as a roundabout link between the ports of Liverpool and Hull, while passing through the busy area of the Potteries and mid-Cheshire, and terminating either in the River Weaver or in the Mersey. Its construction was promoted by Josiah Wedgwood (1730–95), the famous potter, aided by his friends Thomas Bentley and Erasmus Darwin. In 1766 the Trent & Mersey Canal Act was passed by Parliament, authorising the building of a navigation from the River Trent at Shardlow to Runcorn Gap, where it would join the proposed extension of the Bridgewater Canal from Manchester.

The ageing James Brindley was appointed engineer for the canal. Construction began at once and in 1777 the Trent & Mersey Canal was opened. In the total 93 miles between Derwent Mouth and Preston Brook, the Trent & Mersey gained connection with no fewer than nine other canals or significant branches.

By the 1820s the slowly-sinking tunnel at Harecastle had become a serious bottleneck. Thomas Telford recommended building a second tunnel beside the old one. His recommendation was eventually accepted by the company and the whole tunnel was completed in under three years, in 1827.

Although the Trent & Mersey was taken over in 1845 by the new North Staffordshire Railway Company, the canal flourished until World War I. Today it is assured (by statute) of its future as a pleasure cruising waterway. Look out for the handsome cast iron mileposts, which actually measure the mileage from Shardlow, not Derwent Mouth. There are 59 originals, from the Rougeley and Dixon foundry in Stone, and 34 replacements, bearing the mark T & MCS 1977 of the Trent & Mersey Canal Society.

Shardlow

The Trent & Mersey Canal begins at Derwent Mouth, some 2¹/₂ miles upstream of the point where

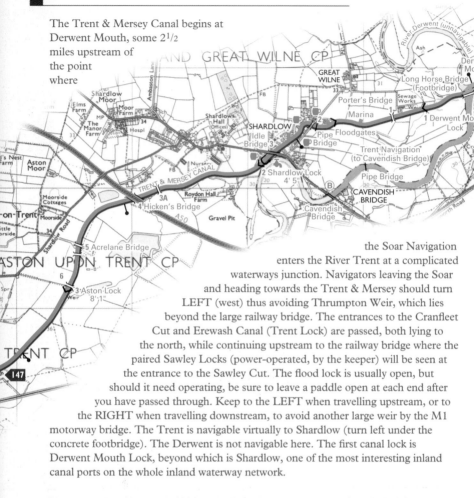

the Soar Navigation enters the River Trent at a complicated waterways junction. Navigators leaving the Soar and heading towards the Trent & Mersey should turn LEFT (west) thus avoiding Thrumpton Weir, which lies beyond the large railway bridge. The entrances to the Cranfleet Cut and Erewash Canal (Trent Lock) are passed, both lying to the north, while continuing upstream to the railway bridge where the paired Sawley Locks (power-operated, by the keeper) will be seen at the entrance to the Sawley Cut. The flood lock is usually open, but should it need operating, be sure to leave a paddle open at each end after you have passed through. Keep to the LEFT when travelling upstream, or to the RIGHT when travelling downstream, to avoid another large weir by the M1 motorway bridge. The Trent is navigable virtually to Shardlow (turn left under the concrete footbridge). The Derwent is not navigable here. The first canal lock is Derwent Mouth Lock, beyond which is Shardlow, one of the most interesting inland canal ports on the whole inland waterway network.

NAVIGATIONAL NOTES

Those heading towards the River Trent should not pass Shardlow floodgates if the warning light shows red.

- **Sawley Cut**
  In addition to a large marina and a well-patronised BW mooring site, the Derby Motor Boat Club has a base on the Sawley Cut where well over 100 boats are kept. There are windlasses for sale at Sawley Lock, as well as the more conventional facilities.
- **Shardlow**
  Derbs. PO, tel, stores, garage. Few canal travellers will want to pass through Shardlow without stopping. Everywhere there are living examples

of large-scale canal architecture, as well as old-established necessities such as canal pubs. By the lock is the biggest and best of these buildings – the 18th-C Trent Mill, now the Clock Warehouse, which has a large central arch where boats once entered to unload. Restored in 1979, it still retains all its original proud elegance.

Shardlow Heritage Centre Adjacent to the Clock Warehouse (01332 792935). *Open Apr-Oct, Fri-Sun 12.00-17.00.* Modest entry charge.

> **The towpath**
> This is generally in good condition throughout.

Boatyards

Ⓑ ✕ **Sawley Bridge Marina** Long Eaton, Nottingham (01159 734278). 🚽 🛢 🔧 P D Pump-out, gas, extensive moorings both overnight and long-term, slipway, crane, boat and engine sales and repairs, telephone, toilets, showers, chandlery, coffee shop, solid fuel, laundrette.

Ⓑ ✕ ♀ **Shardlow Marina** London Road, Shardlow (01332 792832). On the River Trent. 🚽 🛢 🔧 D Pump-out, gas, overnight and long-term mooring, winter storage, slipway, boat sales, toilets & showers, chandlery, licensed bar and restaurant.

Pubs and Restaurants

🍺 **Clock Warehouse** London Road, Shardlow (01332 792844). Mansfield real ale, and food *lunchtimes and evenings every day,* with a vegetarian menu. Children welcome, garden and adventure playground.

🍺 **Navigation** By bridge 3, London Road, Shardlow (01332 792918). Six guest real ales, and bar meals *lunchtimes and evenings,* with a vegetarian menu. Garden with play area and aviary. Regular quiz nights.

🍺 **Malt Shovel** By Bridge 2, The Wharf, Shardlow (01332 799763). Friendly canal-side pub, built in 1779. Marston's real ale. Excellent and inventive food *lunchtimes only (not Sun),* with a vegetarian menu. Children welcome. Outside seating by the canal.

🍺 **New Inn** The Wharf, Shardlow, next to the Malt Shovel (01332 793331). Bass and guest real ales and bar meals *lunchtimes every day, and evenings Tue-Sat,* with a vegetarian options available. Garden and outside seating. Children welcome.

✕ ♀ **The Thai Kitchen** Shardlow (01332 792331). Authentic Thai food in a restaurant haunted by the 'lady in grey'. Children welcome *lunchtimes and early evenings.* Outside seating. *L & D (no L Mon).* B & B.

🍺 **Old Crown** Cavendish Bridge, Shardlow (01332 792392). Bass, Marston's and four guest real ales in a friendly old riverside pub, decorated with old advertsing ephemera. Bar meals *lunchtimes only* and snacks with vegetarian options. Children welcome *at lunchtime only.* Garden with play area. B & B.

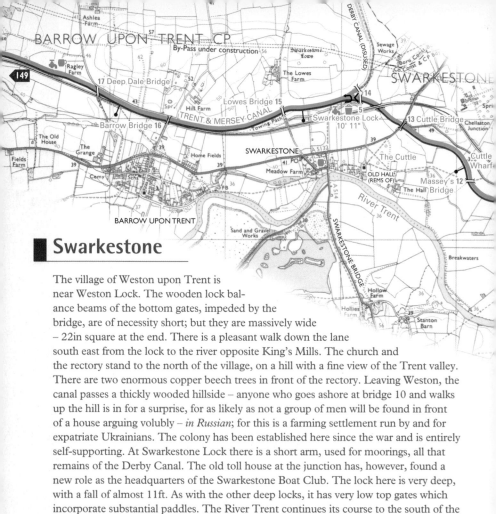

Swarkestone

The village of Weston upon Trent is
near Weston Lock. The wooden lock balance beams of the bottom gates, impeded by the
bridge, are of necessity short; but they are massively wide
– 22in square at the end. There is a pleasant walk down the lane
south east from the lock to the river opposite King's Mills. The church and
the rectory stand to the north of the village, on a hill with a fine view of the Trent valley.
There are two enormous copper beech trees in front of the rectory. Leaving Weston, the
canal passes a thickly wooded hillside – anyone who goes ashore at bridge 10 and walks
up the hill is in for a surprise, for as likely as not a group of men will be found in front
of a house arguing volubly – *in Russian*; for this is a farming settlement run by and for
expatriate Ukrainians. The colony has been established here since the war and is entirely
self-supporting. At Swarkestone Lock there is a short arm, used for moorings, all that
remains of the Derby Canal. The old toll house at the junction has, however, found a
new role as the headquarters of the Swarkestone Boat Club. The lock here is very deep,
with a fall of almost 11ft. As with the other deep locks, it has very low top gates which
incorporate substantial paddles. The River Trent continues its course to the south of the
canal, and can be seen at intervals through the hedges and trees. The countryside is green
and pleasant, with only the occasional freight train rumbling by to disturb the peace.

● **Weston upon Trent**
Derbs. PO, tel, stores. A scattered village that is in
fact not very close to the Trent. The isolated
church is splendidly situated beside woods on
top of a hill, its sturdy tower crowned by a short
14th-C spire. Inside are fine aisle windows of the
same period. The lock gardens make the
approach from the canal particularly attractive.
● **Swarkestone**
Derbs. PO, tel, stores. The main feature of
Swarkestone is the 18th-C five-arched stone
bridge over the main channel of the River Trent.
An elevated causeway then carries the road on
stone arches all the way across the Trent's flood
plain to the village of Stanton by Bridge. It was
at Swarkestone that Bonnie Prince Charlie, in
the rising of 1745, gave up his attempt for the

throne of England and returned to his defeat at
Culloden. In a field nearby are the few remains
of Sir Richard Harpur's Tudor mansion, which
was demolished before 1750. The Summer
House, a handsome, lonely building, overlooks a
square enclosure called the Cuttle. Jacobean in
origin, it is thought that it may have been the
scene of bull-baiting, although it seems more
likely it was just a 'bowle alley'. Restored by
the Landmark Trust, two people may now have
holidays here – telephone 01628 825925 for
details. The Harpurs moved to Calke following
the demolition of their mansion after the Civil
War. The pub in the village, and monuments in
the church, which is tucked away in the back
lanes, are a reminder of the family.

● **Barrow upon Trent**
Derbs. Tel, stores. A small, quiet village severed from the canal by the busy A514. A lane from the church leads down to the river. Until recently the old hall stood next to the church, very much the focus of the village. But now bright modern houses stand in its place and the surviving lodge house looks uncomfortably irrelevant. Opposite is a mellow terrace of old workmen's cottages.

Pubs and Restaurants

Old Plough Main Street, Weston upon Trent (01332 700331). An attractive pub serving Marston's and a guest real ale. There is an exciting range of food, with a good choice for vegetarians and children, available *lunchtimes and evenings every day.* Outside seating. Children welcome

Crew & Harpur Arms Swarkestone, by the river bridge (01332 700641). Marston's and guest real ales and bar meals served *all day 12.00–22.00 (21.00 Sun),* with vegetarian menu in this handsome pub. Riverside seating

and garden, and Billy Bear's children's play area.

Swarkestone Tea Rooms The Lock Cottage (01283 790236).

Ragley Boat Stop Deepdale Lane, off Sinfin Lane, Barrow-on-Trent (01332 703919). A large pub 300 yards west of bridge 17, serving Courage and Marston's real ale. Food is available *lunchtimes and evenings and all day Sun.* Extensive vegetarian and children's menu. Outside seating in a 3-acre garden. Children welcome. Good moorings with ⚓.

A HOP, A SKIP, AND A JUMP TO DERBY

The Derby Canal, which left the Trent & Mersey at Swarkestone and joined the Erewash at Sandiacre, has long been disused. One condition of its building, and a constant drain on its profits, was the free carriage of 5000 tons of coal to Derby each year, for the use of the poor.

But one of the most unusual loads was transported on the 19th April 1826, when 'a fine lama, a kangaroo, a ram with four horns, and a female goat with two young kids, remarkably handsome animals' arrived in Derby by canal 'as a present from Lord Byron to a Gentleman whose residence in the neighbourhood, all of which had been picked up in the course of the voyage of the *Blonde* to the Sandwich Islands in the autumn of 1824'.

Willington

Just by bridge 18 is Arleston House, an attractive old building with ground floor walls of stone and the upper tiers of brick. This is followed by Stenson Lock, the last of the wide locks until Middlewich – it has a massive fall of 12ft 4in. Stenson is a small farming centre, always a popular mooring spot and now benefiting from the large marina. After passing through a railway bridge, the canal

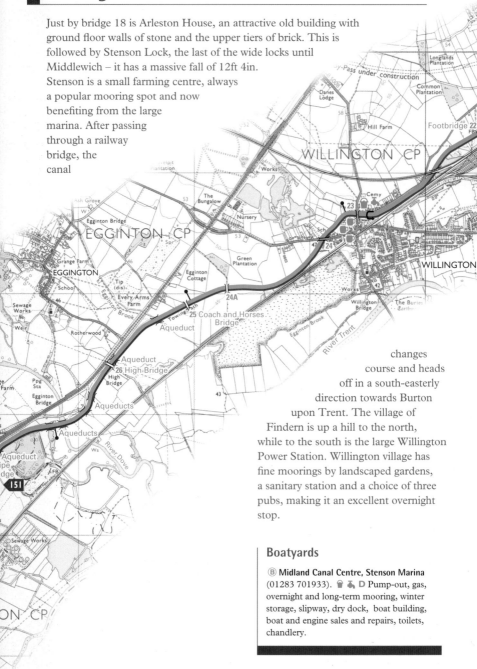

changes course and heads off in a south-easterly direction towards Burton upon Trent. The village of Findern is up a hill to the north, while to the south is the large Willington Power Station. Willington village has fine moorings by landscaped gardens, a sanitary station and a choice of three pubs, making it an excellent overnight stop.

Boatyards

Ⓑ **Midland Canal Centre, Stenson Marina** (01283 701933). 🚿 ⚓ D Pump-out, gas, overnight and long-term mooring, winter storage, slipway, dry dock, boat building, boat and engine sales and repairs, toilets, chandlery.

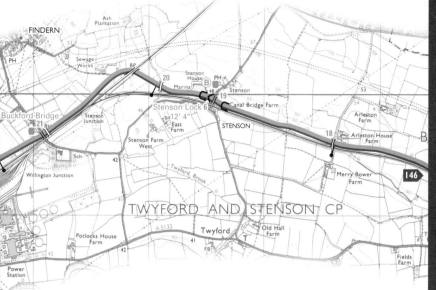

● **Repton**

Derbs. PO. 1½ miles south east of Willington
(over the River Trent) is Repton, one of the
oldest towns in England. It was once the
capital of Mercia and the crypt below St
Wystan's Church was built in the 10thC.
One of the finest examples of Saxon
architecture in the country, this crypt was
completely forgotten until the end of the
18thC when a man fell into it while digging
a grave. Repton public school dates from
1551 and there is much of historical interest
in the school and the town.

● **Willington**

Derbs. PO, tel, stores, fish & chips. The
railway bisects this busy little village by an
embankment, which has three pubs, all
huddled together.

● **Findern**

Derbs. PO, tel, stores. A small, quiet village
where Jedekiah Strutt, the inventor of the
ribbed stocking frame, served a seven-year
apprenticeship with the local wheelwright.
At one time the village green was no more
than a waste patch used by cars as a short cut,
and a parking place. When suggestions were
made to turn it into a formal cross roads, the
indignant Women's Institute galvanised the
villagers into actually uprooting all traces of
tarmac from the green and turfing the whole
area properly.

● **Egginton**

Derbs. PO, tel, stores. A quiet village lying off
the A38. The church, set apart from the village, is pleasingly irregular from the outside,
with a large chancel and squat tower.

Pubs and Restaurants

🍺 **Bubble Inn** (01283 703113) Alongside
Stenson Lock and Marina, this modern pub in
a converted barn serves Marston's and other
Courage real ales and bar meals *all day.*
Children welcome. Garden.

🍺 **Canal Turn** Heath Lane, Findern (01283
701714). Canalside, at bridge 21. A basic but
friendly family pub. Garden.

🍺 **Rising Sun** The Green, Willington (01283
702116). Marston's real ale. Reasonably

priced bar food available at *lunchtimes
(not Sun).* Bar games, and seats outside.

🍺 **Green Dragon** The Green, Willington
(01283 702327). A very popular and
welcoming pub, with plenty of low beams,
serving Marston's, Ind Coope (Burton),
Tetley's and guest real ales. Food available
lunchtimes and evenings every day, including
vegetarian menu. Garden. Children
welcome.

Burton upon Trent

A twelve-arched stone aqueduct carries the canal over the River Dove, beside a handsome four-arched bridge, no longer in use. Factories and car parks herald the outskirts of Burton upon Trent. The canal passes along one side of Burton, without entering the town. Many of the old canalside buildings have been demolished, but the waterside has been nicely tidied up, making the passage very pleasant. The lovely aroma of malt and hops is strongest to the west of the town, where the canal passes between the Marston and Bass breweries. Dallow Lock is the first of the narrow locks, an altogether easier job of work than the wider ones to the east. Shobnall Basin is now used by a boatyard, and visitor moorings nearby are available from which to explore the town. The A38 then joins the canal, depriving the navigator of any peace. The road is mostly a dual carriageway, and this contrasts massively with the narrow canal and its tiny narrow bridges, many with a 2 ton weight restriction. Up on the hills to the north west is the well-wooded Sinai Park – the moated 15th-C house here, now a farm, used to be the summer home of the monks from Burton Abbey. There is a fine canalside pub at bridge 34, and a shop selling provisions, home-made cakes and crafts. It is *open Easter-Oct, daily 09.00–18.00.* The canal enters the new National Forest at bridge 30, and will leave it just beyond Alrewas. The Bass Millenium Woodland, to the west of Branston Lock, is part of this major project.

● Burton upon Trent

Staffs. MD Thu, Fri, Sat. All services. Known widely for its brewing industry, which originated here in the 13thC, when the monks at Burton Abbey discovered that an excellent beer could be brewed from the town's waters, because of their high gypsum content. At one time there were 31 breweries producing three million barrels of ale annually: alas, now only a few remain. The advent of the railways had an enormous effect on the street geography of Burton, for gradually a great network of railways took shape, connecting with each other and with the main line. These branches were mostly constructed at street level, and until recent years it was common for road traffic to be held up by endless goods trains chugging all over the town. Little of this system remains. The east side of the town is bounded by the River Trent, on the other side of which are pleasant hills. The main shopping centre lies to the east of the railway station.

The Bass Museum Horninglow Street, 3/4 mile from Horninglow Basin. All aspects of brewing during the late 19thC. Also a preserved steam engine, café and shop. Conducted tours around the brewery. *Open every day 10.00–17.00 (last admission 16.00). Closed Xmas.* Admission charge.

Marston's Brewery Visitor Centre Shobnall Road, Burton upon Trent (01283 507391). *You must telephone and book in advance* to tour the brewery, see the Burton Union system, visit the cooperage, enjoy some food and sample the beers, which include Marston's Pedigree, Oyster Stout, Banks's Bitter, plus specials such as India Pale Ale and Owd Roger. *Tours Mon-Fri 11.00, 12.30, 14.30 (also Mon-Thu 18.30).* Charge.

Brewhouse Arts Centre Union Street car park (01283 516030). Live entertainment in a 230-seat theatre, plus a gallery and bistro bar.

Tourist Information Centre 183 High Street, Burton upon Trent (01283 516609/508589).

● Shobnall Basin

This is all that remains of the Bond End Canal, which gave the breweries the benefit of what was modern transport, before the coming of the railways.

● Branston

Staffs. PO, tel, stores, garage, butcher, Chinese take-away, fish & chips. Although this is apparently the place where the famous pickle originated, it is a small, unexciting village. Canalside pub and shop.

Boatyards

Ⓑ **Jannel Cruisers** Shobnall Marina, Shobnall Road, Burton upon Trent (01283 542718). In Shobnall Basin. 🛁 🛒 ⚓
D Pump-out, gas, narrow boat hire, overnight mooring, long-term mooring, winter storage, slipway, dry dock, chandlery, books and maps, boat building, boat sales, engine sales and repairs, toilets.

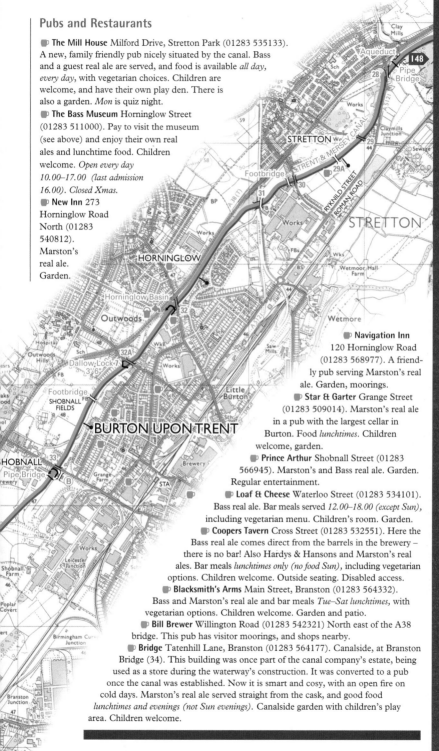

Pubs and Restaurants

The Mill House Milford Drive, Stretton Park (01283 535133).
A new, family friendly pub nicely situated by the canal. Bass
and a guest real ale are served, and food is available *all day,
every day*, with vegetarian choices. Children are
welcome, and have their own play den. There is
also a garden. *Mon* is quiz night.

The Bass Museum Horninglow Street
(01283 511000). Pay to visit the museum
(see above) and enjoy their own real
ales and lunchtime food. Children
welcome. *Open every day
10.00–17.00 (last admission
16.00). Closed Xmas.*

New Inn 273
Horninglow Road
North (01283
540812).
Marston's
real ale.
Garden.

Navigation Inn
120 Horninglow Road
(01283 568977). A friend-
ly pub serving Marston's real
ale. Garden, moorings.

Star & Garter Grange Street
(01283 509014). Marston's real ale
in a pub with the largest cellar in
Burton. Food *lunchtimes*. Children
welcome, garden.

Prince Arthur Shobnall Street (01283
566945). Marston's and Bass real ale. Garden.
Regular entertainment.

Loaf & Cheese Waterloo Street (01283 534101).
Bass real ale. Bar meals served *12.00–18.00 (except Sun)*,
including vegetarian menu. Children's room. Garden.

Coopers Tavern Cross Street (01283 532551). Here the
Bass real ale comes direct from the barrels in the brewery –
there is no bar! Also Hardys & Hansons and Marston's real
ales. Bar meals *lunchtimes only (no food Sun)*, including vegetarian
options. Children welcome. Outside seating. Disabled access.

Blacksmith's Arms Main Street, Branston (01283 564332).
Bass and Marston's real ale and bar meals *Tue–Sat lunchtimes*, with
vegetarian options. Children welcome. Garden and patio.

Bill Brewer Willington Road (01283 542321) North east of the A38
bridge. This pub has visitor moorings, and shops nearby.

Bridge Tatenhill Lane, Branston (01283 564177). Canalside, at Branston
Bridge (34). This building was once part of the canal company's estate, being
used as a store during the waterway's construction. It was converted to a pub
once the canal was established. Now it is smart and cosy, with an open fire on
cold days. Marston's real ale served straight from the cask, and good food
lunchtimes and evenings (not Sun evenings). Canalside garden with children's play
area. Children welcome.

Barton Turn

Beside Tatenhill Lock there is an attractive cottage: at the tail of the lock is yet another of the tiny narrow brick bridges that are such an engaging feature of this navigation. Note the fine National Forest seat just north of the lock – there is another at Bagnall Lock, along with a living willow sculpture. After passing flooded gravel pits and negotiating another tiny brick arch at bridge 36, the canal and the A38, the old Roman road, come very close together – thankfully the settlement of Barton Turn has been passed, leaving the main street (the old Roman road of Ryknild Street) wide and empty. It is with great relief that Wychnor Lock, with its diminutive crane and warehouse, is reached – here the A38 finally parts company with the canal, and some peace returns. To the west is the little 14th-C Wychnor church. Before Alrewas Lock the canal actually joins the River Trent – there is a large weir which should be given a wide berth. The canal then winds through the pretty village of Alrewas, passing the old church, several thatched cottages and a brick bridge.

● **Barton-under-Needwood**
Staffs. PO, tel, stores, bank, garage. Many years ago, when there were few roads and no canals in the Midlands, the only reasonable access to this village was by turning off the old Roman road, Ryknild Street: hence, probably, the name Barton Turn. The village is indeed worth turning off for, although unfortunately it is nearly a mile from the canal. A pleasant footpath from Barton Turns Lock leads quietly to the village, which is set on a slight hill. Its long main street has many attractive pubs. The church is battlemented and surrounded by a very tidy churchyard. Pleasantly uniform in style, it was built in the 16thC by John Taylor, Henry VIII's private secretary, on the site of his cottage birthplace. The former Royal Forest of Needwood is to the north of the village.

● **Wychnor**
Staffs. A tiny farming settlement around the church of St Leonards, which was built in Early English Decorated style. Parts date from around 1200: the tower is probably 17th-C.

● **Alrewas**
Staffs. PO, tel, stores, garage, butcher, chemist, tea room, fish & chips. Away from the A513, this is an attractive village whose rambling back lanes harbour some excellent timbered cottages. The canal's unruffled passage through the village gives the place a restful air, and the presence of the church and its pleasant churchyard adds to this impression. The River Trent touches the village, feeding the old Cotton Mill,

and provides it with a fine background which is much appreciated by fishermen. The somewhat unusual name Alrewas, pronounced olrewus, is a corruption of the words Alder Wash – a reference to the many alder trees which once grew in the often-flooded Trent valley and gave rise to the basket weaving for which the village was once famous.
Alrewas Church A spacious building of mainly 13th-C and 14th-C construction, notable for the unmatching nave arches (octagonal and quatrefoil) and the old leper window, which is now filled by modern stained glass.

Boatyards

Boat Doctor (01332 771622). Emergency marine engineer with *24 hour* emergency breakdown call-out.
Ⓑ **Wychnor Moorings** Wychnor, Burton upon Trent (07778 668388). 🚽 🚿 🔥 Pump-out, gas, long-term mooring, coal.

NAVIGATIONAL NOTES

In times of flood great caution should be exercised along the stretch immediately north of Alrewas lock – keep well over to the towpath side at all times.

Pubs and Restaurants

🍺 **Three Horseshoes** Station Road, Barton-under-Needwood (01283 716268). A quiet pub, with no juke box or pool table, but with extremely friendly staff serving a changing range of real ales and excellent bar meals *lunchtimes and evenings,* with vegetarian options.

Good selection of single malt whiskys. Children are welcome. Garden, and regular entertainment.

✕ **Little Chef** Canal-side at Barton, and very handy (01283 716135). *Open daily 07.00–22.00.* Vegetarian options.

🍺 **Shoulder of Mutton** Main Street, Barton-under-Needwood (01283 712568). A 17th-C pub serving Bass, Worthington and a guest real ale and bar meals *lunchtimes and evenings (not Sun evenings),* with a vegetarian menu. Function room. Children welcome, and a garden with a play area.

🍺 **Barton Turns** Barton Turn, just opposite Barton Lock (01283 712142). A basic but friendly pub serving Marston's real ale and bar meals *lunchtimes and evenings,* with vegetarian menu. Breakfast is also available. Small garden, and occasional live music.

🍺 **Crown** Post Office Road, Alrewas, near bridge 46 (01283 790328). Marston's, Bass and guest real ales and food *lunchtimes and evenings every day,* with a vegetarian menu. Children welcome. Garden.

🍺 **The Old Boat** Canalside at Alrewas, Kings Bromley Road (01283 791468). With a boat-themed and quirky interior, this relaxed and popular pub offers excellent meals *lunchtimes and evenings every day,* with vegetarian options, along with Ushers real ale. Children (and also dogs) welcome. Pleasant garden with play area. Regular entertainment. Moorings. Fishing facilities.

🍺 **George & Dragon** Main Street, Alrewas (01283 791476). Marston's real ale and bar meals *lunchtimes and evenings (not Sun)* with vegetarian menu, in an old village local. Garden. Children welcome.

🍺 **William IV** William IV Road, Alrewas (01283 790206). Marston's real ale, with bar meals *lunchtimes and evenings every day,* with a vegetarian menu. Children welcome. Patio. Regular *Sunday* quiz nights.

✕ 🍷 **Rafters Restaurant** Claymar Hotel, Alrewas (01283 790202). A welcoming and informal restaurant with a fine collection of Royal commorative mugs. Marston's real ale, bar meals and an à la carte menu served *evenings and Sun lunchtimes.* Children welcome, and a garden.

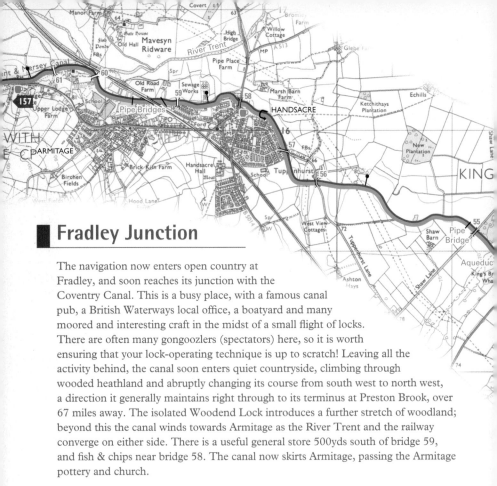

Fradley Junction

The navigation now enters open country at Fradley, and soon reaches its junction with the Coventry Canal. This is a busy place, with a famous canal pub, a British Waterways local office, a boatyard and many moored and interesting craft in the midst of a small flight of locks. There are often many gongoozlers (spectators) here, so it is worth ensuring that your lock-operating technique is up to scratch! Leaving all the activity behind, the canal soon enters quiet countryside, climbing through wooded heathland and abruptly changing its course from south west to north west, a direction it generally maintains right through to its terminus at Preston Brook, over 67 miles away. The isolated Woodend Lock introduces a further stretch of woodland; beyond this the canal winds towards Armitage as the River Trent and the railway converge on either side. There is a useful general store 500yds south of bridge 59, and fish & chips near bridge 58. The canal now skirts Armitage, passing the Armitage pottery and church.

NAVIGATIONAL NOTES

West of bridge 61 the canal is very narrow, due to the removal of Armitage Tunnel, and wide enough for one boat only. Check that the canal is clear before proceeding.

Boatyards

Ⓑ **BW Waterways Office** Fradley Junction (01283 790236). 🚿 🚽 ⚓ Overnight mooring, long-term mooring, toilets.

Ⓑ **Swan Line Cruisers** Fradley Junction (01283 790332). ⚓ D Pump-out (*not weekends*), gas, narrow boat hire, overnight mooring, dry dock, groceries, chandlery, books and maps, boat building, boat sales, engine sales and repairs.

● **Fradley Junction**
A long-established canal centre where the Coventry Canal joins the Trent & Mersey. Like all the best focal points on the waterways, it is concerned solely with the life of the canals, and has no relationship with local roads or even with the village of Fradley. The junction bristles with boats for, apart from it being an inevitable meeting place for canal craft, there is a boatyard, a British Waterways maintenance yard, BW moorings, a boat club and a popular pub – all in the middle of a five-lock flight.

Kings Bromley

Staffs. PO, tel, stores. A village 1½ miles north of bridge 54, along the A515. There are some pleasant houses and an old mill to be seen here, as well as what is reputed to have been Lady Godiva's early home. The Trent flows just beyond the church, which contains some old glass and a 17th-C pulpit and font. A large cross in the southern part of the churchyard is known locally as Godiva's cross.

Armitage

Staffs. PO, tel, stores, garage. A main road village, whose church is interesting: it was rebuilt in the 19thC in a Saxon/Norman style, which makes it rather dark. The font is genuine Saxon, however, and the tower was built in 1690. The organ is 200 years old, and enormous: it came from Lichfield Cathedral and practically deafens the organist at Armitage. The town is widely known for its Armitage Shanks water closets.

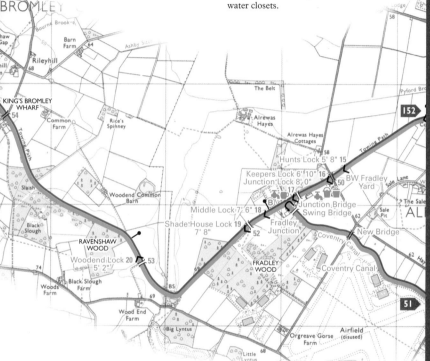

Pubs and Restaurants

Swan Fradley Junction (01283 790330). Canalside, the focus of the junction and justly famous. There is a fine public bar with a coal fire and pub games, a comfortable lounge, and a cellar bar. Ansells, Ind Coope (Burton) and Marston's real ales are offered, and bar meals are served *lunchtimes and evenings every day.*

Crown The Green, Handsacre (01543 490239). At bridge 58. A welcoming 300-year-old pub serving Bass, Marston's and Worthington real ale. Reasonably priced but good bar food *Tue–Sat lunchtimes only,* with a vegetarian menu. Grocer and fish & chips nearby. Family and games room, and a garden. Regular quiz nights. Good moorings.

Tom Cobleigh's Spode Cottage Armitage (01543 490353). A very popular restaurant in a timbered 17th-C farmhouse, sensitively converted. Imaginative menu, vegetarians catered for, and Bass, Marston's, Worthington and a guest real ale to enjoy. *Open Mon–Sat 11.00–23.00, Sun 12.00–22.30.* Booking advisable at weekends. Children welcome *until 21.30.* Large garden.

Plum Pudding Canalside, west of Armitage, Rugeley Road, Armitage (01543 490330). A well kept pub serving Marston's, Tetley's and guest real ales, with bar meals *lunchtimes and evenings, restaurant meals evenings,* and including a vegetarian menu. Outside seating and garden. Children welcome *for meals only.*

Rugeley

The A513 crosses the canal on
a new bridge where the short, 130yds
long, Armitage Tunnel used to run before its
roof was removed in 1971 to combat the subsidence
effects of coal being mined nearby. There is a distinguished
restaurant just across the road here, very much a rarity on canals
in general and this area in particular. To the west stands Spode House,
a former home of the pottery family. The huge power station at Rugeley,
tidied up now, comes into view – and takes a long time to recede. There are
pleasant moorings at Rugeley, by bridge 66, with the town centre and shops
only a short walk away. North of the town, the canal crosses the River Trent via a
substantial aqueduct. The canal now enters an immensely attractive area full of
interest. Accompanied by the River Trent, the canal moves up a narrowing valley
bordered by green slopes on either side, Cannock Chase being clearly visible to the
south. Wolseley Hall has gone, but Bishton Hall (now a school) still stands: its very
elegant front faces the canal near Wolseley Bridge.

- **Spode House** Spode House and Hawkesyard
  Priory stand side by side. The priory was founded
  in 1897 by Josiah Spode's grandson and his niece
  Helen Gulson when they lived at Spode House.
- **Rugeley**
  Staffs. PO, tel, stores, garage, banks, station, cinema.
  An unexciting place with a modern town centre
  and a dominating power station. There are two
  churches by bridge 67; one is a 14th-C ruin, the
  other is the parish church built in 1822 as a
  replacement.

- **Cannock Chase**
  An area of outstanding natural beauty and
  officially designated as such in 1949. The Chase
  is all that remains of what was once a Norman
  hunting ground known as the King's Forest of
  Cannock. Flora and fauna are abundant and
  include a herd of fallow deer whose ancestors
  have grazed in this area for centuries.
  Shugborough Park is at the north end of the
  Chase.

Cannock Chase

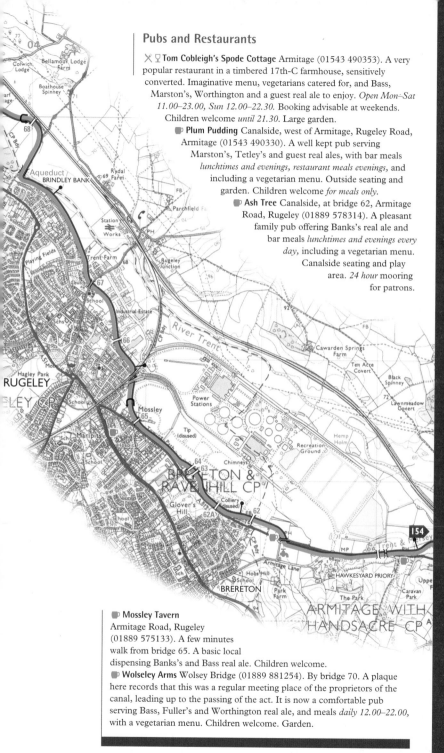

Pubs and Restaurants

✕ ♀ **Tom Cobleigh's Spode Cottage** Armitage (01543 490353). A very popular restaurant in a timbered 17th-C farmhouse, sensitively converted. Imaginative menu, vegetarians catered for, and Bass, Marston's, Worthington and a guest real ale to enjoy. *Open Mon–Sat 11.00–23.00, Sun 12.00–22.30.* Booking advisable at weekends. Children welcome *until 21.30.* Large garden.

Plum Pudding Canalside, west of Armitage, Rugeley Road, Armitage (01543 490330). A well kept pub serving Marston's, Tetley's and guest real ales, with bar meals *lunchtimes and evenings, restaurant meals evenings,* and including a vegetarian menu. Outside seating and garden. Children welcome *for meals only.*

Ash Tree Canalside, at bridge 62, Armitage Road, Rugeley (01889 578314). A pleasant family pub offering Banks's real ale and bar meals *lunchtimes and evenings every day,* including a vegetarian menu. Canalside seating and play area. *24 hour* mooring for patrons.

Mossley Tavern Armitage Road, Rugeley (01889 575133). A few minutes walk from bridge 65. A basic local dispensing Banks's and Bass real ale. Children welcome.

Wolseley Arms Wolsey Bridge (01889 881254). By bridge 70. A plaque here records that this was a regular meeting place of the proprietors of the canal, leading up to the passing of the act. It is now a comfortable pub serving Bass, Fuller's and Worthington real ale, and meals *daily 12.00–22.00,* with a vegetarian menu. Children welcome. Garden.

Great Haywood

The pleasant surroundings continue as the canal passes Colwich. As the perimeter of Shugborough Park is reached the impressive façade of the Hall can be seen across the parkland. Haywood Lock and a line of moored craft announce the presence of Great Haywood and the junction with the Staffordshire & Worcestershire Canal (see page 121), which joins the Trent & Mersey under a graceful and much photographed towpath bridge: just the other side there is a useful boatyard. Beyond the junction the Trent valley becomes much broader and more open. There is another boatyard by Hoo Mill Lock.

● **Great Haywood**
Staffs. PO, tel, stores. Centre of the Great Haywood and Shugborough Conservation Area, the village is not particularly beautiful, but it is closely connected in many ways to Shugborough Park, to which it is physically linked by the very old Essex Bridge, where the crystal clear waters of the River Sow join the Trent on its way down from Stoke. Haywood Lock is beautifully situated between this pack-horse bridge (which is an Ancient Monument) and the unusually decorative railway bridge that leads into Trent Lane. The lane consists of completely symmetrical and very handsome terraced cottages: they were built by the Ansons to house the people evicted from the former Shugborough village, the site of which is now occupied by the Arch of Hadrian within the park, built to celebrate Anson's circumnavigation of the globe in 1740–4. There is an interesting-looking Roman Catholic church in Great Haywood: the other curious feature concerns the Anglican church. About 100yds south of Haywood Lock is an iron bridge over the canal. This bridge, which now leads nowhere, used to carry a private road from Shugborough Hall which crossed both the river and the canal on its way to the church just east of the railway. This was important to the Ansons, since the pack-horse bridge just upstream is not wide enough for a horse and carriage, and so until the iron bridge was built the family had to *walk* the 300yds to church on Sunday mornings!
Shugborough Hall *National Trust property.* Walk west from Haywood Lock and through the park. The present house dates from 1693, but was substantially altered by James Stuart around 1760 and by Samuel Wyatt around the turn of the 18thC. It was at this time that the old village of Shugborough was bought up and demolished by the Anson family so that they should enjoy more privacy and space in their park. Family fortunes fluctuated greatly for the Ansons, the Earl of Lichfield's family; eventually crippling death duties in the 1960s brought about the transfer of the estate to the National Trust. The Trust has leased the property to Staffordshire County Council who now manage the whole estate. The house has been restored at great expense. There are some magnificent rooms and many treasures inside.

Museum of Staffordshire Life This excellent establishment, which is Staffordshire's County Museum, is housed in the old stables adjacent to Shugborough Hall. Open since 1966, it is superbly laid out and contains all sorts of exhibits concerned with old country life in Staffordshire. Amongst other things it contains an old fashioned laundry, the old gun-room and the old estate brew-house, all completely equipped. Part of the stables contains harness, carts, coaches and motor cars. There is an industrial annexe up the road, containing a collection of preserved steam locomotives and some industrial machinery.
Shugborough Park There are some remarkable sights in the large park that encircles the hall. Thomas Anson, who inherited the estate in 1720, enlisted in 1744 the help of his famous brother, Admiral George Anson, to beautify and improve the house and the park. And in 1762 he commissioned James Stuart, a neo-Grecian architect, to embellish the park. 'Athenian' Stuart set to with a will, and the spectacular results of his work can be seen scattered round the park. The stone monuments that he built have deservedly extravagant names like the 'Tower of the Winds', the 'Lanthorn of Demosthenes' and so on.
The Park Farm Designed by Samuel Wyatt, it contains an agricultural museum, a working mill and a rare breeds centre. Traditional country skills such as bread-making, butter-churning and cheese-making are demonstrated.
Shugborough Hall, Grounds, Museum and Farm (01889 881388). *Open late Mar–late Sep, daily 11.00–17.00. Parties must book.*

Boatyards

Ⓑ **Anglo Welsh** The Canal Wharf, Mill Lane, Great Haywood (01889 881711). 🚽 🚰 ⛽ D Pump-out, gas, narrow boat hire, day hire craft, overnight mooring, long-term mooring, boat and engine repairs, toilets, gifts.
Ⓑ **Hoo Mill Boatyard** Hoo Mill Lane, Great Haywood (01889 882611) ⛽ D Pump-out, gas, narrow boat hire, long-term mooring, winter storage, dry dock, boatbuilding, boat and engine sales and repairs, toilets, showers, laundrette, chandlery.

INDEX

Trent & Mersey Canal   Great Haywood

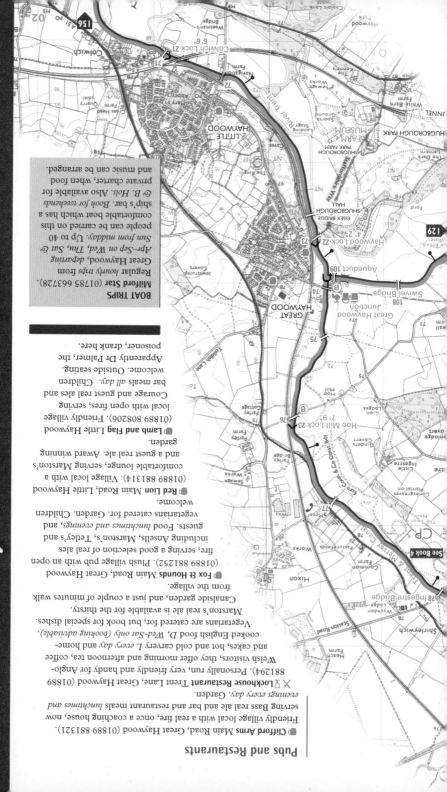

Pubs and Restaurants

Clifford Arms Main Road, Great Haywood (01889 881321). Friendly village local with a real fire, once a coaching house, now serving Bass real ale and bar and restaurant meals *lunchtimes and evenings every day*. Garden.

✗ � **Lockhouse Restaurant** Trent Lane, Great Haywood (01889 881294). Personally run, very friendly and handy for Anglo-Welsh visitors, they offer morning and afternoon tea, coffee and cakes, hot and cold carvery L *every day* and home-cooked English food D, *Wed–Sat only (booking advisable)*. Vegetarians are catered for, but book for special dishes. Marston's real ale is available for the thirsty. Canalside garden, and just a couple of minutes walk from the village.

Fox & Hounds Main Road, Great Haywood (01889 881252). Plush village pub with an open fire, serving a good selection of real ales including Ansells, Marston's, Tetley's and guests. Food *lunchtimes and evenings*, and vegetarians catered for. Garden. Children welcome.

Red Lion Main Road, Little Haywood (01889 881314). Village local with a comfortable lounge, serving Marston's and a guest real ale. Award winning garden.

Lamb and Flag Little Haywood (01889 808206). Friendly village local with open fires, serving Courage and guest real ales and bar meals *all day*. Children welcome. Outside seating. Apparently Dr Palmer, the poisoner, drank here.

BOAT TRIPS

Milford Star (01785 663728). Regular hourly trips from Great Haywood, departing *Apr–Sep on Wed, Thu, Sat & Sun from midday*. Up to 40 people can be carried on this comfortable boat which has a ship's bar. Also available for private charter, when food and music can be arranged. *Book for weekends & B. Hols.*